Greetings from New Nashville

GREETINGS FROM New Nashville

HOW A SLEEPY SOUTHERN TOWN BECAME "IT" CITY

edited by **STEVE HARUCH**

VANDERBILT UNIVERSITY PRESS
Nashville, Tennessee

Library of Congress Cataloging-in-Publication Data

Names: Haruch, Steve, 1974– editor.
Title: Greetings from new Nashville : how a sleepy southern town became "it"
   city / Steve Haruch, editor.
Description: Nashville : Vanderbilt University Press, 2020. | Summary: "A col-
   lection of journalism and essays that traces the transformation of Nashville
   over the last two decades through journalistic essays about specific facets of
   that transformation"— Provided by publisher.
Identifiers: LCCN 2020005336 (print) | LCCN 2020005337 (ebook) |
   ISBN 9780826500274 (paperback) | ISBN 9780826500281 (epub) |
   ISBN 9780826500298 (pdf)
Subjects: LCSH: Nashville (Tenn.)—History. | Cities and towns—Growth. |
   Nashville (Tenn.)—Social life and customs.
Classification: LCC F444.N24 G74 2020 (print) | LCC F444.N24 (ebook) | DDC
   976.8/55—dc23

LC record available at https://lccn.loc.gov/2020005336
LC ebook record available at https://lccn.loc.gov/2020005337

For J.

CONTENTS

INTRODUCTION

IN 1998, ROUGHLY TWO million visitors came to see what there was to see in Nashville. By 2018, the annual number had ballooned to 15.2 million. On some level, Nashville has always packaged itself for consumption, but suddenly everyone wanted a taste.

In that span of two decades, the physical boundaries of Nashville did not change. (The city and county governments had long ago consolidated.) But something did. Or rather, *many* somethings changed, and kept changing, until many who lived here began to feel they no longer recognized their own city. And some began to feel it wasn't their own city at all anymore, as they were pushed to its fringes by rising housing costs.

Between 1998 and 2018, the population of Nashville grew by 150,000. The greater metropolitan statistical area grew by a half-million people, and is expected to cross the two million mark some time in 2020.

But why Nashville? Why now? This book is an attempt to grapple with those questions without offering pat answers. Cities and histories are complex, and there is no single event or factor to credit. What we offer is a series of dispatches aimed at showing the contours, identifying turning points, and more urgently, giving a sense of texture to the life of a place in flux. Roughly half of the chapters are reprints, snapshots of a particular moment in the fast, messy evolution of the city. Others are new essays, written for this book with the benefit of at least some hindsight.

In 2001, the late John Egerton, along with fellow journalist E. Thomas Wood, assembled *Nashville: An American Self-Portrait*, which looked back on recent developments and forward to a new and perhaps newly prosperous century. This collection functions in much the same way Egerton describes his work in relation to the 1979 book *Nashville: The Faces of Two Centuries*: "This is not a sequel to the prior volume, not a direct descendant or even a close relative—but it is a companion, and a kindred spirit."

It is also incomplete, as any document of a transformation still in progress must be.

"IT'S HARD TO PINPOINT the exact moment the sleepy town of Nashville became a real city, but I'll go with 1998—the year the NHL Nashville Predators and NFL Houston Oilers (now the Tennessee Titans) moved here," the singer and songwriter Marshall Chapman writes in a 2011 story for *W* magazine. "Suddenly everything exploded. You'd look out over the city, and all you'd see were construction cranes."

Like all narrative starting points, 1998 is to some extent arbitrary. But Chapman reminds us that what is old is new again—the construction cranes are back, piercing the sky in every direction, their silhouettes now emblazoned half-jokingly on everything from rock show flyers to public radio station pledge-drive socks. The starting point isn't random, either.

1998 is the year Owen Bradley dies. As much as any artist and producer, Bradley helped define the Nashville Sound, and Music Row was more or less built around the Quonset Hut Studio he operated with his brother Harold on 16th Avenue South where Patsy Cline, Red Foley, Brenda Lee, Marty Robbins, Sonny James, and countless others recorded. Still, as much as the Nashville Sound is now synonymous with what we now might call classic country music, it was a conscious departure from the folksy Bristol sessions that birthed the genre. "Now we've cut out the fiddle and steel guitar and added choruses to country music," Bradley once said. "But it can't stop there. It always has to keep developing to keep fresh."

The same year Bradley passes, the advocacy organization Walk Bike Nashville is formed; in coming years it will be at the table for countless discussions around walkable neighborhoods, pedestrian safety, biking infrastructure—the stuff of urban renewal. The *Nashville Banner*, the afternoon newspaper that shared a building with the *Tennessean*, ceases operation in February after 122 years.

Garth Brooks, Faith Hill, Tim McGraw, and Dixie Chicks (now just The Chicks) rule the country charts, but it is a banner year for Nashville's independent music scene. Lucinda Williams's *Car Wheels on a Gravel Road*, Duane Jarvis's *Far from Perfect*, Kevin Gordon's *Cadillac Jack's Son*, Paul Burch & the WPA Ballclub's *Wire to Wire*, and Lambchop's *What Another Man Spills* are all released this year. To whatever extent it registers in Nashville at the time, a Detroit band called the White Stripes releases its first single, "Let's Shake Hands," in 1998 as well. Jack White will eventually settle in Nashville, establish Third Man Records, and in so doing alter the perception of the city. The honky-tonk revival on Lower Broadway has only recently begun, but already groups like BR549 are breathing new life into a stretch of the city dominated by the coin-operated peep shows and other unsavory goings-on that filled in after the Grand Ole Opry pulled out of the Ryman Auditorium and settled into its new building out near the sprawling Opryland Hotel and Resort.

It is also the year that a 25-foot-tall statue of Nathan Bedford Forrest—slave owner, early leader of the Ku Klux Klan, and Confederate general whose troops were responsible for the massacre of surrendered black Union soldiers at Fort Pillow—is erected on private property in full view of I-65.

Also in 1998, a years-long effort by the Nashville school board culminates in the end of court-supervised desegregation. The consequences of that will be deep and long lasting.

Outside of Hank Williams there is arguably no more iconic figure in country music than Johnny Cash. In 1998, fresh off a Grammy win for Best Country Album, the Man in Black appears in a full-page ad in *Billboard* magazine. It's an older photograph, taken in 1969 at San Quentin Prison. Cash's mouth is drawn up in a grimace, his lower teeth pressed against his upper lip the way one does when producing the *F* sound. He holds up his middle finger emphatically. "American Recordings and Johnny Cash would like to acknowledge the Nashville music establishment and country radio for your support," the caption reads, a reference to the absence of the album from the airwaves Cash once ruled. The sarcasm doesn't come cheap; producer Rick Rubin reportedly shells out $20,000 for the ad.

On April 15, a little more than a month after Cash's flipping off of Music Row, a tornado touches down a mile west of where Charlotte Pike meets I-440. It tears across the city, injuring dozens of people, one of whom later dies. It blows out 100 windows in the Tennessee Performing Arts Center and, after crossing the Cumberland River, topples three of the 10 cranes that are on site for the construction of the new NFL stadium. Then it keeps going, through the residential sections of East Nashville.

On that day, as the funnel cloud twists through the neighborhood, Joe Goller huddles inside the walk-in cooler in his restaurant on Eastland Avenue. When he finally emerges, the cooler and a few walls are all that remain of Joe's Diner. A photograph of then vice president Al Gore standing amid the rubble, where the front window had once been, subsequently goes the pre-Y2K equivalent of viral. As Kay West would write in the *Scene* the following year: "Between all the free publicity and a major insurance settlement, it soon became clear to Goller that the tornado had perhaps been the best thing that could have happened to his fledgling business."

In some ways, this is true of the entire East Side. As Nate Rau writes in the *Tennessean* on the 20th anniversary of the outbreak: "The popular bars, pizza joints and upscale restaurants came from entrepreneurs who invested in East Nashville after the tornado hit." Then mayor Phil Bredesen creates a tornado recovery task force; the American Institute of Architects dispatches an R/UDAT (Regional/Urban Design Assistance Team).

"It is hard to debate the fact that an enormous amount of insurance money came in to assist with what became case-by-case redevelopment," attorney Mike Jameson tells the *Tennessean's* Rau. "That's not to say it was without heartache. Months passed with tarps on people's roofs. But, the money eventually did pour in. It's just hard to debate that the tornado was, if not a turning point, a boost for East Nashville in the long term."

And it will be the East Side that, in many ways, leads the way in Nashville's reimagining of itself. This is partly out of necessity; rebuilding means grappling with city codes, and though residents had already begun thinking about and organizing around such things, it means engaging in a real way with planning, zoning, and preservation. But out of the wreckage a new vision of the city rises, a vision of somewhere a little more modern and worldly.

THE VIDEO FOR THE song "Won't Keep Me Up at Night," by the Nashville band Sun Seeker, opens with a shot of a modest single-story brick house. A sign out front reads: "Coming Soon: Luxury Condominiums; 32 Residential Units—8 Ground Floor Retail Spaces."

A van pulls into the driveway and a gaggle of shaggy twentysome-things piles out, armed with crowbars, hatchets, and hammers. They hop the fence, pry open the back door, then proceed to party. As the song progresses in gently lilting chords, a growing mob of young, interestingly dressed people perform prodigious and sometimes athletic acts of alco-hol consumption as they simultaneously tear the house apart—literally.

They smash holes in the drywall, toss beer bottles at mirrors, sledge-hammer the countertops, hang from ceiling fans in an attempt to rip them free. At one point someone brings a motorcycle into the living room and burns rubber on the hardwood floor; onlookers cheer and pump their fists as the spark plugs fire inside the bloom of smoke like lightning bolts in a storm cloud. It's a ritual of catharsis, one last hurrah before the wrecking claw accomplishes in a few hours what would take days to finish by hand.

Walking among the partiers is someone everyone seems to know. He's greeted with hugs, beers raised high, and hearty slaps on the back. But as the celebration descends into bacchanalian chaos, his smile fades. He pauses to run his hand down a section of wall, and on the jamb we can see telltale pencil lines: a series of dated hash marks charting a child's height through the years. Now the young man that child became gazes out a window he's looked through thousands of times, standing in a house that's no longer his, bracing for the end and knowing it's already here.

"Won't Keep Me Up at Night" betrays no evidence that it's an homage to the Gillian Welch song "Wayside/Back in Time." But it's a spot-on visualization of her oft-quoted line from that song: "Drink a round to Nashville, before they tear it down."

Bobby Allyn, now a reporter for National Public Radio, surveyed the city's fast-changing landscape in a 2013 cover story for the *Nashville Scene* titled "Demolition Derby" (reproduced in this volume). "It's not just low-income families or native Nashvillians who are singing the It City Blues as teardown fever reaches epidemic proportions," Allyn writes. "It's also the people who came here long before the recent wave of national press, lured by the city's downhome charm and deep roots."

You could count Welch among those pre-wave transplants, drawn by the rich musical tradition of a city where many of her most cherished albums were recorded. Although, looking at it that way, she had missed a previous wave as much as she had landed ahead of the next one. The logo of Acony Records, her label with musical partner David Rawlings, still adorns a storefront in the Five Points section of East Nashville. It's the same stretch of Woodland Street that was made up to look like a small-town Main Street in the 1991 film *Ernest Scared Stupid*. (Jim Varney, the actor who played Ernest P. Worrell, was a longtime Nashvillian; he died of cancer in 2000, at age 50.)

The "wave of national press" Allyn alludes to crested in January 2013 when Kim Severson, writing in the *New York Times*, asserted it was Nashville's turn to be "the nation's 'it' city." The phrasing was ubiquitous on arrival. Hence the "It City Blues" and a hundred other iterations, applied with varying levels of irony and spite. People wielded "It City" as both honorific and albatross, and whether one's eyes rolled while saying it or not, the notion of Nashville's new status, conferred by the paper of record, became a yardstick for just about everything. "We're the 'It City' because X." "We can't really be the 'It City' if we don't do Y." "The arrival of Z just goes to show we really are the 'It City.'" Or that we really aren't.

Albeit tongue-in-cheek, the *Nashville Scene* dedicated an entire cover story to the build-up preceding that moment in January—a timeline that's "full of it," according to the introduction (written by an uncredited Jim Ridley). By 2018, the *Tennessean* had worked the nomenclature into the title of dozens, if not hundreds, of news stories, op-eds, slideshows, videos, and whatever else they could dream up—a fact that, in a click-based advertising environment, was likely analytics-driven. Give the people what they want. Or at least what they love to hate.

A common scene in the early 2010s involves Nashville residents observing a new construction going up and wondering aloud, "Who's *buying* these?" It's one thing for a developer to buy a modest home, tear it down, and slap up some bigger, open-floor-planned, and importantly, more expensive house in its place. But someone has to *want* the damn thing. (Or, as often was the case, *both* of the damn things.) Perhaps part of the answer lies in two factors: one, what a house is to a certain class of people; and two, what kinds of investment opportunities were available in the murky waters of post–Great Recession America.

"All these people out there that have so much money, it's sitting in some stupid money-market account making 2 percent or 3 percent or whatever their horrible rates are right now," Steve Jones told the American Public Media show *Marketplace* in December 2014. "And so for me, I have to present to these people, like look, here's an opportunity for you. I can make you X percent on your money." After a pause, Jones added, "And I have made these people a lot of money."

Jones is known as the "Hipster Flipper" of Highland Park, a neighborhood in Los Angeles that he has helped gentrify, intentionally and at a terrific profit to himself and his backers. At the time of the *Marketplace* interview, Jones and his associates had bought, remodeled, and sold more than 50 houses, many of them foreclosures. The foreclosures were casualties of the housing market crash, which resulted in stricter lending standards. That, in turn, meant that the only people able to buy houses were just the kind of affluent customers Jones was trying to sell on the neighborhood and its "transition."

In Nashville, there were plenty of speculators jonesing to run the exact same game, bending toward their project in the local equivalents of Highland Park—those neighborhoods where the once-maligned "inner city," long synonymous with poverty, was becoming the "urban core," now synonymous with upscale living. (It's worth noting here that the phrase "It City" replaced as the most widely derided was the early-2000s T-shirt mainstay "Nashville: the new L.A." Whoever had the shirts printed either didn't know the old Scorchers song or had missed the irony.)

"Every city changes, and walking through a slowly changing city is like walking through an organic landscape during various seasons; leaves and even trees fall, birds migrate, but the forest stands: familiarity anchors the changes," Rebecca Solnit writes in *Hollow City: The Siege of San Francisco and the Crisis of American Urbanism*. "But if the pace of change accelerates, a disjuncture between memory and actuality arises and one moves through a city of phantoms, of the disappeared, a city that is lonely and disorienting," she continues. "To have your city dismantled too rapidly around you is to have the relationship between mind and place thrown into disarray."

In 2014, I wrote a rather melancholy op-ed for the *New York Times* about the pace and haphazardness of change in Nashville. It garnered enough interest that another journalist published my address and a photograph of my home in order to make some kind of point, I suppose, about people who can afford glass houses throwing stones at the idea of gentrification. An editor at a glossy men's magazine emailed me shortly after my essay was published and asked if I'd write a story—"less of a bummer," he hoped—about the good things Nashville has to offer. I wanted to say no, but it was the best money I'd ever been offered to write. I harbor no illusions about how much impact, economic or otherwise, my chipper endorsement of various restaurants and bars had on the growth of the city; at least one of them was closed within the year. But it did feel, on some level, like complicity.

"The story of Nashville's current prosperity is a case study in how to make the most out of organic advantages," the historian Jon Meacham wrote in *Time* that same year. "The specific factors behind its rise aren't readily transferable, but the larger lessons about what works are. Chief among the takeaways from the Music City's revival: culture is commerce."

Some bristled at the last part, about culture as commerce. It seemed so *transactional*. But hasn't it always been the case? While Bristol, Tennessee, is arguably the birthplace of what we call country music, Nashville is its capital—thanks to what we might today call a tech start-up: a radio station whose 50,000-watt signal carried the *Grand Ole Opry* for hundreds of miles in all directions, letting listeners as far away as Canada know that this is country music, and it's all happening in Nashville. Where you should come visit some time, see the show live, and part ways with some of your money. It was on some level an early form of sponsored content. The radio station call letters, WSM, stand for "We Shield Millions," the slogan of the National Life and Accident Insurance Company. The "Music City" appellation would come later, and many—especially those who felt "The Athens of the South" needed no improvement—would resist. In the Chamber of Commerce–produced promotional film *For the Love of Music: The Story of Nashville*, Charlie Daniels says: "It wasn't, 'We're gonna be the country music mecca of the world.' They were trying to sell insurance. But it caught on."

Later in 2014, Meacham told the crowd at a Chamber of Commerce event: "Every other city . . . wants to know [the secrets] of what's happening here." Nashville, Meacham said, was "in its golden hour." In photographic terms, the "golden hour" refers to the time near day's end when the light conveys a honeyed, almost otherworldly glow—the hour just before the sun sets. And indeed, there was darkness to come.

One aspect of Kim Severson's story that got lost in the shuffle was that, as with its linguistic forebear "it girl," the gilded "It City" tiara was never meant to be worn forever. It was Nashville's "turn"; to be the "It City" is to stand in the winner's circle at a pageant held at capricious intervals. But even among those who smirked at the new nickname, there were plenty who drank the sweet tea. It was easy to groan at all the new attention, and just as easy to enjoy its fruits—interesting new restaurants and bars, bands that used to skip the city making tour stops, friends from around the country suddenly eager to visit.

The wider world was waking up to Nashville's charms, but there was a nagging sense developing that the story, like so many American stories, lacked perspective—or rather, was dominated by one point of view. Responding to Meacham, Betsy Phillips wrote an essay for ThinkProgress titled "Whose 'It City' Is Nashville?" A very simple accounting lies at the heart of her discomfort: "In the *Time* article, here is a list of everyone mentioned by name and their race," Phillips writes. Of the 24 people named, all are white.

The coming months and years would see a slew of essays wondering aloud whether the next-leveling of the city had gone too far, too fast. A sampling: "Airbnb Has Taken Over Nashville"; "Is Nashville's 'It City' Reputation Getting Frayed around the Edges?"; "As U.S. 'Superstar' Cities Thrive, Weaker Ones Get Left Behind"; "Nashville: A Boomtown in Bust."

After the flood of 2010, which claimed 18 lives in Middle Tennessee and caused billions in damage, Nashvillians were fond of presenting a united front—"We Are Nashville," the title of a rallying-cry post by *Section303* blogger Patten Fuqua, became a widely reproduced slogan. There was also a sense that the tragedy had been largely ignored by national media in part because Nashville had so quickly and quietly set about doing what it does: taking care of its own. There was no looting, the argument went, because Nashville is not *that kind of place.*

In 2017, when a white Metro Police officer fatally shot a black man in the back as he fled, Nashville was faced with a harder truth: that it is still part of the United States of America, and the United States of America is still that kind of place. Jocques Clemmons died in the James Cayce Homes, a compound of dilapidated public housing units wedged between the interstate and some of the most expensive real estate in the city—a place where the average household income is less than $8,000 a year, and where almost every resident is black. The shooting and its subsequent investigation forced Nashvillians to peer behind our beautiful forevers and confront the neglect at work there. The "goofy grin of the newly popular," as the *Times* had described it, felt difficult to bear. The slogans splashed on murals and T-shirts across the city—"I Believe in Nashville"; "Nashville Looks Good on You"; "Spread Love It's the Nashville Way"—looked different, if not hideously self-congratulatory, under this light. Who was the "we" in "We are Nashville," and could it be redeemed?

In the same essay that minted the "It City" moniker, John Egerton calls Nashville "a big unfinished song." In a less-often cited passage, he tells Severson, "People are too smug about how fortunate we are now. . . . We ought to be paying more attention to how many people we have who are ill-fed and ill-housed and ill-educated."

The first iteration of "If we're It City, then why . . . ?"

IN SOME RESPECTS, 2018 is as arbitrary an ending point as 1998 is an arbitrary place to begin. But it is a tumultuous year in Nashville, and the end of at least one era.

In March, Mayor Megan Barry resigns after an improbable scandal. She had carried on an extramarital affair with the head of her security detail, and later pleaded guilty to felony theft of more than $10,000. The story gets even weirder than that—it involves clandestine rendezvouses at a cemetery, among other details—but the upshot is that the city's first woman leader, hugely popular and widely considered a rising political star, steps down in disgrace.

At a Waffle House in Antioch, in the city's southeast quadrant, a 29-year-old man opens fire with an AR-15 rifle, killing four people and injuring four others. James Shaw Jr. disarms the man barehanded, preventing further bloodshed and becoming a local and national hero in the process. In a truly bizarre turn of events, an anti-transit group posts news of the shooting to its Facebook page, adding: "We are sorry to post this, but 'transit' will bring more crime like this."

We will never know how much of a difference her resignation makes, but in Barry's absence the $5.4 billion transit bill she had willed into existence and subsequently championed—which would have added light rail, a downtown tunnel, numerous new transit centers, and other improvements to a traffic-choked city—fails spectacularly at the polls. Anti-transit activists, after cutting formal ties with the Koch Brothers' Americans for Prosperity, raise nearly $1 million, the majority of it from undisclosed donors.

An expansion Major League Soccer team gets the go-ahead from the Metro Council to build a new soccer-only stadium in yet another deal sweetened by tax incentives. But in a rare slowing of the New Nashville machinery, a planned development at Fort Negley, headed by a developer and music producer T Bone Burnett, is called off after an archaeological survey finds it "highly likely" that the formerly enslaved people who helped build the fort are still buried there.

In July, Metro Police Officer Andrew Delke shoots and kills Daniel Hambrick, a 25-year-old black man, as Hambrick flees the scene of an attempted traffic stop. The next month, Sheila Clemmons Lee, the mother of Jocques Clemmons, who had been killed by a different MNPD officer the previous year, delivers a petition to put a community oversight board for police on the fall ballot. It contains more than 8,000 signatures. Amendment 1 passes.

The statue of Nathan Bedford Forrest had been doused in pink paint in 2017, but a year later—20 years after its installation—it's still standing on the side of the interstate, in defiance of Nashville's self-image as a cosmopolitan blue dot in a red state. A bust of Forrest remains in the state capitol, despite renewed efforts to have it removed, and a state law requiring that Forrest be honored every year remains on the books. (The State Capitol Commission will vote, in July 2020, to recommend moving the bust, and two others, to the Tennessee State Museum.)

The teardowns continue. In the caption to an Instagram post showing a large tree in her neighborhood that was about to be cut down—a tree that had stood for 50 years on a piece of land that had recently sold for $1.1 million—the singer and songwriter Caitlin Rose describes the on-going redevelopment of the city this way: "A bunch of millionaires trading other people's neighborhoods around until they find the right idiot to build something no one actually wants and it's the only option left in a city where everyone wants to live. The greed just never ends."

Speaking of millionaires, Taylor Swift, who started her career as a teenager in Nashville, still maintains a home here and has become an international superstar above and beyond the confines of country music, does something unusual (for her): She endorses former Nashville mayor Phil Bredesen for Senate. "In the past I've been reluctant to publicly voice my political opinions," Swift writes in an Instagram post, "but due to several events in my life and in the world in the past two years, I feel very differently about that now." She doesn't mention Bredesen's support for Supreme Court–nominee Brett Kavanaugh, who is accused by several women of grotesque sexual misconduct. But she does mention Bredesen's Republican opponent: "As much as I have in the past and would like to continue voting for women in office, I cannot support Marsha Blackburn. Her voting record in Congress appalls and terrifies me." The post garners more than 2 million likes. Blackburn wins easily. Kavanaugh is confirmed to the Supreme Court.

After watching cities from coast to coast bearing piles of filthy lucre that it couldn't possibly need grovel at its feet, Amazon announces that, while it won't be building its HQ2 in Nashville, it *will* be installing something called an Operations Center of Excellence. Nashville—a city where first-year public school teachers spend, on average, more than half their salary on rent—offers $17.5 million in incentives to a company that is just the second in US history to cross the $1 trillion market cap benchmark. In 2018, Amazon paid no federal taxes on $11.2 billion in profits.

Depending on who you are, this is a sign that Nashville has leveled up yet again, or that it has jumped the shark entirely. *Are you sure Hank done it this way?*

At the Johnny Cash Museum on Third Avenue, the video for his rendition of "Hurt"—which features the gutted display cases and shattered memorabilia of another, long-since shuttered Johnny Cash museum—plays on a loop as tourists file by. Though it's one of the few Cash-branded items not for sale in the museum gift shop, the middle-finger photo is now a ubiquitous image, 20 years after its publication in *Billboard*. It's like Nashville's version of the Che Guevara poster, and somehow, through the miasma of time, it has come to represent both Cash's rebel spirit and the good old days of country music. It's caught in a sort of context collapse where the man and what he railed against have become part of the same nostalgia.

Something similar might be said of the city itself. For all its celebrations of openness and egalitarianism—we defeated the xenophobic English Only bill in 2009—Nashville and its glittering progress has begun to feel increasingly closed off to an ever larger segment of its less affluent citizenry. And the Barry scandal, which became a closely watched national story, strikes a tremendous blow to the city's ego—not only because she embodies the hopes of a progressive Nashville that has loved seeing itself reflected in her warmth, charisma, and confidence, but because it also serves as a stark reminder that we can have everything we think we want and yet, below the surface and out of view, it is not what we think it is at all.

Nashville's Band of Outsiders

ANN PATCHETT, 2007

This is my confession: I live in Nashville and I don't listen to country music. It is not such an uncommon state of affairs. Carrie Underwood's album has sold over six million copies, and yet I don't know a single person who owns it. Of course I like the old country music—Patsy Cline, Johnny Cash, Hank Sr. But I cannot connect the dots, in fact I believe there are no dots, between Patsy and Carrie.

That said, if you poke around anywhere in my hometown you will discover an endless assortment of small clubs and cafes where musicians prove nightly that the coolest music scene today is in Nashville. In the same way that ingenious independent films get made in Los Angeles, the city that is at this very moment no doubt working on *Die Hard 15*, Nashville in its spare time is making, dare I say it, art—unexpected and darkly fascinating music whose renegade spirit has been learned from everybody and is beholden to no one.

Maybe you didn't notice; it's easy to move under the radar when the radar is set by Tim McGraw and Faith Hill. But Nashville is a place where musicians of all kinds come to work and to live. Like New York and Los Angeles, it's an American city of dreams—where you go when you decide to put everything on the line and bet on yourself. For that reason, it's also a city with plenty of pawnshops and cheap bars. Seven nights a week the downtown strip is a weird combination of tourists, T-shirt shops and truly inspired singing. Finding a good music club in Nashville is about as challenging as finding good pizza in Sicily. Throw a rock in any direction, you'll hit one: the Mercy, the Basement, the Station Inn, the Bluebird Cafe.

I learned to see all this when I ran into an old college friend of mine in the gym not long ago. Diana Jones and I went to school in New York, and when I knew her she was the coolest girl around. She played guitar and sang rocking Joan Armatrading covers in the coffeehouse. Now she lives in Nashville and writes her own songs, which she sings in such a haunting high lonesome that one can't help but wonder if she isn't the lost daughter of the Carter Family. "You can't live as cheaply in Austin or any of the artsy centers anymore," she said when I asked why she'd moved here. She used to live in Austin. She used to live in a lot of places. She came here from Northampton, Mass. "I'm a songwriter. I go to bed at 2 a.m., I get up at 10. The community wasn't there."

Diana lives in East Nashville; it's where she bought what may well be the last $38,000 house in history. In fact, most of the people who are making the music I've come to love are living in East Nashville. It's what you'd call up-and-coming, which is to say there are lots of fabulous old brick manses that look like they belong on the cover of a Lemony Snicket novel, all turrets and bell towers and leaded windows, and in between those fabulous manses (some renovated, some not), there are plenty of ratty bungalows. It isn't the side of town where people tend to play (although I hear there are quite a few secret recording studios, hiding behind closed doors because of zoning laws). This is where they sleep and go to the grocery store and hang out in bars and coffee shops like the Family Wash and the 5 Spot, working on songs. There's now even a CD of those songs, called *The Other Side: Music From East Nashville.*

It's where Todd Snider came to live 10 years ago. "When I got here, it felt like Austin in the '70s," he told me. "Everybody on your street's a musician, too. It's as close as I'll get to Greenwich Village, or that fantasy I had about it when I was a kid. We talk about songs. We don't talk about the money around songs."

Everybody, in my opinion, should be talking about Todd Snider's songs. The man is the troubadour for our times, an inventive cross of Dylan and Kristofferson with just the right dash of Tom Petty thrown in. He likes to play the Belcourt, an old theater that often hosts music while showing art-house films.

It is possible to walk back and forth between the two theaters and see a local band like Brother Henry and a showing of *The 400 Blows* at the same time.

It's hard to know exactly what to call this genre that sounds sort of like old country music and nothing like the new country music. But in the last few years, most of it has gotten swept together under the heading of Americana, a label that is broad and blurry enough to welcome everyone who isn't getting played on mainstream radio. Jed Hilly, the new executive director of the Americana Music Association, says the music honors, and is derived from, the traditions of American roots music. That, he tells me, encompasses everyone from Gram Parsons and the Band to Lucinda Williams and Lyle Lovett. People who you would think are the very cornerstones of country music—Willie Nelson and Johnny Cash—are now called Americana, and in that case Americana is what we'd loved all along. Of course it's also what Nashville has made for decades, and it's the reason this city keeps drawing in talented folks from the fringes of the radio dial.

Jeff Burke and Vida Wakeman of the Jeff and Vida band came here from New Orleans to try and make it big, and even if that hasn't happened yet (and it should happen soon), Nashville is working out fine for them. In a city that values its rhinestones, they are managing to make music that is real and true, the thing itself as opposed to a parody of the thing. Theirs are the songs you long to hear late at night on the interstate, in pool halls and smoky whiskey bars. Jeff and Vida like to play at the 12 South Taproom and Norm's River Road House, the kind of bars that sound like they could be names of their songs.

Ketch Secor, who plays in the band Old Crow Medicine Show, has moved back to Nashville after a few years away. When I talk to him, he's sitting in his backyard in East Nashville listening to Woody Guthrie. He says he's glad to be back. If it was up to him, he thinks his music should be called country and country music should be called Americana. "I think the small and belittling label should be given to country music," he says. That, of course, is a genius solution. The word Americana seems to fit Carrie Underwood (Americana Idol?), whereas country would be a better fit for Old Crow, which is doing something that has all the raw energy and seeming spontaneity of the Smokey Mountain Boys but with the archness of the Rolling Stones singing "Far Away Eyes."

It feels like the music that happens when talented country folk get together, as opposed to the music that happens when talented producers hire pretty girls. When I ask him where he likes to play, Ketch points out that the Grand Ole Opry House, the bastion of that other country music, "has one of the best-sounding stages I've ever been on." It surprises me that it would be his kind of place, but when I mention it to Gillian Welch, she concurs. "That stage loves Ketch's harmonica," she says.

Every stage loves Gillian Welch and David Rawlings, from the bluegrass heaven of the Station Inn to the brand-new Schermerhorn Symphony Center. Gillian and David are the universal donors; no matter what genre of music you like or don't like, you'll love what they're doing. Gillian was the person who was able to explain to me why Nashville came to be Music City, USA, something I should have known, seeing as how I've been here most of my life. It turns out it was all a matter of geography.

"It's amazing where you can get to in a car in 12 hours," she said. "Hank Williams knew this. You can go out, play your gigs, and still get to the Opry. Of course that's not why I came. I had this really romantic notion of the music that was being made here. Little did I know I'd be arriving 30 years too late."

Even so, I give Gillian the most credit for turning back the clock, or taking it way ahead, depending on how you look at it. And whether she's really too late or positively cutting-edge all depends on how you're listening on any given night. After all, the best of Nashville is so out-of-date it's new again.

Author's note: Funny how times change. All across Nashville, sprawling expanses of new condos have sprung up like mushrooms after a rain. There are no $38,000 houses anymore but there are still plenty of dreams. Some of these people I wrote about here went onto great careers, others vanished, and most have held remarkably steady. The new kids became the old guard overnight. When I read this now the thing I regret is taking such a needless swipe at Carrie Underwood. She never needed my love but she certainly has it now. I have joined her legions of fans. That's the nice thing about having something reprinted. It gives me the chance to say I'm sorry.

Miracles and Ice

J. R. LIND, 2019

THE UNUSUAL TORNADO THAT ravaged Nashville on April 16, 1998—
mere days after a local television meteorologist explained how unlikely
it was that a twister would form and sustain itself in an urban area—
tumbled three construction cranes and destroyed four trailers at what
was then known as the East Bank Stadium site.

It had been nearly a year since ground breaking, and opening day was
still 18 months away. But among the many worries Nashville faced in the
days after the storm was whether the stadium would stay on schedule.

Nashville had been waiting for years for big-time professional sports.
Minor league baseball had been part of the city since Reconstruction. A
handful of minor league hockey teams had played at Municipal Auditorium since the 1960s. The Arena Football League's Nashville Kats began
play at the new Nashville Area in 1996. Of course, Nashville's myriad
colleges had big followings.

But Metro Nashville Mayor Phil Bredesen wanted to be a big-league
city, and that meant big-league sports.

He took a chance first with indoor sports, shepherding through
approvals for a new downtown arena. In the mid-1990s, the conventional wisdom was that sports facilities should sit far from city centers,

surrounded by parking lots and interstate exits. According to this line of thinking, amenities—restaurants, hotels, and the like—would come to arenas and stadiums.

Bredesen, though, had another idea: What if the arena was smack in the middle of an entertainment district that already existed? Nashville's Lower Broadway wasn't exactly the shimmering made-for-TV Neon Canyon it is now. There were, though, venerable honky-tonks and an under-renovation Ryman Auditorium. Sure, the massage parlors and adult bookstores and strip clubs were there, and those who worked downtown made sure to clear out shortly after sundown. But the bones were there. The arena, in Bredesen's thinking, would be the jumpstart.

It opened its doors in 1996, and by that time Bredesen had already tried to woo numerous teams as prime tenant.

The mid-'90s were a time of raucous reshuffling in professional sports. The National Hockey League saw two Canadian franchises—the Winnipeg Jets and Quebec Nordiques—move south of the border to Phoenix and Denver, respectively. The Minnesota North Stars dropped the adjective and became the Dallas Stars.

In 1995, even as the team was on a run to a Stanley Cup, rumors plagued the New Jersey Devils that they'd be the latest hockey team to pack up the moving truck. The rumors were so persistent and seemingly so credible that sportswriters asked various Devils stars how they felt about country music during locker room interviews just minutes after they'd won the Cup. In Nashville, local media ran stories about whether "Devils" was an appropriate name for a team based in the Buckle of the Bible Belt (and that would play its home games just yards from a Baptist church).

The Devils deal fizzled, but Bredesen stayed after it. Pro basketball was seemingly a better fit for the Music City anyway, so flirtations were made in efforts to bring in the Sacramento Kings or the Minnesota Timberwolves. Nothing came of those plans either.

Bigger than basketball and hockey, though, would be scoring an NFL franchise. While not yet the cultural behemoth it is today, pro football was muscling up, bolstered by TV deals that put every game on television and a 16-week schedule that was far more easily digestible than the 82-game seasons of basketball and hockey.

Luckily for Nashville, eccentric oil man K. S. "Bud" Adams was foundering in his efforts to get a new stadium deal in Houston for the Oilers and said, in no uncertain terms, he'd move the team elsewhere if he didn't get one. The city of Houston called his bluff and found out Adams wasn't joking. After the 1995 season, he said the team would move to Nashville in 1996, pending approval of a stadium deal. He got his wish in May 1996 when voters overwhelmingly approved a $144 million plan, the funds raised on the back of an increase in water tax and a property tax increase. The state kicked in some money on the condition the team be geographically denoted as "Tennessee," rather than Nashville, something Adams had already planned to do.

While the Nashville stadium was under construction, the Oilers played in Memphis, pleasing no one. Memphis had tried and failed numerous times to secure an NFL team, and Memphians certainly weren't inclined to support a team that'd soon be off to old rival Nashville. On the other side of I-40, Nashvillians didn't feel the need to drive three hours every week to see a team that would be in town soon enough anyway. After just one season, the Oilers moved to Nashville to play out the string at Vanderbilt Stadium.

The twister's interference with construction prompted a brief wave of support for the idea that the renamed Oilers should honor the event by naming themselves the Tennessee Tornadoes or Twisters or the like, but Adams liked "Titans," a nod to Nashville's reputation as "Athens of the South." The franchise's marketing arm claimed—and continues to do so in various ways—that the Titans were greater even than the gods. That's fudging things a bit—the Titans lost their war to Zeus and his Olympians—but no one, even those forced to endure Edith Hamilton in junior high, minded the mythological exaggeration much.

Meanwhile, the $20 million bounty Nashville offered to NHL franchises to move to town never bore fruit, but it did put the city on the league's radar. Commissioner Gary Bettman often noted the Music City would be a top candidate in the next round of expansion and, sure enough, a group led by Wisconsin businessman Craig Leipold was awarded a franchise in a round that also brought new teams to Atlanta, the Twin Cities, and Columbus, Ohio. Taking its inspiration from a saber-tooth cat skull found during the construction of a downtown skyscraper in 1971, the team would be called the Predators and begin play in the 1998–99 season, a full year before the Titans would kick off across the river.

Both teams embraced the sudden youthful exuberance the city itself had developed. The Titans would be coached by Jeff Fisher, who had been the Oilers head coach since 1994, taking the reins at the age of 36. The Predators signed Barry Trotz, then just 35, as the team's first coach.

The Titans moved to town seemingly on the verge of greatness. Quarterback Steve McNair and former Heisman Trophy–winning running back Eddie George paced the offense, which had high hopes for a young receiving corps as well. (The Titans would continue to have high hopes for their young receiving corps for the next two decades.) The team boasted a stout defense to go along with their grinding offense, and had played .500 football in the three seasons before they stepped on the field at the stadium—originally dubbed Adelphia Coliseum, starting an unfortunate Nashville tradition of selling naming rights to doomed companies.

The Predators were a mix of young and old, castoffs and has-beens, fairly standard stuff for expansion teams. But goalie Mike Dunham, who was named to Team USA's Olympic squad in 1994 and 2002, always kept things close. And while they were never truly in contention for a playoff spot, the Predators were a respectable 28-47-7, avoiding the cellar of the Western Conference.

Unfortunately, Nashville fans were a bit of a punching bag for the rest of the league. Not knowing what else to do, the crowd cheered for nearly everything, including relatively mundane offsides and icing calls and face-off wins. A couple of stalwart fans up in Section 303—dubbed "The Cellblock"—began the tradition of chanting and reminding various opponents of their . . . ineptitude . . . in decidedly PG-13 language. Hockey observers, particularly those from Canada, derided the antics as creating a "college atmosphere," but in a town steeped in college sports, what was meant to be an insult turned into an inspiration. Eventually, the fuddy-duddies took notice: Opposing players started talking about how loud the Predators crowds were, and more than one opposing goaltender became visibly crestfallen at the reminder that a goal was "all your fault." "College atmosphere" turned from castigation into calling card.

Across the river, the home atmosphere for football was intimidating, too. In their inaugural season, the Titans were undefeated at home and finished the year 13-3, the best record in team history and rewarding the long-waiting Nashville fans with a home playoff berth.

And that's when miracles happened.

In that first playoff game, the Titans found themselves down 16–15 to the Buffalo Bills with 16 seconds left. Bills kicker Steve Christie launched a high pooch that fell into the hands of—inexplicably—fullback Lorenzo Neal, certainly not the Titans' first option for returns. Neal handed the ball off to tight end Frank Wycheck, who coaches had seen throwing during practice and thus added various gadget plays that involved him passing to the playbook. Wycheck ran a few steps to his right before pirouetting and throwing a reasonable facsimile of a spiral to wide receiver Kevin Dyson. Dyson, it should be noted, learned how to run the play during the TV timeout before the kickoff. But he caught the ball—just barely a lateral as everyone outside upstate New York agrees—and had nothing but open field in front of him. He raced 75 yards while then radio color commentator Pat Ryan told his broadcast partner Mike Keith repeatedly: "He's got something. He's got something." On that gray January day, a crescendo rose from the crowd; footage shows various people leaping in the air on the sidelines, including an unknown Tennessee Highway Patrol officer, pumping his fist joyously as Dyson scored the winning touchdown.

"There are no flags on the field," Keith screamed on the radio.

"It's a miracle!"

And it was, and it is, the Music City Miracle. Seemingly touched by angels, the Titans defeated the Indianapolis Colts in the next round and rival Jacksonville in the AFC championship, punching their ticket to the Super Bowl in Atlanta against the St. Louis Rams.

This time, Dyson was out of miracles. Catching a pass from McNair, he was tackled One Yard Short of a Super Bowl title as time expired.

Disappointed, sure, but Nashville didn't let the sadness consume it for too long, throwing a raucous parade downtown two days later. It was a sports scene unmatched in Nashville, until the Predators decided to one-up their big brothers across the river more than a decade later.

While the Titans thrived early on, the Predators struggled, not making the playoffs until their fifth season and not winning a postseason series at all until 2011. Worse than that, the team was plagued by relocation rumors almost from the moment the franchise came to town. (In fact, there was talk that Leipold would take his expansion franchise to Edmonton and the Edmonton Oilers would move to Nashville; all this before the team had any players.) Leipold finally had enough after the lockout cancelled the 2004–05 NHL season and put the team up for sale before the 2007 season.

BlackBerry impresario Jim Balsillie made no secret of his desire to own an NHL team in his hometown of Hamilton, Ontario. So confident was he that he'd own the Predators, he began selling season tickets. Predators fans, predictably, revolted, holding a Save Our Team rally at the arena that resulted in the iconic photo of Bredesen's wife, die-hard Preds fan Andrea Conte, holding a sign handed to her by a fellow fan that read "Get Your Damn Hands Off My Team." A group of low-key local businessmen came together, scraped up enough capital and kept the team in Nashville, though the rumors of a relocation still hounded the team as it struggled to meet the attendance benchmarks in its lease with the city.

But something changed for the Predators in the summer of 2010, when the ownership group hired Jeff Cogen, a former circus executive who had worked for the Dallas Stars, and Sean Henry, formerly of the Tampa Bay Lightning, as CEO and COO, respectively. Instantly, the attitude changed. Cogen all but prohibited the team's employees from even suggesting the Predators would move if this or that benchmark wasn't met. Coincidentally, the team's play improved as well. And bolstered by more than a few freebies and steep discounts, attendance at the arena got better, a phenomena buoyed by the fact the first generation of Nashvillians who grew up only knowing the town as a big-league city were now old enough to buy tickets themselves. A series of ho-hum seasons by the Titans, who suddenly looked aimless, led people to look back at the Preds as a viable sports option. The team inked a naming rights deal with Nashville-based Bridgestone, which just so happened to be one of the NHL's major sponsors.

A couple of disappointing seasons on the ice, though, cost Trotz his job in 2014. He was replaced by Peter Laviolette, known for an up-tempo style that thrilled fans.

In 2016, the Predators were finally able to one-up the Titans, hosting the NHL's All-Star game. The event became a citywide party with concerts outside the arena and beer flowing freely at Lower Broad's honky-tonks, now revitalized in large part because of the guaranteed crowds at the arena. It was lauded as the best All-Star weekend in league history by those same blustery Canadian media types who had derided Nashville a decade earlier, some asking how feasible it would be to hold the event in Nashville annually.

"How can they follow this up?" they asked.

And they found out one year later when the Predators, the conference's eighth seed, swept the hated Chicago Blackhawks in the first round of the playoffs, vanquished the tough St. Louis Blues in the second, won a Western Conference title by knocking out the Anaheim Ducks, and brought the Stanley Cup Final to Nashville. If the All-Star game the winter previous was a showcase for what Nashville had become, the Cup Final was an extravaganza, bolstered by the fact that the first weekend of home games for the Predators coincided with the CMA Fest.

Hundreds of thousands of people poured downtown, cramming Lower Broad to watch the game on big screens, sometimes cheering so loudly they could be heard inside Bridgestone Arena, where the once-chilly relationship between the Preds and Titans thawed as the NFL team's offensive linemen became the Preds' chief cheerleaders, shirtlessly pounding beers and heaving gargantuan catfish. Because in Nashville there's always a side hustle, knockoff T-shirts were being sold from stands outside the arena and even in places as far flung as White Bridge Road. The Preds, like the Titans nearly 20 years before, fell short of the ultimate prize, losing in six games to the Pittsburgh Penguins. But their once tenuous relationship with the city had been firmed up, with Predators gold now nearly as common a sight as two-tone Titans blue.

So how did the Titans answer? They drew the NFL draft to town in the summer of 2019, packing Broadway much as their on-ice pals had done three years earlier.

It's not all been sunshine and rainbows for the two teams that were the harbingers of It City Nashville, of course. But now they are as much a part of the fabric of the city as traffic complaints and songwriting baristas. Their fans have matured too. Years ago, it would be inconceivable for there to be naysaying of either franchise. *What if someone heard? What if they decided we didn't deserve the teams?* Now, criticism—loving criticism, but criticism nonetheless—is commonplace.

Sports can teach us all kinds of lessons, and the one the Titans and Preds could teach Nashville is that acknowledging a shortcoming and addressing it is part of true love. It's possible to believe growth has good aspects, but that it creates problems that need addressing, just as it's possible to say a hockey team is good but needs a much improved power play. A Nashvillian should be able to say our schools are improving but have a long way to go just as easily as they now say the Titans' passing game is better than it once was but could be better.

Some goals—a competent receiving corps, for example, or a functional transit system—are attainable and laudable, and talking about them doesn't mean you love the team or the city any less.

Burned Out

ZACH STAFFORD, 2017

THE FIRST TIME I went to Prince's Hot Chicken Shack, I was 12 years old, and I didn't even eat the chicken. My dad, though, ordered his "hot"—one of six heat levels spicy enough to force beads of sweat from one's brow onto the table, one soft drop at a time. While he ate, he remarked that the heat radiating from the plate didn't just linger in the air or settle on your lips, it sat with you for days afterward. As the old ceiling fans helicoptered above, I sat silently in the pew-like booth, flirting with some fries that had absorbed a whisper of heat from sharing the same cast-iron skillet as the chicken, but never mustering the courage to take a bite.

My dad, undeterred, took me and my sister back again and again over the years. Eventually, we learned to sweat together, and I saw that the world was much bigger than home: Prince's was a visit to "the other side of the tracks," 30 minutes from the mostly white suburb where I grew up. My hometown, just north of Nashville, was the kind of place where the most thrilling food was a cheese-smothered appetizer at O'Charley's

"Burned Out" by Zach Stafford, from *Eater*, first published September 21, 2017. Reprinted with permission of Vox Media, Inc.

and where, when I'd try to explain hot chicken to friends at school, they would ask with a bewildered look if I meant buffalo chicken. Looking back, I realize now that Prince's was one of the few places we'd go and see people who looked like us.

Not too long ago, I was sitting in a restaurant in Chicago that serves hot takes on Southern food; one of those places where whiskey signs blanket the walls and everyone drinks craft microbrews from artisanally hand-blown mason jars. On the menu, next to spare ribs that had allegedly been "slow cooked for days" and cornbread that was probably too dry, was hot chicken. The menu described it as "Nashville hot!" and warned the eater to beware the fire. (I can report that the eater need not worry.) I looked around—surveying the Southern-inspired cocktails gliding across the dining room toward tables of people who'd probably never crossed the proverbial train tracks for chicken—and I wondered: How did hot chicken, a dish that, 10 years ago, was barely known even just a few miles outside of Nashville, get here?

THERE IS A BIT of hot chicken everywhere right now: KFC's Nashville Hot Chicken is a "spicy bird with a savory burn," while Shake Shack has declared "it's getting hot in here" with its Hot Chik'n sandwich, both available nationwide; Chicago and Los Angeles are positively obsessed, with numerous temples to the dish; and if a hot chicken shack hasn't been announced in your city yet, just wait.

Yet nowhere has hot chicken become so conspicuously ubiquitous in recent years than in Nashville, where food has begun to rival country music as the city's premier cultural icon. More than a dozen dedicated restaurants have opened over the last several years, from Pepperfire Hot Chicken to Hattie B's, which, despite an additional location in Birmingham and another on the way in Atlanta, remains *the spot* for any tourist rushing to grab the requisite Nashville 'gram. Some of these hot chicken shacks even have valet parking. A popular local brewery, Tailgate Beer, has created a Hot Chicken IPA; ramen shop Otaku South serves a hot chicken bao; the renowned Indian restaurant Chauhan serves it with ghost pepper sauce; and that's to say nothing of the stream of restaurants slated to open in the next year plotting their own spins on hot chicken. As Danny Chau wrote in the *Ringer* last year, paraphrasing Anthony Bourdain, surveying the hot chicken scene in Nashville is now a multi-day commitment. (Prince's Hot Chicken is on *Eater*'s list of essential Southern restaurants and its National 38 list.)

Maybe the best way to describe what is happening is "hotchicken-frication," a term coined by Timothy Charles Davis in *The Hot Chicken Cookbook*. The word hasn't gained much traction yet—too many syllables, maybe—but eating around town, there's an overwhelming sense of a deliberate effort to give the dish center stage in a Disneyfied version of Nashville. In the process, hot chicken's actual history, its particular origins in a distinct community, has been diluted, transforming it into a pale echo of what it was—a spicy but soulless joyride.

What you might call "hashtag hot chicken" is the kind served at Party Fowl, a restaurant that once provided the official hot chicken of the Tennessee Titans football team. Last summer, over plates of its signature hot chicken with bourbon-glazed beignets—a play on chicken and waffles—and hot chicken lollipops, Bart Pickens, the executive chef, who moved to Nashville from New Orleans in 2006, explained the broad appeal of his menu. "You can take our menu to Chicago; it's got enough reflection," he told me, referring to Party Fowl's wide variety of hot chicken dishes, from poutine to Cuban sandwiches. "If I've got to make a Giordano's deep-dish hot chicken pizza, I can go there." (He has gone there; I've seen the pictures.)

While longtime hot chicken aficionados may cringe, Pickens sees the trend as a natural evolution of local tradition. "Food is up for interpretation," he said. "My philosophy has always been, you have to know the original to go forward with it."

Pickens's views echo those of many of the Nashville chefs I spoke to over the last year. They believe hot chicken is a larger-than-life dish that is fair game for their own interpretations, so they are capitalizing off the trend with a clear conscience despite the dish's singular creation, rooted in a specific time and place in the city. But the history these chefs and new hot chicken dishes refer to is a tall tale, one they often don't even fully understand. "There's nothing worse than a scorned woman," Pickens said, looking over the vast tableau of hot chicken iterations on the table between us. "How does that story go?"

BY NOW, MORE PEOPLE than not have probably heard the origin story of hot chicken. But it is so good that it bears repeating: It begins with Thornton Prince, who, according to his family and the one photograph I've seen of him, was very handsome. Back in the 1930s, he was known to spend his evenings enjoying alcohol and flirting with women, even though he had a "steady girl" at home (a character who always remains nameless when the story is told).

One morning, Prince stumbled into the house after a long night out and went to sleep. Though his lover had long resigned herself to his late arrivals, according to his great-niece, André Prince Jeffries, who now owns the restaurant and goes by Ms. André, something changed that morning—maybe the hint of perfume on his shirt was too strong or there was a smudge of lipstick on his collar. Either way, Prince's lover sought vengeance.

Prince's favorite food was fried chicken, and his lover knew that, making it the perfect vehicle for her pain. While he was sleeping, she went out to the garden behind the house and grabbed a bunch of cayenne peppers she'd grown, then started frying some chicken. As the chicken cooked, she created an unbearably hot spice mix with the cayenne. When the chicken came out of the skillet, still sizzling, she tossed an enormous amount of seasoning all over the bird, thinking it would be agonizingly inedible. Prince awoke and stumbled into the kitchen, almost tripping over the aroma. He took a seat at the kitchen table in front of the pile of chicken; his lover watched, anticipating the first bite of revenge. Her plan was thwarted immediately: Prince loved the chicken so much he wanted more.

The unnamed woman, the mystery mother of hot chicken, left Prince shortly afterward, and his family never saw her again. But he became desperate to replicate the recipe, endlessly experimenting with spices until he was finally able to recreate it. He soon became a hot chicken evangelist and opened his own shack to serve it to the public. According to legend, for decades, he was the only person cooking hot chicken.

Speaking with the Prince family, no one could say how much of the legend is true, though most will readily admit that not every detail is factually accurate. Few other records exist, which has only made this story more essential to the Prince's brand over the years. Despite the story's many variations and exaggerations, one detail remains indisputably and undeniably true: Hot chicken started in the Prince family.

Around 1945, a few years after hot chicken was supposedly created, Prince opened Prince's BBQ Chicken Shack on Jefferson Street and 28th Avenue, in the then predominantly black neighborhood Hadley Park. Despite the restaurant's name, it didn't serve barbecue, just hot chicken. It was only open in the evenings, after Prince finished his day job, and on Friday and Saturday nights it was open until 4 a.m. The late-night hangout quickly became a neighborhood institution for anyone with a taste for heat. After a few years, Prince moved the restaurant downtown to an area known as Hell's Half Acre (named for gunfights that occurred in the 1800s), only blocks away from the Ryman Auditorium, a legendary concert hall that was home to the Grand Ole Opry.

Over time, the clientele expanded, and Prince's became especially popular amongst the country music singers who frequented the Ryman, exposing it to a new audience: white people. Word spread, and as white audiences left country shows on Friday and Saturday nights, they wanted to try the underground restaurant they'd heard about, which was also one of the few late-night eateries in the area. "It was a secret in Nashville," Ms. André told me. "They came in through the backdoor and had their own place." Throwing back her dark, feathered hair and sipping on a soda, she laughed as she described the space, a "room with no windows," that she visited a handful of times as a child.

Ms. André's smile grew wider as she recounted the story: At Prince's, black people ate in the front while white people ate in the back, a radical inversion of Nashville's Jim Crow laws at the time. It's no wonder that hot chicken remained an underground dish, exclusive to Nashville's black community for decades: White people in Tennessee didn't want to be seen eating it in public.

After Thornton Prince died in the 1970s, the shack was run by different members of the Prince family before it wound up in the hands of Ms. André in the early 1980s. A government worker who'd recently gone through a divorce, she never considered running the restaurant until her mother—Prince's niece—urged her to take over the shack. For the last 30 years, she has spent nearly every day at Prince's, except for Sundays, when it's closed.

In 1988, Ms. André moved Prince's to its current location on Ewing Drive in Nashville's north side, the heart of the city's black community at the time. She also dropped "BBQ" from the name. A few years later, she started tweaking the offerings. At first, she left the legendary chicken untouched, simply adding french fries and dessert to Prince's bare-bones menu. But then she had a revelation and decided to expand Prince's palette from a single note (the current "medium" heat level, also called "original hot") to six levels of fire, the two spiciest of which she won't even eat.

For the next 20 years, Prince's flourished. There were few imitators and no real competition except for Columbo's, a hot chicken shack opened in the late '70s by Bolton Polk, a former Prince's cook, miles away in downtown Nashville. Things were relatively quiet, and the heat was under control in Ms. André's kitchen—until it wasn't.

THE CREATION MYTH OF hot chicken as Nashville's culinary staple isn't as well known as the origin story, but it's getting there (Rachel L. Martin's version in the *Bitter Southerner* is a particularly complete one). That overwhelming sense of a deliberate plan to make the dish a city icon? It's not a conspiracy theory; it's true.

In the late-1990s, Nashville began construction on a new football stadium meant to lure an NFL team to the city. Columbo's, the only hot chicken shack in downtown Nashville, was razed to make room for the Adelphia Coliseum (now the Nissan Stadium), which opened in 1999 as the home of the Tennessee Titans and the Tennessee State Tigers. Bill Purcell, a state congressman and lawyer who worked nearby, ate at Columbo's nearly every week before it was leveled, having fallen deeply, madly in love with hot chicken. (The Polk family has since opened Bolton's Spicy Chicken and Fish down the street from the original shack.) One day, after Columbo's demise, Purcell's unsatisfied cravings got the best of him, and he found himself driving miles from downtown to eat at a place he had heard about but never experienced: Prince's Hot Chicken Shack.

To his incredible delight, Prince's chicken was even better than Columbo's. The flavors were more complex, the heat more agreeable, and the chicken much juicier. The chicken at Prince's was and is the best he's ever had, something he continues to tell anyone who will listen as hot chicken begins to sprout all over the city. Sitting with him in the same booth I'd sat in as a child, on a Friday afternoon last year, I could see the love spread across his face as he recounted the tale in between nibbles on a leg (original hot) and sips of a soda.

One of the first things Purcell did to show his dedication to Prince's was ensure that the shack remained within his district. "I was involved in gerrymandering," Purcell told me with a smile. "I did insist, if at all possible, that in the new maps Prince's Hot Chicken would be in my district." He went on to clarify that the gesture was harmless, because the area was commercial and he didn't garner any additional votes in the process. "It just made me happy knowing that I represented Prince's Hot Chicken," he said. Represent it he did: On the day he retired from the Tennessee House of Representatives, in 1996, he put through a resolution declaring Prince's Hot Chicken Shack the best restaurant in Tennessee—a surprise to the Prince family, as well as the many people in the state who had never heard of it.

After a short stint at Vanderbilt, Purcell became the mayor of Nashville in 1999. He maintained his "fanboy" status with regular visits while in office (Prince's set aside an official seat so he didn't have to wait in line). In 2007, as his second term was coming to a close and the city's 200th birthday approached, he had a realization: Nashville's only "indigenous food," to his knowledge, was hot chicken. "There was no better or more appropriate thought than to have a hot chicken festival," Purcell said.

The festival was meant to introduce locals to a dish that had been under their noses for years and to establish hot chicken as *the* food of Nashville. As Purcell began planning, Ms. André agreed to anchor the event. Though Prince's had never even put out advertising, the offer to reach thousands of new customers seemed too good to pass up. "Most of Nashville at the time hadn't eaten it before or had access or found themselves here," Purcell said.

On July 4, 2007, the inaugural hot chicken festival took place in East Nashville, not too far from Prince's original shack in Hadley Park. Prince's, as well as a couple of vendors who had emerged over the years, served their takes on hot chicken amid live music. "We had half as many vendors as we do now, but thousands of Nashvillians appeared," Purcell said as he took a swig of his diet soda. "We gave out free samples. People came early, people stayed late. They had a good time." For Prince's, the plan worked as billed: After endless lines at the festival, the restaurant saw an influx of new customers who had never experienced hot chicken before.

The festival was so successful that Purcell decided to keep it going after the bicentennial. Since leaving office, he has spearheaded the event, helping it grow into one of Nashville's largest annual festivals. In recent years, the hot chicken competition has become a proving ground for chefs looking to make their own mark on hot chicken. Winning is an instant stamp of approval from the hot chickenerati, a virtual guarantee that a recipe can stand on its own. Both Hattie B's and Party Fowl credit the competition as the crucible in which their own, now-famous versions of hot chicken were forged. In this creation myth, the festival has become the birthplace of hot chicken, the Nashville icon and viral phenomenon, for better or for worse.

LAST YEAR, WHICH *FOOD Republic* dubbed "the year of hot chicken," the publication made another, more remarkable declaration: that John Lasater, the executive chef of Hattie B's, was "the man who launched the Nashville hot chicken craze." Immediate backlash tore through Nashville's tightly knit hot chicken community. "If, at this point, you're still writing articles where black people have been doing shit for years, going mostly unnoticed by white people, and it's only when the white people come in and decide to monetize it that you declare it cool," Betsy Phillips wrote in *Nashville Scene*, the local alt-weekly paper, "then you are the problem with America."

Many others rallied behind that sentiment. The articles bounced from private Facebook group to private Facebook group, where the debate seemed unending. Follow-up essays were written by other food experts to provide context. Hot chicken had transformed from a food consumed on the other side of the tracks to an emblem of a major city. As intrigue blossomed around the politics of hot chicken, it was clear how divisive the dish had become.

Hattie B's stayed silent in the face of the controversy, which eventually passed by. "You have to wait in line," a young white woman who recently moved to Nashville from Mississippi told me outside of its midtown location, not long after the blow up last year. "It's like Disney World, but not as expensive and just as hot." She and two friends had been waiting for 30 minutes and weren't even halfway through the parking lot.

When I initially reached out to Hattie B's to chat with either Lasater or the Bishop family, who owns the restaurant, they seemed cautious. There was some back-and-forth on what exactly I'd ask and why, and a spokesperson eventually confirmed an in-person interview with a member of the Bishop family. But as the day drew closer, she asked if we could conduct the interview over email. After I sent my questions, some of which addressed the controversy, the spokesperson stopped responding to my emails.

AROUND THE TIME OF the Hattie B's controversy, Prince's opened a second location, called Prince's Hot Chicken South, as well as a food truck. (Hotville Chicken, the acclaimed Los Angeles pop-up launched by Ms. André's niece, has no affiliation with Prince's beyond familial relation.) Ms. André was initially against opening a new location, but as she watched the dish her family created sweep the country, making corporations and other people rich, she became convinced that expansion was the only way to fight for the Prince's legacy.

When I spoke to Ms. André last fall, it was clear that she was nervous about the new venture. "It's so personal," she told me as she looked around the busy restaurant. "If you franchise something like this, you miss all of that intimacy." Still, she finds herself flirting with the idea of creating a Prince's franchise, which is the brainchild of Mario Hambrick, a businessman who has worked for Ms. André for so long that she calls him "son."

Hambrick, a local entrepreneur with a handful of businesses, including Free at Last Bail Bonding, is the primary investor in the new restaurants, having acquired the food truck and negotiated the deal for the new space. Ms. André hopes that her grandchildren will take an interest in the family business when they're older, like her daughter has in recent years, but it's clear that Hambrick is vying to be next in line—and that he has a clear vision for the future of Prince's.

"I could remember when we first started allowing other hot chicken restaurants," Hambrick told me, recounting the first years of the city's hot chicken festival and the booths that have since become perpetually packed restaurants all over the city. "They passed out fliers—they had 10 people in their line and we had 500. They would then invite people to their tent," he said, explaining how other vendors used the lines at Prince's to attract people to their tents, which had shorter waits.

As Hambrick talked, his resentment toward everyone who has capitalized on the Prince's legacy, especially from outside of the community, became palpable. Unlike Ms. André, who maintains a regal confidence in Prince's reputation as first and best, he is aggrieved. "Everybody wants to take the torch and run with it," he said. There is, for instance, no small amount of irony in the ad campaign for KFC's hot chicken, in which the dish is portrayed in the same manner as rock and roll in the 1960s—rock and roll being a cultural touchstone that was pilfered from black creators and then whitewashed so that it could be sold to white America.

So, it's here, miles from downtown, that Prince's has started its fight for the future of hot chicken. Prince's South is a model for how Ms. André and Hambrick could franchise the brand as hot chicken goes global—even if it means more work for Ms. André, who had begun toying with the idea of retirement. "Sometimes I think about what it'd be like to be on vacation every day for the rest of my life," she said, referring to the fact that she wouldn't need to work if she just sold it all. "But then I know I'd get bored after a while, and I stop thinking about it."

Prince's South is quite different from the original: A mural of Thornton Prince on the back wall, based on previous signage at the original, is the only real similarity between the two. Large televisions cover the walls, while a full bar—a first for Prince's—juts out near the cash register. The tables, missing the signature picnic tablecloth, have a shiny wood finish. It looks a lot like the inside of a Buffalo Wild Wings.

I brought my dad to get his opinion of the dish he introduced to me more than 15 years ago. We ordered medium, the original spice level. Less than 10 minutes after our order was placed, the food arrived, which made my dad perk up immediately—it's widely quipped that the longer you wait for hot chicken, the better it is, because you know it hasn't been sitting under heat lamps all day. As we dug into the chicken thighs, our hands took on that familiar fiery red tint. We stopped talking for a moment to take a bite. I looked to my dad as he stared down at the chicken. Without taking a breath or looking up, he said, "It's just not the same."

Editor's note: In December 2018, a car crashed into the commercial strip on Ewing Drive that was home to the original Prince's Hot Chicken Shack, setting off a fire that eventually reached and damaged the restaurant. In July 2019, after waiting for months for the building's landlord to make repairs, André Prince Jeffries announced the Ewing Drive location would not re-open, and that she would seek out another space somewhere in North Nashville.

An Open Letter

BEN FOLDS, 2014

DEAR NASHVILLE,

Last week, on the day that would have been Chet Atkins' 90th birthday (June 20, 1924), my office received news that the historic RCA Building on Music Row is likely to be sold. This building, with the historic Studio A as its centerpiece, was Atkins' and Owen Bradley's vision and baby, and had become home to the largest classic recording space in Nashville. Word is that the prospective buyer is a Brentwood, TN-based commercial development company called Bravo Development owned and operated by Tim Reynolds. We don't know what this will mean to the future of the building.

First off, kudos to the estates and descendants of Atkins and Bradley for doing their best to keep the building alive. They've owned the property all these years and could have at any point closed it up or mowed it down. Sadly, it's what happens in the name of progress.

Studio A, which turns 50 years old next year, has a rich history. Here are just some of the artists and groups who have made hits here: Peter

Bradley Adams, Gary Allan, Brent Anderson, Anika, Arlis Albritton, Asleep at the Wheel, The Beach Boys, Ben Folds Five, Tony Bennett, Amy Black, Jason Blaine, Blind Boys of Alabama, Joe Bonamassa, Wade Bowen, Eden Brent, Jim Brickman, The Brothers Osborne, Rachel Bradshaw, Brentwood Benson, David Bullock, Laura Bell Bundy, Ken Burns, The Canadian Tenors, The City Harmonic, Steven Curtis Chapman, Chocolate Horse, Brandy Clark, Brent Cobb, Jesse Colter, Elizabeth Cook, Wayne Coyne, Margaret Cho, Billy Currington, Matt Dame, Danae, Ilse DeLange, Rebecca de la Torre, Steve Earle, ESPN, Jace Everett, The Fabulous Headliners, Dani Flowers, Danny Flowers, Colt Ford, The Frog Sessions, Eleanor Fye, Cami Gallardo, Billy Gibbons, Sarah Gibson, Vince Gill, Alyssa Graham, Peter Groenwald, Harlan Pepper, Harper Blynn, Connie Harrington, Hunter Hayes, John Hiatt, Faith Hill, JT Hodges, Adam Hood, James House, Sierra Hull, Alan Jackson, Joe Jackson, Casey James, Jenny Jarnigan, Jewel, Jamey Johnson, Josh Jones, Kristin Kelly, Kesha, Anna Krantz, Ben Kweller, Lady Antebellum, Miranda Lambert, Sonny Landreth, Samantha Landrum, Mark Lanigan, Stoney LaRue, Jim Lauderdale, Frank Liddell, LIfeway, Meagan Lindsey, Longmont All Stars Jazz Band, Lyle Lovette, Luella and the Sun, Tayla Lynn, Amanda Palmer, John Pardi, Rich Parkinson, Alan Parson, Charlie Pate, Kellie Pickler, Pistol Annies, Pretty Lights, Mike Posner, Sean McConnell, Scotty McCreery, Kate Miller Heidke, Ronnie Milsap, Miss Willie Brown, Danny Mitchell, Allison Moorer, Kacey Musgraves, Musiq Soulchild, David Nail, the Nashville Symphony, Jerrod Neimann, Willie Nelson, Joe Nichols, Sierra Noble, Natalie Noone, The Oakridge Boys, Jake Owen, Rainfall, Johnny Reid, Thomas Rhett, Lionel Richie, The Robertson Family, Henry Rollins, Shannon Sanders, Jader Santos, Alejando Sanz, Mondo Saez, Kate Schrock, Bob Seger, Sera B., Brian Setzer, Nikki Shannon, William Shatner, SHEDaisy, Jordyn Shellart, Joel Shewmake, Sleeping With Sirens, Jake Shimabukuro, Mike Shipp, Kevin Shirley, Anthony Smith, Joanna Smith, Dr. Ralph Stanley, Chelsea Staling, Steel Magnolia, Tate Stevens, Jay Stocker, Rayburn, RED, RockIt City, Jeff Taylor, Justin Towns Earle, Josh Thompson, Those Darlins, Josh Turner, Bonnie Tyler, Carrie Underwood, Keith Urban, Ben Utecht, Phil Vassar, Venus and the Moon, Andy Victor, Amanda Watkins, Chuck Wicks, Hank Williams Jr., Williamson County Youth Orchestra, Alicia Witt, Lee Ann Womack, Word Entertainment, and Charlie Worsham.

I had no idea of the extent of the legacy of this great studio until I became the tenant of the space 12 years ago. Most of us know about Studio

B. Studio A was its grander younger sibling, erected by Atkins when he became an RCA executive. The result was an orchestral room built to record strings for Elvis Presley and to entice international stars to record in one of these four Putnam-designed RCA spaces in the world. The other three RCA studios of the same dimensions—built in LA, Chicago, and New York—have long since been shut down. I can't tell you how many engineers, producers, and musicians have walked into this space to share their stories of the great classic recorded music made here that put Nashville on the map. I've heard tales of audio engineers who would roller skate around the room waiting for Elvis to show up at some point in the weeks he booked, stories about how Eddy Arnold recorded one of the first sessions in the room that included the song "Make The World Go Away," about Dolly Parton's recordings and mixes here ("Jolene," etc.), of The Monkees recording here, and so on. Legendary songwriter John D. Loudermilk and his bride were serenaded by a session orchestra hired by Atkins who were recording there for an artist. He recalled that they danced all the way to the loading doors and into their wedding limo, reminiscing about the beautiful floor tiles which still line the entire space. He co-wrote countless numbers of songs with Atkins and many others in this studio.

To this day, Studio A remains a viable, relevant, and vibrant space. In recent years these artists and filmmakers have recorded or worked here, to name a few: Sara Bareilles, William Shatner, Kacey Musgraves, Jewel, Brian Setzer, Ken Burns, Kesha, The Beach Boys, Wayne Cohen, Tony Bennett, Willie Nelson, Kellie Pickler, Hunter Hayes, Charlie Worsham, David Nail, Jamey Johnson, Joe Bonamassa, Word Music, Gary Allan, and me.

While we Nashvillians can feel proud about the overall economic progress and prosperity we're enjoying, we know it's not always so kind to historical spaces, or to the legacy and foundation upon which that prosperity was built.

My motivation for spending over a million dollars in rent and renovations over these past 12 years was simple. I could have built my own space of the same dimensions with that kind of investment. But I'm a musician with no interest in development or business in general. I only want to make music in this historic space, and allow others to do the same. I've recorded all over the world and I can say emphatically that there's no recording space like it anywhere on the planet. These studio walls were born to ring with music. I just wanted to keep it alive.

Before the news of the sale I had been in recent talks with other entities on how we could collaborate on allowing visitors to Music City to see the space firsthand and hear its rich history, while also making sure that it stays busy making music history of tomorrow. No one can say now what will become of that idea.

Selfishly I'd like to remain the tenant and caretaker of this amazing studio space. I love it. But if I must let it go in the interest of change, my only hope is that it remain intact and alive. A couple of years ago my co-manager, Sharon Corbitt House, promised the late, great producer Phil Ramone, while he was in town recording Tony Bennett and an orchestra LIVE in this space, that she would do what she could to keep the studio doors open. Ramone had watched the former New York RCA studio transform into office space for the IRS and couldn't bear to see the last of this incredible acoustic design fade away.

So here's where we're coming from. Historic RCA Studio A is too much a part of why such incredible business opportunities exist in 2014 in Nashville to simply disappear. Music City was built on the foundation of ideas, and of music. What will the Nashville of tomorrow look like if we continue to tear out the heart of the Music Row that made us who we are as a city? Ultimately, who will want to build new condos in an area that has no central community of ideas or creatives?

We are Music City—the only city in the world truly built on music.

My simple request is for Tim Reynolds or whoever the next owners might be of this property, before deciding what to do with this space, to take a moment to stand in silence between the grand walls of RCA Studio A and feel the history and the echoes of the Nashville that changed the world. I'd like to ask him and other developers to listen first hand to the stories from those among us who made the countless hit records in this studio—the artists, musicians, engineers, producers, writers who built this rich music legacy note by note, brick by brick.

I don't know what impact my words here will have on anything. But I felt the need to share, and to encourage others who also care about preserving our music heritage to speak up as well.

I believe that progress and heritage can co-exist in mutual respect. Maybe this time we can at least try to make the effort.

Yours,
Ben Folds

Editor's note: Harold Bradley, brother of the late Owen Bradley, fired back with an open letter of his own, in which he said many things, among them: "Music City isn't about making a perfect room, or hanging just the right baffling. Turns out, the architecture of Nashville's evolving sound is a synergy of creative energy. That's still here, and it has nothing to do with this building." In October 2014, a mystery buyer swooped in at the 11th hour to purchase Studio A from Bravo Development for $5.6 million. It was later revealed that the buyer was Leiper's Fork philanthropist and preservationist Aubrey Preston. Soon after, Preston announced he would be joined by health care executive Charles "Chuck" Elcan and record executive Mike Curb in ownership, operating under the name Studio A Preservation Partners, LLC. Ben Folds got to stay. In 2016, the Nashville Metro Council placed a moratorium on new developments on Music Row.

Demolition Derby

BOBBY ALLYN, 2013

JAMES DOBSON HAS LIVED in the same brick ranch house in Edgehill, a historically black neighborhood a stone's throw from Belmont University, since the Eisenhower administration. For five of those decades, the same man lived next door in the same modest home. "He was my neighbor and my paperboy," Dobson says, and together they sat in the shadow of a three-story condo constructed nearby.

But now Dobson has a new neighbor: a mound of rubble where the late owner's house once stood, and out front a lawn sign that reads, "We Will Buy Your Home."

That message has been broadcast to Dobson and scores of Nashville homeowners, who are seeing the value of lots far outpace that of the homes built on them decades ago. Ever since his neighbor's home was razed, developers have been hounding Dobson about giving up his own.

"They keep asking me how much I want for my home, and I always say, 'Nothing. I ain't moving,'" says Dobson, 97, who remains sharp and confident in his abilities. "I raised three kids here, and I want my last days to be my best days."

"Demolition Derby" by Bobby Allyn, first published in the *Nashville Scene* on December 19, 2013. Reprinted with permission of FW Publishing.

But as Dobson can attest, real estate investors and speculators are joining the gold rush for new living spaces and the rising value of dirt. In Nashville's hottest neighborhoods, come-ons from companies seeking to purchase are arriving faster than spam.

The correspondence can look official, blaring "notice" in all-caps. "Our company is now seeking to purchase several homes in your neighborhood..." reads a pitch recently taped to an East Nashville door. A Sylvan Park resident who asked not to be identified says he has received "about a dozen" mailers this year from developers looking to buy his property.

"There's such a surge of opportunity for builders to come into Nashville," says Jim Spangler of Hidden Valley Homes, which posted the sign next door to James Dobson. The company expanded into Nashville this summer from Brentwood, where it builds mostly high-end homes. "We're going to go where the demand is going to be. You're seeing a lot of it in Nashville." Asked how he thinks the city's landscape is evolving, Spangler replies, "I call it revitalization."

That's not the word opponents use.

A DEBATE IS CATCHING fire in neighborhoods across the city. On one side are residents who say the imposing new properties hoisted on the graves of former homes—many almost comically larger than what came before—are blighting communities. On the other side are developers, investors, and builders like Spangler, who spy opportunity.

Spangler is eyeing lots adjacent to Dobson's where other houses and apartments sit. His company has already leveled three other homes in the area. On all of them, he plans to build cottage-style condos. To show the amount of money at stake, each of those will run about $400,000—nearly triple the appraised value of Dobson's dwelling.

Call this another verse of the It City Blues: a booming metropolis outgrowing its capacity. According to a statistic often cited by city planners, the Nashville area is poised to add a million more residents in coming decades. The current and expected influx is bringing new business prospects and creative minds to Nashville, showering the city with national attention.

But that only makes longtime Nashvillians more worried about their town losing its unique qualities. Bursts of new activity from Charlotte Pike to Inglewood are reviving age-old debates about the tradeoff between preservation and development. How will we lure newcomers with our "big city with small-town charm" label, teardown opponents argue, when we're bulldozing older homes and replacing them with generic lot-busters?

"Once the ball gets rolling downhill, it can roll extremely quickly," says Vanderbilt urban sociology professor Richard Douglas Lloyd. "We're going to experience some unwelcome consequences: traffic, disruption of fabric of established communities and neighborhood identities, and all of us feeling like it's not easy to live here anymore.

"This is the new paradigm for urban renewal. In a city that's not as vertical as Manhattan, this level of growth can create a fractured and incoherent landscape."

Citizens may be divided over whether they think the next phase in Nashville's growth will be better than the last. On teardowns, however, they seem united—in opposition. Residents argue that teardowns are affecting the rhythm and flow of streets and altering the character of neighborhoods. To be sure, not every house deserves to be saved, and new construction often helps prop up property values (along with property taxes) while attracting new investment.

But every time a bulldozer revs into gear on a quiet residential street, the misgivings get louder. So far this year, developers have spent more than $3 million to tear down 549 residential properties. That's more than double the number of demolitions five years ago, according to records from Metro Codes. Home demos started to pick up around 2011 as the economy recovered and the city licked its wounds from the 2010 flood. They've risen steadily ever since.

"We have a tremendous demand for infill development, and that reflects the changing demographics," says Rick Bernhardt, director of the city's planning department. (In other words, that means more affluent people are moving to Nashville and want to live within the city.) "Neighborhoods are changing because land is becoming so valuable."

Detractors say public officials like Bernhardt are biased toward development. To them, this is a replay of the shortsighted planning that razed much of the city's historic downtown in favor of parking lots back in the last century. Advocates say adding properties translates into more tax dollars, which can lead to improved services.

In the middle, most residents see only the short-term growing pains. They wonder if the teardowns, and the boom they embody, will only make existing city ailments worse.

HAVING LIVED IN THE same small white house in Sylvan Park nearly her entire life, Cynthia Newlon has witnessed her share of change. Most of it, she says, has required little adjustment. Neighbors and businesses have come and gone. Gradual growth has been noticeable, but not disruptive.

Adapting to the latest changes has been much more difficult. The house next to hers was demolished recently. In its place stand two slender homes that dwarf her own.

For Newlon, the intrusive new buildings have cut into her quality of life.

"It makes me sick to look out my kitchen window and not be able to see the sky," says Newlon, a retired office administrator approaching 70. "They have a window facing my deck, so there's no more privacy there. And everybody just stares when they go down the street. It doesn't look right next to my little house."

Developers, who stand to gain the most, portray the teardown phenomenon as inevitable. As older homes fall into disrepair or fixing up older properties becomes too costly, they say, it makes more sense to start from scratch. They add that current buyer preferences skew toward new construction—a kind of insurance that there are no hidden quirks or dormant structural issues.

With demand soaring, therefore, and space up for grabs, many areas of the city are now targets for outside developers.

"You're seeing tons of teardowns in 12South, Belmont, Sylvan Park, and all over," says real estate agent Christie Wilson. "A lot of people have a sort of love-hate relationship with them. People want neighborhoods to keep their charm and cool character, but the land, many times, has become more valuable than the homes sitting on it. And for some buyers, a new small home in a cool neighborhood is far more affordable than a historic one."

What Newlon sees when she looks out her window represents the current hot trend with Nashville developers. It consists of two buildings attached like conjoined twins on one lot. Indeed, the units, often called "skinny duplexes," are connected by a shared space developers call an "umbilical cord."

The trend springs from a quirk in the city's code, which leaves the definition of a duplex rather ambiguous. In neighborhoods around the city's core, any builder can put two structures on a single residential lot as long as they are connected by an 8-foot umbilical cord. When buyers move in, the units are owned separately but the land is owned jointly.

"During the rewrite of the code some 15 years ago, the planning commission unintentionally left out that a duplex had to have a contiguous interior," says former Metro councilmember John Summers, who has done two stints on the city's planning commission. "Nobody caught it. A couple of years later, an interpretation said two-on-one is OK as long as they're connected."

In some areas, such as Green Hills, two-on-one lots can exist without the umbilical cord. Pro-development Metro councilmember Charlie Tygard is among those trying to sway city officials to get rid of the connector altogether. He says the structures it creates are eyesores.

"I don't know there's anybody that has the unique interpretation of a duplex that we have in Nashville," Bernhardt says. "And there are some problems with that." In some cases, he explains, the skinny duplexes are far taller than the homes that abut them, and thus they sometimes look out of place with surrounding neighborhoods.

One solution, he says, is for city planners to make the definition of a duplex clearer to regulate their proliferation, something Bernhardt and his colleagues have discussed. For developers, though, the code quirk often means a two-for-one profit margin. For that reason, there would be fierce resistance from real estate forces in the event of a proposed change—at least one that would limit one structure to each residential lot.

"The two-on-one trend is the wave of the future," says real estate investor Jeff Livingston. "It pencils"—i.e., pays—"for me to build two-on-one all day."

Such talk rankles residents in East Nashville's Eastwood section. On a Friday evening in October, a canary-yellow Victorian home was torn down. The home was nearly a century old; it was demolished in a matter of hours. The demolition struck a nerve with neighbors—especially photographer Gregg Roth, who owns the 1925 Craftsman next door. According to Roth, it was done so hastily that the process broke three side windows on his house and damaged his HVAC unit.

The windows have since been repaired. But Roth and other neighbors remain incredulous at how quickly the home came down. They're even more perplexed by what will soon rise from its rubble: a two-on-one duplex.

"We just thought that if it was that old, you can't just knock it down," Roth says. "It's going to look ridiculous. There's a reason we moved into these houses. This new thing can potentially ruin the reason why we moved here. It's so wrong for the neighborhood, and nobody wants it."

Other neighbors are just as irate. As in 12South, they feel they took a chance on a troubled neighborhood when no one else would, only to have outside developers swoop in to profit.

"The people did a lot of work to turn this neighborhood around, and we didn't do it so a developer can come in, tear down a home, and make

$200,000," says Dave Jacques, a musician and Eastwood neighbor. "These new duplexes are all over the city now. They're going to look like the brick duplexes of the past. They're going to eventually think: Why did they do that? Whereas the houses being torn down have real shelf life."

As with every teardown story in Nashville, developers and neighbors have different viewpoints. The developer, two-on-one advocate Livingston, says the home had fallen into ill repair, and the financially distressed homeowner did nothing about it. Livingston's first intention wasn't to bulldoze the property, he says, "but it would have cost me extreme amounts of money with an engineer to make it work."

So he purchased, cleared the lot, and made plans for something new, to a chorus of protest from neighbors. But Livingston says he did get one note of approval. "I got a personal phone call from the codes department thanking me very much," he says, "since the home had so many codes violations for so long."

Hoping to stave off future developer conquests, Roth and other neighbors say they will ask city preservation officials to include their street in a protected area, known as a historical overlay, which places restrictions on development to maintain historic character. They plan to meet with their councilmember, Peter Westerholm, to discuss their next steps.

"These are rough conversations, because not everyone appreciates the same things, or values the same things," Westerholm says. "I don't mind density, but what's being built tends to be larger and out of scale with the neighborhood, and some people think that's too much."

EASTWOOD NEIGHBORS AREN'T THE only ones concerned. According to Tim Walker, who heads the Metro Historical Commission, eight other neighborhoods are now exploring new or expanded overlays. These include Lockeland Springs, Hillsboro-West End, Sylvan Park, and Woodmont.

In most cases, historical overlays in Nashville come in two forms: a preservation overlay, which affords the strongest protections, and a conservation overlay, a type of zoning introduced in the mid-1980s that protects properties but is less rigid. Homeowners have been using them increasingly as a way to react to the city's growth.

"It is a response to several issues," Walker says, "including the loss of historic buildings, which can change the character of a neighborhood, and the construction of new homes that are out of scale and not in the character with the existing neighborhood fabric."

Being placed within a historical overlay doesn't freeze future tear-downs or development. It simply places another step in the process: having to gain the blessing of historic zoning officials.

But to some developers, that's trouble enough to look elsewhere. Real estate agent Price Lechleiter says he was involved in one redevelopment project where the historic zoning step added about two months to the process. "For some developers, that would not have fit into their timeline expectations," he says.

Generally, homes built before World War II are considered historic. In order for a community to gain an overlay, though, the homes have to reflect an important architectural style or contribute in some meaningful way to the historic character of the neighborhood.

John Summers, the former councilmember and planning commission member, introduced preservation zoning 30 years ago as a way to regulate demolitions. He feels the current makeup of the commission lacks a community advocate.

"The planning commission has gone from the concept of neighborhood preservation to neighborhood development," Summers says. "They've always been pro-growth, but it's really accelerated.

"We have places in Nashville that need new development, but builders only go to the high-dollar areas. They overbuild in those parts and impact the environment. Take, for example, Green Hills."

Former Metro councilmember Ronnie Greer, who represented Edgehill, is a vocal opponent of the city's brisk infill development. He said some homeowners, especially older ones on Social Security, often face different outcomes than Dobson when confronted by developers. As new homes start popping up, residents with fixed incomes or limited means sometimes can't afford the accompanying property-tax increases and are effectively pushed out—an almost textbook example of gentrification's perils.

Homeowners caught in this bind commonly accept offers from developers. According to Greer, a friend got an offer from one developer, with a caveat attached: The friend had to convince his neighbors that selling was a smart idea.

"Some of these developers, these new folks with all kind of money," Greer says, "are vultures."

Such transactions have stoked arguments about the effect of rising property values on transitional neighborhoods from East to North Nashville—and whether the teardowns are a symptom or the disease itself. Yet one nuance often missed in these conversations is that opposing gentrification shouldn't be lumped in with opposing development, according to James Fraser, a professor of human and organization development at Vanderbilt.

Fraser has studied low-income communities surrounding downtown Nashville, and he recently met with planning director Bernhardt to discuss how the department can make development more equitable. At the same time affluent newcomers are clamoring for living space within the city—the demand behind the teardowns and two-on-ones—Nashville must figure out how not to take it away from those who have less.

"The 'back to the city' movement that we are experiencing comes at a cost to people who have lived in low-income neighborhoods that are targeted for gentrification," Fraser says. "Largely because we have so few planning tools to use in order to maintain affordable housing stock."

The problem, Fraser believes, isn't development itself. Rather, he says it is that "we have not been intentional about creating truly mixed-income neighborhoods where those who are less affluent can live in desirable places in the city."

Specifically, Nashville lacks policies that encourage low-income housing: units owned by nonprofits or land trusts, working in conjunction with private developers. What's needed is a process that essentially connects real estate people with groups whose main concern is generating quality housing for the underserved, not profit. Such relationships can help keep communities economically diverse, Fraser says.

Planning officials counter that similar regulations have been proposed many times over the past several decades, but they have not passed the 40-member Metro Council. That development-friendly body is better at handling short-term crises, they say, than long-term problems.

Whatever the case, housing advocates warn that rapid development is producing a dire consequence: a growing number of low-income residents getting bumped out of their neighborhoods. According to the Census Bureau, anyone spending more than 30 percent of their annual income on their mortgage or monthly rent is considered cost-burdened. The last time they surveyed Davidson County, census officials found approximately 100,000 households fit that description.

"We need to look at what we can do to preserve affordability," says Paul Johnson, executive director of the nonprofit Housing Fund. "The trick is always how do we make sure we save the housing choices of people who already live there as we anticipate new growth?"

Many advocates point to inclusionary zoning as part of the solution. It's a zoning model that makes developers devote a percentage of new housing units to low-income residents. Developers, in turn, usually receive incentives like looser density limits and other relaxed zoning requirements. In Montgomery County, Md., just north of Washington, DC, for example, up to 15 percent of new housing has to be affordable. The requirement has spawned around 11,000 affordable units over several decades.

Asked about the prospect of adopting inclusionary zoning in Nashville, Bernhardt says he would welcome it, though state and local politics stand in the way.

"I believe that the time is right to try it, and we probably will in the upcoming year," he says, noting that other cities have passed inclusionary zoning that applies to developments of 50 units or more. That would not have much effect in Nashville, he says, since much of the city's new construction is scattered lot development.

Nashville has had affordable housing requirements in some of its redevelopment districts. The Gulch, for instance, took advantage of tax increment financing, in which property taxes in a specific area are dedicated to redevelopment. One of the stipulations of using TIF money is that developers include low-income set-asides.

The practice, however, is far from meeting the city's need. "Nashville is seeing a growing gap in affordability," The Housing Fund's Johnson says. "And people are going way out to get affordable housing, but then they just tripled their transportation cost."

FROM SYLVAN PARK TO Green Hills, as plus-sized houses squeeze into ill-fitting lots like a cartoon hippo in a chorus line, teardown opponents are finding other ways to push back. The Metro Historical Commission's Walker says that in neighborhoods where bigger homes are being constructed, as in some parts of Belmont-Hillsboro, neighbors have started citing lists of ways such structures reduce the quality of life for the entire area. Things like the lack of green space, the absence of sky.

That has become a selling point for smaller units promoting "sustainable" living, which claim that their smaller environmental impact helps retain open spaces. But city researchers like Vanderbilt's James Fraser question the logic behind the messaging.

"The term 'sustainable' does not mean much by itself," Fraser says. "So we have to ask the question: 'Sustainable for what people?' More often than not, pro-growth coalitions of developers, city officials, and the business community think sustainability is driving up land value as far as it will go by building housing products that are out of reach for low-income families."

But it's not just low-income families or native Nashvillians who are singing the It City Blues as teardown fever reaches epidemic proportions. It's also the people who came here long before the recent wave of national press, lured by the city's downhome charm and deep roots. Among them is Bob Bernstein, founder and owner of the city's Bongo Java coffeehouses, who moved to Nashville from Chicago about 25 years ago, drawn by a certain, perhaps erstwhile, quaintness.

"For years, I would say I love Nashville because it's an easy place to be," Bernstein says. "Now it's an exciting place to be, but it's far less easy."

That unease recently manifested itself two doors down from his 12South home. There, a home was demolished to make way for a two-on-one structure that, as he sees it, "is going to look like the oddball" on the block.

"It's so out of line with the historic homes on my street," Bernstein says. "It really pushed people over the edge."

Out of frustration, Bernstein, a born sloganeer, started a mini grass-roots campaign in the form of yard signs that read: "Build Like You Live Next Door." He's passed them out to about a dozen neighbors, and plans on passing out more. Some developers have profit-maximizing tunnel vision and don't care enough about what neighbors think of what they're building, Bernstein says.

"I don't think development is bad, but the town is changing so fast that there's no discussion about it," he explains. "I'm a business guy. I'm not against growth. But at what cost?"

Bernstein says he moved to 12South from East Nashville once the 15-minute commute to his Hillsboro Village office stretched to a half-hour. Now he's finding that longer and longer traffic delays on the way to his kids' school are the new norm. Like the teardowns and the two-on-ones, it's a sign that where status is concerned, Nashville should sometimes be cautious what it wishes for, or how quickly it arrives. Because when some things are demolished, they can't just be replaced—no matter how big you try to build.

"The city is growing like crazy," Bernstein says. "It's exploding. Being here and being 50 years old makes me wonder, 'What kind of lifestyle do I really want?' It's a decision I'm always wrestling with."

Gimme Shelter

BOBBY ALLYN, 2014

WELL, THAT WAS FAST.

A week after I wrote a story for this newspaper documenting the city's spectacular pace of home teardowns ("Demolition Derby," Dec. 19), I became one of the statistics. My landlord informed my roommate and me that our Edgehill apartment is scheduled for demolition. We can be out by the spring or confront the wrecking ball.

In many ways, we saw this coming. The homes of our neighbors have in recent months been leveled for new units; a new police precinct is rising from the ground right down the street; and our all-too-cozy living quarters nestled comfortably between 12South and Hillsboro Village always seemed too good for the price. And yet holding my landlord's letter telling us that it's been a pleasure having us as tenants and that "it is with regret that we have to notify you" still provokes a feeling of angry helplessness. Having to uproot to clear the way for posher residents feels unjust.

At the same time, though, my roommate and I were part of the gentrification wave that made our displacement possible, just as Jane

"Gimme Shelter" by Bobby Allyn, first published in the *Nashville Scene* on January 9, 2014. Reprinted with permission of FW Publishing.

Jacobs and her intellectual compatriots unintentionally pushed out the working class from Greenwich Village in the '60s by making it a cool place for young urbanites. When my roommate, who runs the creative space Fort Houston, and I relocated to the neighborhood, our dollars poured into the purveyors of funky-fusion tacos and 1950s-throwback coffee shops that blossomed here to serve guilt-wracked newcomers like us. We unwittingly drove up assessed values and rents and culturally gentrified the corners of a community that is at once a beneficiary and casualty of its location.

The outcome for the other eight or so tenants on my block is more dire. Nearly all of them are middle-aged African American bachelors who have called their modest brick apartment units home for many years. Saul, who lives with his elderly mother, is moving back to Chattanooga to be with family. Next door, Wayman, who moved in around 2006, is moving to North Nashville with his mom until he finds his own digs. "Moving back in with your folks at age 47 is a hard thing, dude," he told me.

Living with low rent in a nice neighborhood gets comfortable quickly. But once market forces disrupt that leisure, equal replacements prove elusive. A Craigslist search for comparable apartments in my neighborhood yields units going for three to four times what my roommate and I now pay every month. Affordable rent is a reality if you're willing to venture to the city's spread-out periphery—though once the hike in transportation cost is calculated, the real savings can seem insignificant.

When I rang Paul Johnson of the Housing Fund recently about my situation, he assured me that it's a predicament a growing number of middle-class Middle Tennesseans are facing. "Once you get above a certain income level, there's not a lot of advocacy and lobbying," he explained. "There's a gap for those who are moderate income and maybe could have been homeowners in the past, but right now are being priced out of that." In Edgehill, Johnson calls the current development moment "second-wave gentrification." The neighborhood has what developers cheerfully call a "mixed community," which in reality means that condo-residing yuppies live next to blue-collar folks who have far deeper roots.

A marketing pro might say this blending creates a "dynamic" neighborhood with real "grit." Day to day, though, it can set the stage for fraught class wars over parking availability and the practicality and usefulness of boutiques and bistros, not to mention large swaths of the community that still don't have sidewalks.

Cathie Dodd, who heads the Woodbine Community Organization, which invests in affordable housing and educates lower-income residents on issues of financial literacy, says everyone hears displacement stories, but few people think it'll ever happen to them. "We can't prevent it because we don't have the money developers do, but we can advise them about their rental options, and how things like slowing building can help avoid homelessness," she says. "But a real question Nashville has to ask is where the city's factory workers and service providers are going to live when nearly all options seem unaffordable."

The site of my apartment, one of two shotgun triplexes built in 1966, will be demolished in March. The property was purchased by John Eldridge, who built the townhome-style condos that sit on the corner of Wedgewood and 14th. Reached by phone at his Manhattan home, the 71-year-old owner of my apartment, who is now a professional body coach, said he built the apartments for $36,000 some four decades ago. The latest assessment puts the tax value at $271,000. How much did the property fetch this year? A whopping $850,000.

Which is to say, if I want to move into another cheap spot around here, it might be smart to unpack just half my bags.

Black Nashville Now and Then

RON WYNN, 2019

"I CAME UP IN an era where you didn't mess around on Lower Broadway, and now it is one of the central hubs of the city—especially for tourists."

That's jeff obafemi carr, talking about the city he's called home his entire life, save for a stint in New York in the 1990s. Now 52, carr—trim, bespectacled, sporting a clean-shaven head and goatee—has, over the decades, established a presence as one of the city's most outspoken citizens.

Jeff and I met soon after my arrival in Nashville in 1995. At the time, he was doing a show on Fisk's radio station, WFSK-FM, called "The Third Eye" and publishing an independent newspaper with that same name. We initially bonded over radio, then I later discovered that he was also an accomplished actor and equally interested in writing for both the theater and film. We're also both big sports fans.

Our friendship blossomed to the point that, several years later, I asked him to help me launch a talk show on the same station where he'd formerly been a host. I envisioned "Freestyle" as a free-flowing panel show that could smoothly move through multiple topics we both enjoyed discussing, while also being open, some weeks, to having guests. Jeff was a regular as well as a producer the first few years, but eventually became too busy with other activities. He was also in demand nationally, lending his commentary to various NPR shows. And he was always working on something.

I once wrote a cover story about him for the alt-weekly *Nashville Scene*: He and former Tennessee Titans running back Eddie George had teamed up to stage a local version of the Pulitzer Prize-winning play *Topdog/Underdog*. He's been an actor, theater owner, film producer and director, talk show host, radio commentator, journalist, and community activist. It seems no category can contain him.

When we talk about Nashville, carr expresses his love for the city, especially its rich black heritage. There are three HBCUs in Tennessee State, Fisk, and American Baptist, plus one of the nation's premier black medical colleges in Meharry. He's equally fond of landmarks like Mary's BBQ, Woodcuts, and other establishments along Jefferson Street, the main thoroughfare of the city's African American sector in North Nashville, as well as historically crucial institutions like the Fisk Jubilee Singers. Part of what fueled his on-campus political activity as a student was the role Fisk and TSU students played in Nashville's lunch counter sit-ins and in the broader Civil Rights movement.

Yet while he treasures the city's legacy, he's wary of the recent hype and quite concerned about Nashville's future direction.

"I've seen a lot of growth here, and it makes sense: Nashville borders five states, the climate is mild, and taxes are relatively low," carr says. "Almost a decade ago, the rest of the world discovered this, we got named the 'It City,' and things started to expand rapidly. We grew up really fast. Some might say too fast."

But with all the talk, not nearly enough of the discussion has involved key segments of the population. In particular, there are many in the city's sizable black community (estimated to be as low as 20 percent and as high as 29 going into the 2020 census) who feel either alienated from this talk or left out of it entirely.

A number of Nashville's African Americans feel like they have mostly experienced the ongoing chatter about the city's evolution from the outside. There's a sense of disaffection and dissatisfaction that sets in, seeing promos and advertising presentations about Music City that fail to mention its historic black institutions—or any past or present establishment in North Nashville.

Likewise, with all the discussion of the city's undeniable importance in the emergence of country music as a major piece of America's cultural fabric, they don't hear similar status given to Nashville's prominence in such black-dominated idioms as jazz, soul, blues, or gospel. Jimi Hendrix once played the R&B clubs along Jefferson Street, but for the most part it's not a selling point. For that matter, the impact of blacks in country music was, until recently, either treated as a footnote or ignored altogether.

A married father of five children, carr is in many ways emblematic of middle-aged black adults who represent both the city's past and future, and who view it with a mixture of pride, disappointment, and stubborn hope.

Carr cites his father and mother as primary influences, and like many blacks from the past couple of generations, uses their struggle as inspiration. "They had a sixth- and 10th-grade education between them, but they were all about family and supporting their kids' dreams," carr says. "They somehow managed to instill in me the notion that I could do whatever I set my mind to, and I've held to that positive attitude throughout some challenging situations." One of carr's grandfathers worked his way out of sharecropping—"no minor miracle," as carr puts it—and the other was an independent farmer. "I'm sure that's where I get my entrepreneurial sensibilities from," carr says, testifying to the power of these family stories.

GROWTH AND TRANSITION CAN be a tricky thing, particularly when it comes to politics. Carr's have evolved—some might say dramatically— since an essay of his appeared in the 2001 book *Nashville: An American Self-Portrait*. His contribution, "Black Nashville Now," begins:

> Just as James Weldon Johnson dared to take a sobering look at the state of race in America during his time, so must I embrace this opportunity to peer into the window of the house of African Americans in Nashville as the city makes a wide, sweeping turn into the next phase of its history. Let me warn you that not much has changed since Johnson's day—at least insofar as Nashville's African-American citizenry is concerned.

Further down in the essay, carr excoriates the Metro Council and outgoing mayor Phil Bredesen for "a wave of lavish spending" on "huge taxpayer-funded capital projects, such as the new arena and football stadium," adding that the same officials "also doled out a variety of subsidies to Dell Computer, HCA, the Country Music Association, and other private enterprises."

He cites the "wealth of quality art being created by African-American artists" across the country, then asks pointedly: "Do we see it in Nashville,

on the stages of the larger arts companies—the Tennessee Repertory The-
atre, the Nashville Opera, the Nashville Ballet—or even from any of the
fledgling companies whose stated purpose at first was to expose the city
to new and avant-garde art? Nope."

He continues by listing a number of African American theater groups
doing what he considers important work in changing this landscape.
"Nonetheless," carr writes, "these ventures don't receive a proportional
share of community support, even though African American Nashvillians
pay their proportional share of taxes. Money is the acid test of fairness."

Not one to sit by and do nothing, carr took on the task of starting
a theater company. He founded Amun Ra Theater in 2001, locating it
on Clifton Avenue. The name came from ancient Egypt, and translates
as "The Hidden Light." Amun Ra was established as a nonprofit professional arts ensemble, and at one point it spawned several entities under its
wing. These included choral, dance, and jazz ensembles, a series of events
featuring works by new playwrights, a youth Performing Arts Academy,
and several plays produced and presented by carr and other playwrights
and directors, both at Amun Ra and other North Nashville locales.

Over its 11-year history Amun Ra presented or helped launch such
works as Langston Hughes' *Black Nativity*, carr's one-man show celebrat-
ing Nat King Cole, and productions presented in other venues, including
God's Trombones and *Before the People Came*. During that same time
there were several other Amun Ra initiatives, most notably one to raise
scholarship money for its arts academy students.

One year, budgetary problems resulted in a shortfall in funds for a
planned summer scholarship program. Carr had to decide whether to
cut enrollment or try something more radical to raise money quickly.
He opted for the latter. So he pitched a tent on the theater's roof to draw
attention to its plight. Over an eight-day period, carr lived atop Amun
Ra and raised nearly $30,000 in the process. The summer program did
indeed go on. Some later carr efforts included fundraising for victims
of hurricane disasters in Haiti and rallying support for more affordable
housing for the homeless through the construction of tiny houses. (The
latter effort garnered national attention, including a story in the *Atlantic*.)
In other words, carr didn't just preach—he put in the work.

Yet with time often comes change. In 2018, carr took what some would
call a major philosophical turn, though he maintains his decision was
based on the same values he's always held dear: speaking on behalf of the
less fortunate and underserved.

That year, a $5.4 billion transit bill came up for public vote. The plan called for the creation of 26 miles of light rail spread over five new lines and a transit tunnel underneath downtown. In addition, the plan called for 19 transit centers, new bus rapid transit lines, and new crosstown bus routes, plus a variety of improvements to traffic signals, sidewalks, and bike infrastructure. This would be paid for by an increase in sales tax. Factoring in that tax increase, plus interest, the plan was projected to cost $8.9 billion overall.

Given carr's extensive background in the arts, and by extension what are often thought of as liberal or progressive circles, many in the city were surprised to see him align with No Tax 4 Tracks, the lead group opposing the transit measure, which had a solidly conservative pedigree.

In February 2018, the car-dealership owner and anti-transit activist Lee Beaman had stepped down as the group's treasurer. In the eyes of some, this was a way to distance the group from the idea that it was being funded by the conservative activist Koch brothers. That's because Beaman had previously helped defeat a 2015 bus rapid transit plan known as The Amp, thanks in large part to aggressive campaigning by Americans for Prosperity, the Koch-funded political advocacy group. Early on, Americans for Prosperity had also been leading the effort against the 2018 transit plan. Then Beaman stepped down, and a 501(c)(4) nonprofit called Nashville Smart provided the bulk of the No Tax 4 Tracks funding—$750,000 out of almost $950,000, according to one disclosure. At one debate, carr brought a copy of the disclosure onstage to showcase the absence of the name "Koch." Nashville Smart was not required to disclose its donors.

For his part, carr insists he took no money from anyone other than disclosed donors. In any event, he was a calm and confident spokesman, deftly presenting a case against the plan and never losing his cool even when the debates got intense. His community bona fides and long history of working for African American causes also helped shield No Tax 4 Tracks from the most obvious criticism—that it mainly represented outlying areas and their overwhelmingly white, affluent residents.

And while Nashville's progressives tended to see the transit plan as a necessary next step in the city's progress, carr successfully put doubts in the minds of those who had misgivings about how uneven the city's rapid recent progress has been. New trains and tunnels were all well and good for the people who would be served by them, and the developers who stood to cash in on new development corridors. But as carr said many times from the debate stage, the rest of the city—those who depend on public transportation most—would be left "with the bus and the bill."

The measure was defeated by a two-to-one margin.

AFTER THE DECISIVE WIN in the transit referendum, carr somewhat unexpectedly added another item to his long and varied resume: candidate. "Running for mayor was an amazing experience," he says. "I felt it was important that the average person in Nashville have some representation at the table."

He says that after former mayor Megan Barry left office in the wake of a scandal involving an extramarital affair with her head of security, "the city fell into instability." A court ruled that with Barry's resignation a special election had to be held mere weeks after the referendum vote. It certainly didn't hurt carr's cause that he had been a steady presence in the media over the course of the transit debate and had come out on the winning side. Even so, it he faced long odds: "In essence, I had 22 days to run a mayoral campaign."

In that tight time frame, carr was able to raise only about $20,000. "I had people from all backgrounds and parties, though, and I was going up against the sitting vice mayor, David Briley, who had the full force of the business community with him," carr says. "I think he had around $800,000 at the time." Without much money but energy to spare, carr hit the streets with volunteers. "I came into the race as the 13th person in, and I was able to finish sixth, which was a huge victory in my mind," he says, "considering the city was caught up in election fatigue."

As someone who ran for office—an experience he says he's grateful for, regardless of the outcome—carr doesn't dismiss electoral politics in the manner some do. But he's not thoroughly convinced that it represents the best path to change, locally or otherwise. "Electoral politics have their place," he says. "They are not a panacea, however. Look at the national landscape. We've got a president who was not popularly elected, but somehow, he's in the White House. How's that work?"

He says concern about the city's future and ongoing direction were a big part of the reason why he decided to run, and the process, in some ways, reflected some of the problems he hoped to address. "Locally, we have people who have a lot of money, who can afford to do what is needed to influence the electorate," he says. "That's a real issue: how much funding people need to participate in an election." He wonders aloud how differently things might have turned out if he had been the one sitting on $800,000, and David Briley went knocking on doors with $20,000 in the bank.

And while he's not entertaining another run any time soon, carr did get directly involved in mayoral politics again—joining at-large council member John Cooper's 2019 campaign as a senior advisor. "He was one of the only voices within the government questioning the [transit] deal," carr says of Cooper, calling him "a smart voice, with watchdog energy." For all his misgivings about the financial means necessary to mount a successful mayor bid, carr says he isn't disillusioned.

"Getting into positions where you can make systemic change—however small—is a good thing, and something we shouldn't abandon."

THESE DAYS, WITH THAT goal of an equitable society still in his sights, carr is heading a rather unusual church, though he doesn't call it one: The Infinity Fellowship. He doesn't use the term "minister" or "reverend," and he describes his role as "Chief Spiritual Officer."

"I left the traditional 'church' years ago," carr explains. "It was too exclusive of people who were different. I studied various religions and spiritual traditions, from ancient African to eastern to First Nations traditions. I always saw how things fit together; I just didn't have any place to call home."

Now he does. He calls Infinity "one of the most diverse spaces I've ever been in, and it's why I love it so dearly. . . . We've got black, white, mixed, Eastern, male and female, LGBTQ, and people who just don't like to be boxed." While carr avoids labeling himself an "activist," a desire to work for positive change remains a driving force in his life. Ultimately, he sees a connecting thread running through all his past experiences and leading him to his present position.

"Spirituality has always been an important foundation of my living," carr says, in his measured, forceful way. "I always saw what people had in common as opposed to difference, and when you look back over my writings, my art, my plays, films, and the institutions I've been blessed to build, there is a common theme: How do we push through discomfort to find our higher purpose and work together to heal the world? So yes, from a nerdy, polymathic perspective, it all fits together for me."

Eventually, our conversation swings back to Nashville's future, and carr sees equality, in particular economic opportunity, as the major issue facing Music City in the coming years.

"When I grew up, there were pockets of people who pretty much lived, worked, and played in their own parts of town, but there was a common spirit of everyone knowing each other," he says. "We were a mid-major city with a small-town feel. I think we've moved away from that some."

Now, given what carr calls "the rapid gentrification that has hit many of our historic corridors," he sees a divide between an "Old Nashville" and a "New Nashville." The challenge, as he sees it, is "how to reconcile the two so that we can grow together in a way that is beneficial and equitable for all of us."

For carr, the most pressing issues facing Nashville all center around fairness. "We've got an expanding population, but the resources are still not equal," he says. "Because of gentrification, the wealthier neighborhoods have the resources, and the neighborhoods with higher areas of concentrated poverty don't. That's a savage inequality that we still are not addressing adequately." This connects to carr's somewhat unusual alliance with the conservative-led No Tax 4 Tracks.

"I was engaged with a PAC that was fighting a very burdensome referendum on transit that would have harmed the poor and elderly with higher taxes for no real benefit," he says. And while politics makes strange bedfellows, in this case the stances carr took could easily be linked to his long-held beliefs. "That was the issue with transit," he explains. "The failed proposal was basically a downtown development density deal with shiny new trains that didn't serve the neglected parts of town. We've got to spread the love as a city."

For carr, equity in infrastructure support is key: "That means sidewalks, traffic lights, stormwater—the basic things we pay taxes equally for." It's an echo of his essay in *Nashville: An American Self-Portrait*, especially the part where he calls out "a town that is being touted by government and industry and the image-makers as a progressive community" for corporate handouts and for not supporting African American–led endeavors.

"We need to make sure that African American businesses share in the prosperity and growth of the city," carr says today. "Getting less than 5 percent of city contracts is not something to boast of, and it keeps us away from realizing the strength of true diversity."

Though no longer part of the day-to-day arts world, carr hasn't totally abandoned it. "I plan to keep telling stories," he acknowledges. "It's a part of everything I do, and I couldn't breathe without it." But he's equally excited about other things happening at the Infinity Center, calling its creation, which took three years, "the journey of a lifetime." Last summer, the center re-launched a Youth Performing Arts Academy—a program that started at carr's Amun Ra Theater years ago. In a way, it's carr coming full circle. "We're committed to keep being the change we want to see in the world," he says.

Dish Network

STEVE CAVENDISH, 2019

THERE IS NOT MUCH Randy Rayburn hasn't seen.

Over coffee at his Midtown Cafe—where a walk through the packed dining room at lunch will find politicians, business leaders, and more than a few members of the music industry—Rayburn enjoys regaling an audience with stories about the city and, specifically, the dining *scene*. What's left of his hair is silver now, but with his five decades in Nashville restaurants, there are few more expert.

"Nashville was a chain town from the 1950s through the 1980s," Rayburn says. He's right. During that stretch, people like Ray Danner built an empire out of Shoneys, Fifth Quarter, and Sailmaker. Mrs. Winner's and Kenny Rogers Roasters were based here, and other chains like J. Alexanders used Nashville as their launch site. As Paul Hemphill notes in his 1970 book *The Nashville Sound*, "So many of the stars were sinking their money into fast-food franchises (Minnie Pearl's Fried Chicken, Tennessee Ernie Steak 'n' Biscuits, Tex Ritter's Chuck Wagon System) that some people were touting Nashville as the franchise center of the nation."

And while there were a few independent standouts like Julian's or Mario's, there was little to differentiate Nashville dining from Columbus or Charlotte. In fact, Nashville's relative acceptance of everything is what led longtime West End staple Houston's to land here in 1977. (That location—which like Midtown Cafe is often crowded with elites—is now home to one of BrickTop's eight southeast franchises.)

"Contrary to revisionist history, there were actually excellent restaurants and top-notch, acclaimed chefs in Nashville in the late 1990s and throughout the 2000s," Rayburn says. Deb Paquette got national mentions for her work at Zola and Bound'ry. And Rayburn still beams a bit when he mentions being named wine marketer of the year by the influential *Wine Enthusiast* in 1998 while his Sunset Grille was at its peak in Hillsboro Village.

But Nashville didn't truly arrive as a culinary destination until the new millennium, the culmination of factors as diverse as tourism growth, a rise in disposable income, and good old-fashioned dumb luck. The Nashville metro area passed one million residents in the mid-1990s, making it a target for larger corporate entities to relocate or put big operations here, including Nissan and Dell. Large numbers of the employees who came to work at those new arrivals wanted to live in the city, not a county away in the suburbs. Those new residents brought with them new tastes and sometimes a desire to recreate them, like in the case of Sarah Gavigan, a music industry transplant whose love of LA izakayas led her to open a couple of ramen shops and a gleaming, Tokyo-inspired bar in the Gulch—a neighborhood that until the mid-2000s had been a mostly industrial strip bisected by train tracks, holding little more than a couple restaurants, the bluegrass club The Station Inn, and a blocks-long refrigeration plant.

In many ways, too, the city's dining scene has mirrored tastes across the country that have become more sophisticated thanks to multiple cable channels devoted to fetishizing food and chefs—or, to put it more simply, we knew what we were missing and we wanted it in Nashville. If an Iron Chef could make a shabu shabu on TV, couldn't a chef here make it as well? Some of those celebrities on TV relocated to Nashville, like *Top Chef* finalist Dale Levitski and *Chopped* star Maneet Chauhan, whose Morph Hospitality group now includes four restaurants. Even those TV chefs who didn't relocate became regular visitors, thanks in part to the massive Music City Food and Wine Festival, started in 2006—a glitzy, gawky sort of event put on by a perhaps unlikely group of event planners that includes chef Jonathan Waxman and rock band Kings of Leon.

Other Nashville chefs have found national notoriety in the pages of *Food + Wine* and other national publications, like rising star Julia Sullivan, a Nashville native who returned from the line at Franny's in New

York to open Henrietta Red, a wood-fired, seafood-first place she opened with Max and Benjamin Goldberg. It was hailed by *Bon Appetit* as one of the country's best new restaurants in 2017.

And while Rayburn is right that there were some quality restaurants here before the late 1990s, there was nowhere near the number of talented chefs and restaurateurs that compete for attention and dollars today. Much of that is fueled by tourism—those extra five million visitors we added between 2012 and 2018 have to eat somewhere, right?—but both the quality and quantity of our offerings has changed.

Nashville chefs regularly appear on nomination lists for the prestigious James Beard Award—Josh Habiger, Matt Bolus, Hal Holden-Bache, Sullivan, Margot McCormack, the Goldbergs and others have been nominated at various points—and Tandy Wilson, the proprietor and force behind the acclaimed City House, won one in 2016. City House, in many ways, was the culmination of all of those forces in a Nashville restaurant, a restaurant built by a local talent who saw the world, returned with an idea, and then set a standard others had to live up to. Along the way, the quality of restaurants was elevated as well as our expectations for what a good dining experience should be.

I would argue there are four elements that have been enormously, though not exclusively, responsible for elevating the city's dining scene in the last two decades.

First, there needs to be an anchor, a restaurant of immense quality that paves the way for others to follow. A single restaurant's sustained excellence can elevate an entire city. Don't believe me? Look at what Frank Stitt and Highlands Bar & Grill have done for Birmingham, wowing local and national diners for more than three decades and spinning off talent to open places of their own. In Nashville, that place is Margot, the Southern-ingredients-by-way-of-France stalwart at Five Points in East Nashville.

Margot McCormack set out to be a writer and worked in kitchens to support her academic habit. When she moved to New York after college, she thought she could split her time between the two vocations until she made it as a wordsmith. Instead, kitchen life became all-consuming, and she realized a passion for food that eventually led to the Culinary Institute of America and then back to Nashville. The radical idea at her eponymous Margot was that the offerings shouldn't just change quarterly or even weekly, but rather daily, depending on what was available. Asparagus is out of season? Well it wouldn't be on the menu.

Margot opened the door for the flood of restaurants that would eventually open in East Nashville, and her kitchen became a breeding ground for talent, including another returning Nashvillian, Tandy Wilson, who had been cooking in California.

Second, Nashville needed entrepreneurs who were willing to push the boundaries of what the city's food scene could be. If the only places brothers Max and Ben Goldberg had ever opened were places like Paradise Park, Merchants, and Pinewood Social—to name three of Strategic Hospitality's very successful restaurants—they would be well respected. But with Patterson House and The Catbird Seat the Goldbergs changed how Nashville would drink and eat, with the former turning cocktails into more than a couple of shakes and a garnish, and the latter deliberately creating provocative dishes that diners may love or hate, but would never forget.

Third, we needed someone to pay more attention to our core cuisine. For Southerners, the word "barbecue" might mean different things but it is ubiquitous throughout the region. In Tennessee, the tradition is pork, and for most aficionados, West Tennessee and Memphis have produced the state's best barbecue for decades. In Nashville, there were a few decent outposts, but there was never someone who stood out the way Pat Martin did. Embracing his whole-hog roots, Martin brought a dedication to technique that was previously unseen, and it made the commissary pork sitting in local chains seem bland. At his restaurants, Martin has fought the perception of barbecue as a cheap dish unworthy of the care that more expensive restaurants might provide.

And finally, we needed a signature dish to call our own. Of course, it had been here all along: André Prince Jeffries, the matriarch of Prince's Hot Chicken, had bubbled beneath the surface for decades while the rest of Nashville discovered and then embraced the cayenne-soaked goodness of her family's famous product. Sitting in a nondescript strip mall off Dickerson Pike, Prince's inspired imitators (many of them delicious) and accolades, including a Beard Award for Jeffries and her crew. And while cynics might look at a certain Colonel's appropriation of hot chicken as evidence that it's a fad, a bite into the original with its perfectly crispy skin and atomic glow will dispel that notion quickly. You might get tired of "Nashville-style hot _____" showing up everywhere, but ask yourself this: Has there ever been a Charlotte-style anything?

What follows are the voices of some of the people who have propelled Nashville's dining scene forward, from a place better known for chains and meat-and-threes to a city full of surprising, challenging, and often amazing cuisine.

ANDRÉ PRINCE JEFFRIES

It is impossible to consider food in Nashville today without two words: hot chicken.

Whether or not you believe the apocryphal story of Thornton Prince's girlfriend taking revenge on the womanizer by putting a cayenne seasoning on his fried chicken—and the way his great niece André Prince Jeffries tells the story, you will want to trust that it's true—there can be little doubt that the dish is universally recognized as the city's signature food. Prince's Hot Chicken Shack was named one of the country's most important restaurants by the James Beard Foundation, and the trend (and imitators) that it inspired, both locally and nationally, has been a real phenomenon for something that is, essentially, just a twist on Southern fried chicken. Ask Jeffries about it, and she'll tell you that hot chicken fans love a little bit of pain (but not too much) with their dinner. Ask Bill Purcell, the former mayor and one of Prince's most loyal customers, and he'll tell you that people have a hard time going back to plain after they've tried hot chicken.

And ask almost any resident and they'll tell you that hot chicken *is* Nashville.

Let's go back into the mid '90s. How popular was the restaurant? How did it get to this point?

Well, this restaurant has been going for a while. I took over in 1980, and of course back then, it was my great uncle that's right there on that picture on the wall, that started it. Of course, that was the first one on 28th and Jefferson, over there by Tennessee State. After Will Prince passed, his wife, Maude, took over. When Maude came down with ill health, she asked my mother, who was dying of cancer at the time, if she knew anybody who wanted to take over, and my mother suggested me because I was the only one in the family, the immediate family, that was divorced. My mother and father were helping me with my two children, making ends meet. So she suggested that I take over.

It was a shock to me. I had only been to the restaurant twice, because it was a late-night place. It opened up at 6 o'clock in the evenings, and stayed open until midnight. My father took us down there only when it was closed. So I knew nothing about the operation of the restaurant. But again, my purpose was to keep something in the family. Try to keep something a mom-and-pop place, which it's always been, in the family. I can't pat myself on the back for something that was already established.

When I took over, I renamed it for the family, because I wanted the family to get the recognition. And that's why I renamed it in August of 1980, to Prince's Hot Chicken.

How hot was it?

It was one way back then, and I do give myself credit for changing it to the different variations. To the plain, because people wanted their children to eat it, so I started serving the plain. The mild was the regular chicken way. It was the only way that they served it, when I started. That was all mild, which is our mild today, but I changed it [because] some people wanted it hotter. Medium, plain, mild, medium, hot, extra hot. But, I give myself credit for those. That is what I changed in the '80s, along with changing the name.

As far as we knew, for a long time, there was no other place called Hot Chicken. No other place. Mayor Purcell always ate it. That's the only way he eats it, is a one-leg order hot. He always has.

When he left as being mayor, he was no longer mayor of Nashville, he got a job. He got a job. He was over at the Kennedy Center at Harvard. And while he was there, he did research on hot chicken. When he came back to Nashville, he told me about this research that he had done, and he said, "Andre, I found out that you all were the first to cook and serve chicken hot in the country." I said, "What?" He said as far as this research could go, he could find no other place that served any hot chicken. I said, "Oh, my goodness. What a compliment!"

So that's why when that got out, the mayor, like I said, Mayor Purcell is the one that really took the lid off the box in a persistent way. He had it put in the airline magazines, about Nashville's hot chicken, on the main airlines. People were telling me, "Hey, I read about—" They were coming straight from the airport to the new place on Ewing and saying, "I read about it on American Airlines, Southwest." I couldn't believe it, I said, "What?" I said, "Mayor Purcell."

And you started noticing people from all over?

Oh, people come in from all over the world. I couldn't believe it. A lot of Australians. Italians, European. Camilla's son—the Camilla that's married to who?

Prince Charles.

Yeah, her son comes all the time and I didn't know it, of course. Mayor Purcell had to tell me. He said, "You know, Camilla's son is coming here and he's sending his friends here." I don't know him. I think I had talked to him on the phone, because he would send his buddies to Prince, and the deal was they had to call him, call him when they got to Prince. Of course, he didn't announce himself. But I couldn't believe it.

All of those publications, them talking about it . . . Now of course, they were coming in, even from Dubai. They wanted me to come to Dubai and to Europe, put a place in Europe, but I'm just too old to travel. But Lord have mercy, it is just amazing. So I don't know what year it was, but progressively every year, it has gotten more and more popular.

A lady I met somewhere, and she had come up to me when she found out that I owned Prince Hot Chicken, and she said, "I am 82 years old," and she said, "I grew up in East Nashville and still live in East Nashville. I would always come to your uncle's place, old Charlotte." It was very popular, old Charlotte, when it was on 17th and Charlotte, over there by Krystal. And she said, "I told my friends that I had come here on Charlotte, and it's so because I couldn't go home drunk." That was the late-night stop.

And the people from Grand Ole Opry would always come down. Back then, of course, during my uncle's time, my great uncle's time, they had segregation but they had a backdoor for them to come into. If they came into the front door, they'd come through the kitchen into that, I remember, a green room, my father showing us. And it was for whites only. Can you imagine? Have mercy.

What makes hot chicken better?

It's different, that's all. I tell a lot of my people I have interviews with, I said, "If you have a boring date, or somebody who you're on your first date or something, and they're not talking, it's, 'Where you get some hot chicken?'" They're going to open up. So it's a conversation piece, because somebody is going to have an opinion after they taste it. Some people think they can eat it hot, and hey, they find out, hey, they can't. More women eat it hot than men, though.

Do they really?

Yes, more women maintain hot.

Do you think women can take it a little better?

Yeah, yeah, yeah, they maintain it. They maintain it. Men will try it, because they don't want to be known as wimps. They're going to try it, but women maintain. And once they start getting it hot, that's it. They don't change. But men will come on back down, but hey. Those women, I don't know how they do it.

How often does somebody come in here to try it for the first time, and they look up at that board, and they say, "Very hot"?

Oh, yeah. They do that all the time. Then, they get to hollering, and then they get to sweating, and then they're putting their fingers in the ice water.

What'd you think the first time you heard that Kentucky Fried Chicken was going to do a Nashville hot?

Well, I was surprised, you know. My great uncle said a long, long, long time ago, when Colonel Sanders was living, that he wanted to buy it. Nothing was in writing that we've found out, but anyway, he wanted to, Colonel Sanders wanted to buy his recipe when my great uncle first went into the business. But like I said, it's been going on almost 90 years. So, it's about time, them catching up. Everybody else has gotten it.

Now, if you want to tell me what the recipe is right now, I would love to hear it.

I can't do that, I've got to stay in business. I've got bills to pay.

But that recipe is protected.

Well hey, it's protected in my heart. But like I say, I have expanded it to include the medium hot, extra hot. That is what I did do. I have expanded it, but I have a real, real, real thing in my heart. Have mercy.

A lot of people and publications have asked you about it over the years. Do you think holding onto that recipe gives it a little bit of mystique?

Of course it does. You know, people love that. People are always going to be curious, and some of them are so bold. They just go all in, back there into the kitchen. That's why we had to put the sign up. Have mercy, they just go stand right there in the doorway, just looking.

You've had everybody in the world come into that shop on Ewing. I mean everybody.

From all walks of life, have mercy. As my mother always said, you need to go into a restaurant business, because everybody eats. And that's true. Everybody eats. Have mercy. So of course, I wasn't paying any attention to mama when she was talking about, way back then, but that is the truth. I think the most startling, of course, you know Shaq? Shaquille O'Neal has been over here twice. He is so down-to-earth, he is such a lovely person.

Jerry Seinfeld came in one Friday night. He just came in and stood there at the window, and I looked up. I was in my little old favorite seat, and I looked up, and I thought he was [*The Today Show*'s] Matt Lauer from Channel 4, but yeah. And I said, "Maybe I'm seeing things." And he said, "Hi." I don't know where the cashier was at that moment, but he said, "Hi, I know you." I said, "Oh, you do?" And I kept looking, and looking, and looking. It was Jerry Seinfeld. I couldn't believe it. But he had done a show downtown at TPAC, and he had his driver, his agent, bring him over there to that little hole in the wall. He came up and ordered it. He said, after he was sitting there eating, it was so funny. He stayed there and ate. He stayed there about an hour, over an hour or so, talking. People thought they were seeing things.

I think he got it medium, but his agent got it hot, and his agent was having conniptions, and Jerry Seinfeld said, "That hot is for suicide."

MARGOT McCORMACK

Maybe East Nashville's dining scene—now replete with ramen shops, tasting menus, and artisanal butchers—would have exploded without Margot, the eponymous restaurant helmed by Margot McCormack. But it's certainly impossible to imagine without it. At a time when fine dining still meant heading across the river to a tonier part of town, McCormack proudly planted a flag for French-inspired cuisine among the hipsters on the East Side. Her menu didn't just change with the seasons, it changed every day, forcing diners to eschew ordering the same favorites and trust the chef. Along the way, her kitchen became the proving ground for several of the city's best chefs and she would be nominated several times for a prestigious James Beard Award. As the restaurant closes in on its third decade, Margot remains one of Nashville's finest places and still at the forefront of chef-driven restaurants.

You had done some time in New York, I believe?

Yeah. I started working for Jody Faison, in Nashville, in 1996 after I graduated from [the University of Tennessee]. And I had come back to Nashville to sort of get my bearings, figure out what I wanted to do. And I was now working for him and a few weeks into the job he promoted me to being the chef, kitchen manager. I didn't really feel like I was a chef then.

Restaurants were something that I found comfortable, and I guess I was pretty good at it. Then Jody introduced me, at some point, to somebody from the National Restaurant Association, and Jody was very keen on me going to culinary school, and I'm like "I just got out of school, and I don't have the money to go to another school. I'm not sure if this is what I want." He was like, "You're really talented, and if you stay in Nashville you're not going to learn anything." So I got a scholarship and I went to CIA. And after I graduated, New York was definitely my destination. I thought that I could cook and write at the same time, and it was a miscalculation. New York kitchens are just all-encompassing. You really can't do anything else.

So yeah, I worked for 10 years-ish there and then decided I can't sustain life in New York. Well, I could, but it was a decision. Because I was like 30-ish. I was like you're either all-in in New York or you have to make some changes. My parents ended up retiring in Nashville. So I moved home and got a job at F. Scott's, and worked there for five years before Margot opened, and it was a good five years. It was really nice to get reacquainted with Nashville and the dining community, trying to figure out what was what.

And finally, the fourth year, I think [the owner] said, "If you stay one more year, I'm going to give you $25,000." He gave me almost like a departing bonus. I said OK, and I agreed to stay 'til the next year. And right about midway through that year, Fred Grgich came along and ate in the restaurant one night, and left me a card. And he was like, "I wanted just to find out what you're doing." I didn't know who he was, and I called him and we started talking and we kind of hit it off right away. And we were like, "OK, let's make a restaurant together." I mean, who does that?

So we start riding around looking for space. And my sous chef was dating a gentleman, a guy in East Nashville, and she would ride around up there and look around. And she said, "I think you'll love this building." So we went over and drove by it. And we just drove by it, because it was so bad. I was like, "We are not stopping." It was absolutely desolate. There was no one on the street. And it looked really scary. I mean, like ghost town. Like, if you get out of the car, you might get shot. I don't know, it was just really like, "No, we're not stopping."

I looked at a lot of spaces. And kept coming back to the corner. The porch had a big banner on the front door, so we called and actually got in to see the building, which just looked like a bomb had dropped on it. And we were like, "Yeah, this is it!" And I think, again, Fred had said that day, "Yeah we can do this." And I just needed somebody to tell me that. I just needed someone to go along with me. You have to jump off the cliff. You have to take the leap. You have to believe in something.

And, so yeah, signed the lease and he really helped us get going. That whole, how do you get a permit, what do you do you about . . . Fred was that person for me. I knew how to cook, I knew how to make the money, I knew how to set up the kitchen. I knew my part of the game. So I was very confident that it was going to be just fine. My turn to be great. And like I was saying, you know in 2001 there wasn't a whole lot going on. Kay West [of the *Nashville Scene*] just really gave us a lot of wind underneath our wings. That sounds corny, but she kept driving by and, "Oh my god, there's something happening. I'm going to report on it." I mean, she really whipped up a lot of interest and anticipation for when we opened. People kept coming. And talking about how hard it was to get a reservation. And we were full for two solid years. Just in and out every day, before we got any sort of little breath. And it was crazy.

You go to East Nashville now, and a bunch of places have opened in the last 12 to 18 months, and it's easy to say, "Well, of course she would do that, because there's a ton of success people have had over there." From the tornado in 1998 until now, the amount of people living over there has increased substantially. There's all sorts of new housing that's going in now. But that was not the case in 2001. Why did you think, "Oh, well we can do this and be successful in East Nashville."

Honest to goodness, that was my vision. I wanted a place that was really outside the pocket of Nashville. I did not want to be—no offense to anybody—but I did not want to be in a mall, in a strip mall. I did not want to be in a plaza. I didn't want to be in a building connected to another building. I actually really wanted to be in a house. I love, love, love that type of experience. If I could've duplicated that, I would have. But we didn't find a house, we found this. And then it just worked. The minute I saw the bones of the restaurant, I was like, "OK, the bar's here, the dining room's here, the kitchen's right there." And we just made it work.

Another huge thing to go along with the first thing is I wanted . . . coming from New York, I really wanted an urban experience. I did not want a suburban place. I wanted people to have to walk, I wanted people to be able to walk, because I really wanted it to be a neighborhood-y vibe. And I also wanted to make Nashville—it sounds aggressive—but it's sort of like, "get out of your car." You might have to park on the street, you may have to park in a parking lot that's down the road. But I wanted to make Nashville less lazy.

I think I'm very happy, I'm very proud of Nashville as a city, as a dining community. For one example, when we went in, they really had to trust me, because the menu changed every day. And they couldn't just go, "Oh, I'm going to go there and have that blah blah blah that I had last time, that I liked so much." And they also had to trust some of the innovations and some of the new things that we brought to the table, like we brought a lot of special cuts of meat. When I got here, people were serving filets and chips, no dip. Maybe a few exceptions, but as a rule, no one has a seasonal menu. It was just the same menu, 365 days a year. We started the seasonal menu at F. Scott's and then we wanted to do a daily menu at Margot. So they stepped up and they ate steak loin. They ate tri-tip and flat iron and things that they had never heard of before. And they're like, "Yeah, OK, that was cool."

Now we have domestic wines and we have beer. But for a long time we only had high-alcohol beer, and we had like basically 100 percent or almost 100 percent European wine list. And a lot of boutique wines that no one had ever heard of. So you have to go out on a limb, you have to really trust it. It's a relationship. When you come to dinner, we have an obligation and our guests have an obligation. So we try to put forth our share every day.

Do you think your menu has changed at all since opening? Are there things that you put on the menu and they didn't sell in '01 versus today or . . . I guess, I've talked to a couple of other people who have said sometimes there's a little education that goes on with your clientele.

Oh, for sure. Yeah, that's where staff comes in. And our staff has been amazing from the get-go and we get a lot of feedback from guests. They're like, "Oh, the people are so awesome and they're so genuine. They're so knowledgeable." And I really think that's what people are looking for in staff. But it's just funny to me that a lot of people don't spend the time, or maybe they think they're spending the time, but maybe they hire the wrong people. I don't know. Education is a huge part of it. I also think 18 years ago, look at all the things happening with Food Network or shows with chefs . . . food has become this really integral part of life.

They're talking about Whole Foods and Trader Joe's and food trucks in public, and where you can get this or that, and even the millennials, young people, food is very much a fabric of their life. And it's great to see some of the stuff in the store that people are buying. They'll say, "Where can you get this chicken?" "Oh, you can get this here." "Where can I get this meat?" "Well, in the farmer's market." We've returned a lot of local producers to our market. The big market, then the neighborhood market. So people are really participating in that. And that's really nice. But now the menu, specifically, it's funny that you mention that, because every year on our birthday, we do the same menu that we opened with. And what I notice more than anything is the impact of global warming. On June 5, 2001, we served soft-shell crabs. News is, this year, I don't think we can get a soft-shell crab.

Really? Wow.

On June 5, 2001, we served like mashed potatoes and some really hot produce. The menu reads really hot. And I'm like, "Was it not hot as hell outside?" Now I'm thinking to myself, "Maybe it wasn't." So June 5, 2001, seems like it was way more spring, which we still have three weeks of spring to go before the summer. And the beginning of the summer. So that's what we notice the most. Is that we had to tailor every year our menu to be way more salad summery, than hot.

I think our palates have also trended toward lighter. Less starch, more vegetables. So a lot of the menu items are the same, but then we'll tweak them with whatever little sets. You want to get a main ingredient in. Now the things that were popular then are still just as popular. We do veal scaloppini. Every night that we have veal scaloppini we sell out of it. Soft-shell crabs are still just as popular. I think we did tuna, same thing. Clams. I think we had linguini with clams. The first linguini was essentially all of my greatest hits. That was one of my strongest dishes at the time. And I think that still holds true. Those are all strong dishes. And we've only added to the catalog of strong dishes that we started out with.

Your restaurant is French, but it's not like a bistro French. How would you describe it?

Well, it's an inspiration. Different. That some of the things I was talking about earlier that, my life literally does revolve around food from the minute I get up until the minute I go to sleep. I'm thinking about it, eating it, cooking it. And I think that's a very French lifestyle. And the restaurant does basically encompass who I am. And what we do there. So the bistro part basically comes in via the hospitality, and the fact that on any given night you look out and you see people talking to the table next to them. And we know a big part of our clientele every evening. And we know, "OK this is so-and-so's birthday tonight." And this dish is not for Reggie because we actually know it. And Mr. X doesn't like raw onion. Things like that, that we take time to know. But I think my style is just, I'm not trying to reinvent food. I'm just trying to reintroduce it to people. And we're still looking for new and different ways to present our local fare into that French way. Whether it be pickling our own cornichons or, gosh, grilling shark fins. I don't know. But I think it's just the, gosh, it's like this inner essence the way we approach food every day. It's not the norm in most places.

PAT MARTIN

If Pat Martin hadn't been busted for beer a few weeks before graduation, we might never have gotten Martin's BBQ restaurants. The man with West Tennessee roots was just about to finish at Freed Hardeman University when he was caught with alcohol—Freed is a Church of Christ institution—and kicked out of school. After transferring to Lipscomb, it took him three more semesters to graduate, and he picked up gigs for fraternities cooking whole hogs the way Henderson pitmaster Harold Thomas had taught him.

Barbecue in Nashville finally stepped out of Memphis' long shadow in the late 2000s largely when Martin and fellow pitmaster Carey Bringle, longtime friends from the competition circuit, decided to open their own restaurants. Martin's specialty is whole hog, and when you step into his places, the smell of wood smoke and pig permeates the air. Over the course of a decade, Martin built his business from a strip mall shop in Nolensville into a multi-state operation, putting Nashville on the map as a destination for serious, well-crafted barbecue.

You didn't start out to be a pitmaster, even though you had been doing it for years. When you graduated from college, you were a bond trader for a while before the internet completely remade bond trading. What did you do after you left the financial industry?

I had two uncles that had sod farms, and this buddy of mine, Matt Merton, was doing some landscaping work. I was out of a job, but I had money, enough that I didn't have to go rush. I'm going to tell you this was around 2001, and we got divorced in '02. Matt wanted to sub out. I was like, "I'll do that for a while." That shit turned into five years. I didn't hate it. I didn't love it. It was good money, not great money. I got through that divorce.

I just worked up. I got remarried, and Martha was like, "You really need to. This is your passion." I was cooking all the time. When I got divorced, I didn't stop barbecuing, but I bought Julia Child's book. I was alone, in Arrington, so I started teaching myself just the classical foundations of cooking, specifically braising. That's how I got started. It was winter time. I didn't want to go outside, so I bought a pot, then pan roasting and all that stuff.

Martha was really encouraging me to go do this. I looked into going to the Culinary Institute. I was like, "I wouldn't mind being a chef, but do I really want to be a restaurateur? I don't know if I want to do that." I felt like I was too old. I was 34. I felt like I was ancient, jeez.

We went down to eat tacos at this little place in Nolensville called Old Texanna, and they had been evicted. I immediately told the guy, "I'll take the lease." I was in a really healthy, I-don't-give-a-shit area in my life. We had no money. I had my house that I owned in Arrington, a little bitty two bedroom, one bath, and I did it and opened with one employee, Bo.

Built my place up myself, went and got the Home Depot 123 Orange book, framed up my little spot and we opened, October 16 of '06, and that was it. I would cook hogs on the weekend, but [the landlord] wouldn't let me build a pit, so I had to go down to Terry Harmon's and get his. I was open five days a week. That's how I got started.

Were you working 20-hour days at first?

Absolutely. It was the 90-hour weeks, but it wasn't terrible. You hear people go, "Well, I work 80, 90 hours a week," and I think the people that bitch about that, one, usually exaggerate, usually, not all the time. If they feel the need to tell you that, they clearly didn't enjoy what they're doing. I never really noticed it. I just went to work, and I got home late, 1:00 in the morning, 12:00, and went to sleep and went back because I fricking actually loved it. It reminded me a lot of the Board of Trade. It was controlled chaos. I have ADD really bad and just everything was about to completely spin out of control. That's my comfort zone. That's what the restaurant business was for me.

What was on that first menu?

I've got a picture of it. It was too much, in the sense that I had a whole section on loaded baked potatoes. You could put barbecue on all these potatoes, all this stuff. I didn't think about what we call mods. So, I've got these meats. You picked the meat. I'd list them all out, so my menu board was the size of that linen truck right there. It was freaking . . . I had étouffée on there. I could make a great roux. So, all that went away. A slugburger was on there originally, believe it or not.

Was it?

Yep. Nobody bought them. My granddad, when we'd come into the farm in the summers, would make them.

How many of those are you selling now?

We have 50 pounds to sell on Fridays, and we usually sell out. It's like Mississippi day on Fridays. Yeah, man, a lot of that stuff, because I wasn't selling it, I started learning more. Before I met Mike Bodnar, who taught me how to run restaurants, I was in business for four years. It was just by the seat of my pants common sense.

Did you make any money?

Yeah, I made money. I wouldn't have lasted four years. In this shit, man, if you don't make money, unless you got somebody backing you, you're done.

It's either hunker up or down.

That's it. There's no gray area. I did not get money from my dad or some rich uncle. We got a $65,000 line of credit. The banker, who's still my banker today, I walked out of there . . . I did ask my dad to sit in on the meeting. It was the first time I'd ever taken a big loan like that. To me, it was a big loan, and I put my house up totally as collateral. I was like, "They didn't even ask me for a business plan. That's freaking great." Dad was like, "Of course they didn't ask you for a business plan. Your house is worth $150,000. They gave you $65,000. They are totally hoping you fail, so they can sell that house and make some money." So, it didn't hurt my feelings, but yeah, that was it. That's how we opened.

OK. Then, you went into that first place, and then you opened the bigger place in Nolensville when, '10?

Yeah. So, around '08, Mike Bodnar comes in, and he literally walked in my kitchen. I had never seen this man. He asked me about my fries. My place was only about 1,000 square feet. I only had 10 tables in there originally.

The entire time before I opened, been scouring the internet on how to run a restaurant. The first time [Bodnar] walked in, he ate my food, and he goes, "I want to meet you. Come out here." I was like, "All right." He came back in, and he started to eat with me. He says, "You've got a cash register, a $99 cash register." He goes, "How many partners do you have?" I said, "None." He goes, "You've got a couple." I said, "No, I don't." He goes, "You do. You just don't know it." He laughed, and he goes, "Cash registers are just that until your employees start feeling entitled. They can slide some money out every now and again. That's what I mean." He goes, "You really should get a POS system. You need to buy an Aloha."

It was so insightful to me. It was free advice. There was no strings attached. I appreciated that. So, I bought the Aloha, and he taught me how to program my recipes in there. This was like porn for me. I was like, "My gosh, I'm learning." Even though it was nothing, it was huge to me. Eventually, we started talking about partnering up because I had to move. I had way outgrown my space. On Fridays, there was people from Nashville driving out. There was a line 50 people long. It was out in fucking Nolensville. So, we leased. This guy bid to build to suit for me across the street. When I moved in there, literally the month after I moved in, Mike and I partnered up. Then, about two years later, he had started doing stuff with Tatziki's. Two years later than that, they formed Fresh Hospitality. That's how it all got started.

I traded him equity. Our deal's on a napkin, and I'm a prideful mother-fucker, too. But, I appreciated when he said, "I'm not going to be your bank. If I sit down and write a check, you're going to write a check." I said, "OK, deal. Here's my deal. You have to mentor me 'til you die." He goes, "I can do that." We wrote it on a fucking napkin, and it's scanned into the hard drive, a copy of that napkin. That's in the database. It's been an incredible relationship. He's taught me so much.

You have rolled your money a couple of times, if I understand this right, to open places on Belmont, and then to open West Virginia, and then down-town.

Well, here's what, we made our money in Nolensville. Mike was a WVU grad. He wanted to open one up, up there. That was the first fight that we had because I was . . . and I'm so glad I dug my heels in because we ended up licensing that store. It was way too risky for me and Martha to put our money in a store that's nine hours away, and I've got 35 employees. It was really stupid on his part. He's Mensa. Mike is literally Mensa. Some guys are just so smart they make dumb decisions. So, I burrowed in, and I was like, "I can't, I'm not going to do this. I'm not going to go for it." So, West Virginia was a licensed store. It opened up very strong, but they ran it like absolute shit.

That's a tough thing when it's long distance.

Yeah, so that's over there, the best lesson I could learn that early, about licensing. That was up here. I took my money, and put it in Mt. Juliet. Mt. Juliet opened up flat and stayed flat. We didn't make any money, didn't lose any money. It was just there. Belmont came along. Took my money again from Nolensville, so Mt. Juliet's over here neutral, doubled down, opened up Belmont. That one made money right out of the gates. Slowly, Mt. Juliet started making money.

You had a big kitchen on Belmont, too, though. You do catering and stuff.

Oh yeah, we started catering and all that out of there. Then, those three, the big thing that nobody understands is that [the downtown location on] Rutledge was the biggest risk, besides doing Nolensville in the first place, because I took everything that we had.

I remember talking to you around this time, and you weren't terrified but you were like, "All right, here we go, we're all in."

It would have wiped me and Martha off the earth financially. We put every dime we had made from the other three stores into Rutledge, and it paid off. That was a game changer for me, personally, and the brand. By that time I really started realizing—well, really, by Belmont—that I couldn't cook the hogs every day and have my hands in it every day. So I started, very informally, apprenticing these guys to cook my hogs and do my food.

How hard was that to do?

It was very hard because that's sexy, so everybody wants to do it. They don't understand that I can sit down and write a brisket procedure for you, a whole hog procedure for you, a rib procedure for you, and on paper, you look at it, and you go, "So, all I've got to do is, do this, do this?" Pretty much, and then, they do it and fuck it up. The thing about barbecue is, it's reps. It's repetitions. It's a skill position. It's not a recipe-driven item. So, you can read some recipe out of a book, but you've got to literally cook it 1,000 times before you can understand the skill-driven part of it, if that makes sense.

Are you just going to keep expanding the empire? You've got 10 in four states.

Let me tell you—my entire focus is to get back to one store. I'm on this train right now, and it's hard. I mean, it's great. My financial life has changed dramatically. It's been great for our family. But, I didn't get in this business to open up 10 Martin's BBQ. I didn't get in it to open up two. I wanted to cook with my hands.

BENJAMIN AND MAX GOLDBERG

THERE ARE TWO VERY clear demarcation points that demonstrate just how Nashville had graduated to a different eating and drinking scene: the opening of The Patterson House in 2009 and The Catbird Seat two years later. The brothers behind the ventures, Nashville natives Benjamin and Max Goldberg, believed the city was ready for a different level of creativity in its cocktails and its food, the kinds of places that the duo had seen in New York and Chicago, but not back home. And most importantly, they believed that Nashvillians were ready to pay the prices necessary to sustain that creativity. At Patterson House, that meant seven different kinds of ice and $12 cocktails that might take 10 minutes to prepare. And at The Catbird Seat, it meant $100 tickets instead of reservations, and a horseshoe-shaped open kitchen that doubles as kind of a food kabuki show. No other restaurant in the city had broached a triple-digit check, and that was without alcohol. Both of them worked for a very simple reason: the Goldbergs' relentless focus on customer experience.

When you opened Patterson House, did you know that Nashville was ready to accept a higher level of cocktail and service and a little more creativity?

MAX: Everybody told us we were idiots, and "why would anybody wait to get in to get a drink that could take 10 or 15 minutes and cost $11 at a time." Benjamin and I have always tried to open up places where we'd want to go, and we've both been exposed to really great cocktails. We were just excited to try and create something that we had seen in other places and thought it would be really hopefully responded well to in Nashville. I'd seen it in Milk & Honey [the cocktail bar, not the comfort food chain with a location in the Gulch] when I lived there in New York. Benjamin had gone into a place called The Violet Hour in Chicago and other cocktail bars, and it turned out to be the same bartender from Milk & Honey and The Violet Hour, which is kind of serendipitous.

BEN: Ultimately, response was pretty incredible. I think what I'm personally more proud of than anything at Patterson House is that you could really have great restaurants in Nashville that clearly existed that had great wine, beer, and spirits menus but didn't necessarily have to have a great cocktail list. Once the Patterson House really opened up the eyes for some folks to see how great a cocktail could be, it really became common practice to see restaurants opening with great cocktails. That was really the team of The Patterson House, and we were just lucky to be a small part of it.

MAX: I think that it really hopefully set the bar to say, "Hey, cocktails can be really great and special, and here's why we pay so much attention to them."

BEN: I will say, just going back to something you said, I will say that any project we do, we have literally no idea of. There is no market research that's going into it. We're creating places that we want to go, and we hope there are more people like us. When I went to The Violet Hour for the first time inside at the bar and had the cocktail, it was unlike anything that I had had, but it was also one of the most special experiences I ever had. To me, getting to know those guys and learning from those guys and interacting with those guys, I was blown away by the passion behind it. We absolutely fell in love with that whole thing. So, I think that, did we know it would work? In no way, shape or form did we, like, ask people, "Would you spend $11 and wait 20 minutes for a drink?"

What we felt like we would have a chance to, if it was special, the cocktail tasted differently, which was everyone's first question. "I can get cocktails on Fridays." And we would be like, "No, no, no. These are different. You don't understand. These aren't like that. These are fresh and—"

MAX: And it's seven different kinds of ice.

BEN: With all of these things, and so it got to the point that we actually made cocktails for people to show them the difference. Yeah, I mean going further we're very lucky that it happened. I think a lot of that is that we were involved. Had to fully buy in to the whole process. If we cheated a step there we would not have worked. But Josh isn't going to cheat a step. Ever. So the fact that he moved to Nashville from Minnesota and was the GM of Patterson, developed the program and all of those things, Josh is probably one of the most talented people I've ever met in my entire life, under any circumstances. That's just a lucky get in a lot of ways. The first night he moved here we helped him unpack his truck. I took them out and we went to some bars and restaurants and people are like, "Josh, what are you eating here for?" And he was obviously excited to tell people. There were several people in the restaurants based in Nashville like, "That is the dumbest thing."

MAX: And I felt bad because this dude has just picked up his life and moved to Nashville. We're a year from opening and now just the fact that he's getting like, "You may not be here tomorrow." And so I think we're lucky that he stuck around.

So, you had the space, but then the Catbird space above it?

BEN: So it was an old attic at the old house and the hair salon was closing. They were moving on to other things. The landlord is awesome and we found out they were leaving. Obviously we sort of cared about who the new tenant was going to be, so we reached out and said, "Hey, we understand they're closing. We don't know what you're doing with it. We just want to be kept in the loop of what's happening because we cared about our neighbors."

Around that time, Josh, Max, and I were just chatting about like, Josh is like, "What are we going to do? What in your head is the next step for your career?" And sort of bantered about the Catbird experience and called the landlord up and said, "We think we've got something we want to do up there if you'll take us."

Not only is there not a tasting menu in town at the time, there's not something at that price point in town at the time. If Patterson House was with people looking at you going, "What the hell do you think you're doing?"

MAX: Even worse in The Catbird Seat.

Was it even worse? Did people tell you that?

MAX: Oh yeah. Absolutely. They still tell us that. You know, hopefully they'll come in and mutter, "OK, we get it now." The whole food TV show was becoming very popular and that caring about where your food comes from, got really lucky with the timing of that, and the layout of the Catbird Seat is very similar to the layout of the Patterson House there. There's no back of the house, we put the chef directly in front of the guests.

The response that we saw from guests is that the food just tasted better for lots of reasons with the team that was working, but when you hear about where your fish came from and the temperature of the water it was caught in, the line it was caught on, what the captain of the boat had for breakfast that morning, that's extreme but you start to genuinely care more about where the product is. The story that's told and the folks that were up there originally, I mean thinking about where they have gone and the team that we had up, it's pretty special.

Our sommelier is now a master somm and working in Australia. Josh is now our partner at Bastion, Erik's going it out in California and Minnesota. It was a really special moment for our little company and for the team that was up there.

BEN: The craziest thing about Catbird was Josh never cooked in town. He was the bartender. So we opened up the Catbird Seat . . . the only way it works is because of Josh and Erik. There is nothing that we could ever do to make that . . .

How did you, I mean you had Josh but how did you get Erik, how did you figure out, "Oh these two guys should do this together." I mean you've done it a couple of different iterations now. How did that come together?

BEN: So Josh and Erik were friends and worked together, so they knew each other. Erik was sort of looking for his next step. He had just either committed to or come back from, I don't remember, a stage with Noma. Or worked a little bit in Noma. Their relationship and the way they viewed food just made sense to do it. Now I would also say it wasn't just the two of them that sort of made it. One of these desserts were ridiculous. Really what we found out early on which we didn't know right away was like. You're living with each other. People don't understand it's four days a week, but it's 80-, 90-, 100-hour weeks. One day off a week, so it's a grind and basically you're a family up there, and so you all had to get along really, really well. Josh and Erik being the two big ones.

MAX: In the early days I would work the door, and Benjamin refilled the water. They were fun.

Tell me if you think this is fair or not. That doesn't work if you don't have talent all the way through that staff, and you guys have had an incredible amount of talent with every iteration of it. Is that fair?

BEN: Yeah, I think so. Unless the chef is talented, not only at food but at people, the whole thing falls flat. I would also say, the more I look back on it, I'm not sure it would've worked if it wasn't above the Patterson House. I just think that the Patterson House got known to be above quality, that when they realized there was the same people doing the Catbird Seat, in people's minds it was like, "It's just food. We're going to trust them." Whereas if we went somewhere else in town I'm not so sure we would have garnered the same trust after that.

MAX: What's really fun about Catbird is it's become this food incubator where we set out to create this really fun tasting menu experience, but the goal would always be pushing and trying to create something fun in the food scene. Watching that progression from Josh and Erik to Trevor and Ryan and Matt, to now Liz and Will, every single Catbird has had a different feel and a real different menu. It's fun to see the chefs really come into their own and create these special experiences but with the knowledge that every couple of years this thing, it's the worst idea ever, right?

There are always growing pains. We're in our fourth iteration of our chef team right now and I think the Catbird is just as fun today as it was when we first opened.

How would you describe the iterations?

MAX: So Erik [Anderson] and Josh [Habiger], I would say were definitely more on that molecular, kind of insane, pushing the limits on that. Trevor [Moran] went back to that foraging, kind of way back to the basics.

BEN: He's going to be so mad you said "foraging."

MAX: That's why I said it. So yeah, foraging. Yeah, Trevor was at Noma [in Copenhagen, Denmark] five out of the six years that they were named Best Restaurant in the World. Trevor was the most playful, fun, still one of our favorite people in the world and we're so excited for his restaurant to open now. Ryan and Matt [Poli] were very influenced by Ryan's time in Asia so there was a lot of really cool kind of Asian dishes and really beautiful pastas and different desserts and it was special. Liz [Johnson] and Will [Aghajanian], they're going for it. I mean they're using ingredients that I never thought would pair well together and they've created a really fun, playful menu and the response at first was very polarizing. You would see the scores and they're all ones or all fives. I kind of love that. Now they've really hit their groove where it is really fun things that you probably haven't tried, but it tastes incredible and the story behind it is super fun, so the response has been great.

I thought they were interesting after Ryan and Matt because Ryan's palate tends to go more comfort and their menu is not. It's uncomfortable sometimes. Great in a completely different way. The ones and fives thing doesn't surprise me at all.

BEN: It's way more fives than ones at this point, but initially I think that they were pushing it so far which was so fun for that creative side of Catbird that it definitely alienated folks, but I'd rather have all ones and fives than threes and fours. It's fun to see what they're doing right now.

MAX: It also takes time. . . . Catbird is tough because every chef has to find their legs and like their vision, exactly what they want to serve because you are under a microscope in that restaurant, unlike any other microscope. It's intense. The iteration changes that we've made have been intentional in that way where like, yeah Ryan's food is comforting. . . . You're going to eat every bite of every single plate. Nothing is going to scare you away from something. Liz and Will are not scared to scare you, so we knew that going into it. So we've made those conscious decisions. I think that's also why Erik and Josh were so interesting because Erik cooked a lot of food that did scare people. Josh would bring them right back to center and they would alternate courses. So Erik's big thing was the pigeon leg with the claw on it. Which was delicious, it was awesome but it was jarring to look at.

BEN: They're like, "You don't want it? Eat a different course." We're OK with that, the next course would be a fish that Josh was cooking. So that's been thoughtful.

MAX: I think what's fun with Liz and Will now is that mentally it's almost as fun as it is to eat. Like the mental process of going through there, experiencing Catbird. The feel, the space, the way that they're putting out dishes. And visually it's stunning. I think it's some of the most beautiful food I ever saw.

Nashville

TIANA CLARK, 2017

is hot chicken on sopping white bread with green pickle
chips—sour to balance prismatic, flame-colored spice
for white people. Or, rather, white people now curate hot
chicken for $16 and two farm-to-table sides, or maybe

they've hungered fried heat and grease from black food
and milk—but didn't want to drive to Jefferson Street or
don't know about the history of Jefferson Street or Hell's
Half Acre, north of downtown. Where freed slaves lived

on the fringe of Union camps, built their own new country.
Where its golden age brought the Silver Streak, a ballroom
bringing Basie, Ellington, and Fitzgerald. First-run movies
at the Ritz and no one had to climb to the balcony. 1968,

they built the interstate. I-40 bisected the black community
like a tourniquet of concrete. There were no highway exits.
120 businesses closed. Ambulance siren driving over
the house that called 911, diminishing howl in the distance,

black bodies going straight to the morgue. At the downtown
library, a continuous loop flashes SNCC videos with black
and white kids training for spit and circular cigarette burns
as the video toggles from coaching to counters covered

in pillars of salt and pie and soda—magma of the movement.
On I-65, there is a two-tone Confederate statue I flick off
daily on my morning commute. Walking down Second Avenue,
past neon honky-tonks playing bro-country and Cash

and herds of squealing pink bachelorette parties—someone
yelled *Nigger-lover* at my husband. Again. Walking down
Second Avenue, I thought I heard someone yelling at the back
of my husband. I turned around to find the voice and saw

myself as someone who didn't give a damn. Again. I turned
around to find that it was I who lived inside the lovely word
made flesh by white mouths masticating mashed sweet potatoes
from my mother's mother's mother—Freelove was her name,

a slave from Warrior, North Carolina, with twelve children
with names like Pansy, Viola, Oscar, Stella, and Toy—my
grandmother. There is always a word I'm chasing inside and
outside of my body, a word inside another word, scanning

the O.E.D. for soot-covered roots: 1577, 1584, 1608 . . . Tracing my
finger along the boomerang shape of the Niger River for my blood.
1856, 1866, 1889 . . . *Who said it?* A hyphen—crackles and bites,
burns the body to a spray of white wisps, like when the hot comb,

with its metal teeth, cut close to petroleum jelly edging the scalp—
sizzling. Southern Babel, smoking the hive of epithets hung fat
above bustling crowds like black-and-white lynching photographs,
mute faces, red finger pointing up at my dead, some smiling,

some with hats and ties—all business, as one needlelike lady
is looking at the camera, as if looking through the camera, at me,
in the way I am looking at my lover now—halcyon and constant.
Once my mother-in-law said *Watch your back*, and I knew exactly

what she meant. Again. I turned around to find I am the breath
of Apollo panting at the back of Daphne's wild hair, chasing words
like arrows inside the knotted meat between my shoulder blades—
four violent syllables stabbing my skin, enamored with pain.

I am kissing all the trees—searching the mob, mumbling to myself:
Who said it?
Who said it?
Who said it?

Welcome to Bachelorette City

STEVEN HALE, 2017

ON A FRIDAY NIGHT at WannaB's Karaoke Bar on Lower Broadway, a blond bride-to-be named Nicole—white dress, black sash—dances on-stage, flanked by a crew of girls shouting along to the end of "Fergalicious."

To the D to the E to the L-I-C-I-O-U-S.
To the D to the E to the L-I-C-I-O-U-S.

Amid scattered applause, Nicole grabs the penis-shaped whistle hanging around her neck, brings it to her mouth—throwing her head one direction and her hips the other as she does—and blows it. Almost instantly a shrill chorus of whistles rises from the crowd. Turns out there are three other bachelorette parties in the bar, and a number of the women are equipped with these pink, plastic, disturbingly detailed phallic instruments. It's like one car alarm setting off a dozen others. Soon, hands in the air, they let out a *"woooo!"* and are out the door.

"Welcome to Bachelorette City" by Steven Hale, first published in the *Nashville Scene* on August 3, 2017. Reprinted with permission of FW Publishing.

Outside, asked what Fergie's 2006 hit means to them, Nicole and her fellow Kansans are all talking in unison. They were in sixth grade when it came out. They rocked out to it then, so they rocked out to it now.

Why'd they come to Nashville?

"Because. It's. Bachelorette. Central!"

These are the girls you've heard of—the girls you've literally heard. These are the Woo Girls, and they are everywhere, even on a suffocating July night like this one.

In less than two hours of observation on Lower Broadway, I count 33 clearly identifiable bachelorette parties. They're from all over the country. Two parties are from Kansas City, two are from Ohio, and there's even one from San Francisco. The true number of such parties on the street is almost certainly higher than that; not every pack of young women hittin' the honky-tonks is so obviously decked out and coordinated. The serious ones can generally be seen in one of two types of ensembles. Some opt for custom-made T-shirts—"Last Bash in Nash" or "Getting Shitty in Music City." Others are a little fancier, with the squad wearing black dresses and the bride-to-be clad in white, with a sash reading "Bride to Be" or "Future Mrs. So and So." On this night there's even a party whose trappings are Harry Potter-themed.

To walk into Honky Tonk Central up the street is to crash one big bachelorette party. There are three of them just on the first floor of the three-level tourist trap. Morgan Frazier, a singer who performed under the tutelage of Blake Shelton and Pharrell on Season 9 of NBC's *The Voice*, is onstage shouting them out. She points to one group on the VIP balcony that floats above the bar—and can be rented by bachelorettes for $75 per person—and calls out to the girl in white.

"You said you wanted '90s rock?"

Her band's lead guitarist launches into the indelible opening riff of Lit's "My Own Worst Enemy," and soon the bachelorette is leaning over the railing, pumping a fist as if she's throwing the lyrics at the stage.

Can we forget about the things I said when I was drunk?

Minutes later, Frazier has invited another bachelorette onstage to sing with her. The girl's name is Abby, and when she leaves the stage, she is hyped.

"We fucking love Nashville!" she says when asked why she chose our fair town as her party destination. She's explaining that the group has a reservation on the Nashville Party Barge the next day when one of her friends decides this interview is over, stepping between Abby and the reporter's recorder. Maybe that's best.

To longtime Nashvillians, these citizens of Broadway are strange visitors who represent a bizarre and relatively new phenomenon. But on a night like this, from Fifth Avenue down to the Cumberland River, this town is theirs.

THINK OF THE BACHELORETTE-PARTY industry—and it is an industry—like a remora that attaches itself to a growing whale, depending on the huge mammal for survival. The boom years have benefited a number of commercial enterprises—coffee shops, craft breweries, mural artists—and Nashville's success as a "bach destination" (pronounced "batch") is one such outcome. But now the little remora is big enough to swim around and eat on its own. If you're not careful, it will bite you.

In recent years, Nashville has earned automatic inclusion on the sorts of internet lists that funnel bachelorettes to town. In 2015, *Travel + Leisure* named Nashville the N°. 1 spot for a "girlfriend getaway," and *Glamour* included it on a list of the nation's Hottest Bachelorette Party Destinations. Earlier this year, Nashville was ranked the N°. 3 Best Bachelorette Party Location by something called Betches.com.

It is an overwhelmingly white phenomenon, which is not all that surprising. Nashville's political and cultural power structure has historically been white, and after all, so has country music.

It's not quite right to call the arrival of our new bachelorette overlords an organic development, but at the same time it is not a creation of the city's official tourism infrastructure. When the *Scene* requests an interview with Nashville Convention & Visitors Corp.'s president, Butch Spyridon, he is unavailable but sends a response through CVC spokesperson Bonna Johnson.

"The city's popularity with them speaks to Nashville's strength as a destination," Johnson says, relaying Spyridon's sentiments. "We've never done anything to attract bachelorette parties, but we would never apologize for groups that want to travel here."

If you detect a defensive posture in that statement, that tells you something about local attitudes toward the surge in bachelorettes and a general assumption that the topic has negative connotations.

So how did this all happen? The answer, generally, is a cocktail of contributing factors that tasted good going down for businesses and party-minded entrepreneurs, but now has some locals feeling a hangover. Among those factors: the boom years on this side of the 2010 flood that positioned Nashville as the hot new thing—think *GQ*'s "Nowville" feature in July 2012, or the (in)famous January 2013 article in the *New York Times* that birthed the "It City" moniker—years that saw Nashville, or a version of it, take center stage in a prime-time TV drama; the explosion of short-term rentals through Airbnb and others, which has made a group trip to Nashville relatively affordable; and the cottage industry that has sprung up to cater to the constant flow of bachelorettes coming through the city, creating ample opportunities for Instagram-able memories and making the whole notion of Nashville as a bachelorette destination a self-perpetuating reality.

But those factors alone wouldn't necessarily guarantee that a city will end up with hundreds of 20-something girls descending upon it for "Nashlorette" weekends. To figure out how that happened, it's worth taking a ground-level look at what's changed on Lower Broadway, a living ecosystem of sorts to which various creatures adapt.

"My mom happily reflects on the downtown Nashville of her youth," says Freddie O'Connell, a Metro Council member who was raised in Nashville, and whose district includes Lower Broadway. "She grew up in Dickson, and when they would come into town, downtown was streetcars, department stores. It was the expansive, post-industrial town square. And then that went away, and it kind of became a commercial district purely where after 5 p.m. on any given day of the week, there wasn't anything. And that was the Nashville of my youth. If you came downtown after 5 p.m. you probably weren't supposed to be there."

Following the Grand Ole Opry's departure from the Ryman Auditorium the decade before, Broadway in the '80s was marked by peep shows, adult bookstores, and nondescript bars. What is now Robert's Western World was a liquor store then.

But toward the end of O'Connell's high school years, through the mid to late '90s, things started to change. Kids started cruising Second Avenue, to the point that the city posted "No Cruising" signs on the street. A transformational moment came in 1996, when Bridgestone Arena, then known as the Nashville Arena, opened its doors.

Until then, Lower Broadway was not fully embraced by the surrounding infrastructure. Because of its architectural orientation, the old Nashville Convention Center was said to "turn its back on Broadway." It didn't engage the downtown strip. But the arena, with its large entrance plaza opening up toward the honky-tonk district, did just that, and made the center of Nashville a destination for many more people. In the years that followed, new honky-tonks, boot stores, and Western-themed karaoke bars began to pop up—the makings of a never-ending block party.

Nashville's rising prominence, the popularity (and proximity) of the Tennessee Titans and the Nashville Predators, and the ubiquity of country music didn't hurt, either.

One could theorize about any number of moments when Nashville took a turn toward becoming "Bachville." But one event in particular stands out to O'Connell, something he seems to lament. In 1992, the legendary letterpress print shop Hatch Show Print moved from its Fourth Avenue South location, where it'd been since 1925, to make way for the AT&T tower, and reopened on Lower Broadway. For more than 20 years, visitors could walk into that cavernous, ink-stained space and find someone making the kind of concert prints that made the shop famous. For O'Connell, it was a landmark with a true, authentic connection to Nashville's past. And then in 2013, it left Lower Broadway for a slick new location attached to the Country Music Hall of Fame—good news, in that the shop survives to this day. But it was also an illustrative change in the ecosystem of Lower Broadway.

Today, 316 Broadway is home to Tin Roof, a honky-tonk-styled bar like all the others. On a recent weekend night, while the band takes a break, three separate bachelorette parties bob along to Ed Sheeran's "Shape of You" blasting through the speakers.

I'm in love with your body
Oh—I—oh—I—oh—I—oh—I

One group, gathered around Morgan—the one in white—is from Cleveland. They came to Nashville, they say, because it's "better than Vegas."

They say they'll be taking a pole-dancing class the next day. And they have the penis whistles too.

"Couple [the departure of Hatch Show Print] with the arrival of Honky Tonk Central," O'Connell says. "It's almost like, to drop a physical manifestation of a reality show about honky-tonking on Broadway."

The three-level tower of tipsy on the corner of Fourth Avenue and Broadway opened in 2012, and it's true: It doesn't just seem on the nose—it's a punch in the nose. It is a honky-tonk called Honky Tonk. And the Epcot-ification of the Broadway scene is only intensified by the opening earlier this year of FGL House, a multilevel establishment from Florida Georgia Line, the duo who found a lucrative career making vaguely country-adjacent noises behind lyrics about partyin', truck beds, beer, and bikinis. The place features massive portraits of each band member and joins other celebrity-branded downtown bars from the likes of

Dierks Bentley—not to mention Blake Shelton, who plans to open a $20 million palace.

If affiliation with country music is one of Nashville's major appeals, consider the sort of mainstream country music Nashville is affiliated with, and ask yourself, Are the penis whistles really surprising?

There's also reason to suspect another tourism factor is at play: Nashville is perceived—rightly or wrongly, for better or worse—as a safe place to get blind drunk in public. (There is a whole other story to be written about how much this presumption of safety may be racialized—connected to Nashville's perception as a white town.)

Chase Humphrey, a hot dog vendor with more than a decade's worth of experience working on Lower Broadway, put it like this when he spoke to the *Scene* for a 2015 article on the sausage-slinging scene: "Back in the day, people would come here to really listen to the music. Now people just come to just get wasted."

Not all of those bachelorettes are staying downtown, of course. There isn't yet a party bus that offers beds for the night—we'll have to wait on that one. In October, as reported by the *Tennessean*, average hotel rates in Nashville, at least temporarily, surpassed those in New York and Boston. Bachelorette parties on a budget are tapping into a thriving network of houses available for rent through companies like Airbnb. Whereas some hotels blocks from Broadway will set you back $400 for a single room, a party of eight (with a little planning) can find an Airbnb in East Nashville to accommodate the whole party for less than that.

But it's worth noting that many Airbnb hosts prohibit parties—and some even single out bachelor and bachelorette parties.

"No bachelor parties, no bachelorette parties," reads one description of a house listed on Airbnb in East Nashville. "No rowdiness. If you're looking for a property to stay in where you have the intention of consuming large amounts of alcohol, there are other properties in town that are a better fit for your time in Nashville."

Indeed there are, although hosts are keenly aware of the line they might be walking with their neighbors. The *Scene* reached out to hosts who specifically court bachelorette parties in their descriptions. One host responded to say that they'd had positive experiences with bachelorette parties and maintain good relationships with their neighbors, but they declined to speak on the record.

"There are those in Nashville that are looking for hosts to attack," wrote the host. "So I must protect myself by staying off the radar."

Another host agrees to talk on the condition of anonymity, hoping to avoid attracting the attention of people pushing for tighter regulation of short-term rentals. Asked about her specific rental description, she laughs.

"It's every weekend," she says. "I wasn't planning to do that, but that's what was happening, so I switched up my description, because I was like, 'This is the main group that I'm getting.'"

She insists her neighbors don't have a problem with what goes on at her property, but not everyone is thrilled about having what can amount to a sorority house—or frat house, as the case may be—on the other side of the fence.

O'Connell has lived in his house in the Salemtown neighborhood for 10 years, on a street that is entirely zoned residential. He and his wife have a 6-year-old daughter and a newborn baby—facts that were no doubt going through his mind two weeks ago, when he says he was woken around 3 a.m. by a group of girls moving their party to the back porch next door.

"We've had the doorbell rung at that hour, multiple times, from people too drunk to know which house they're supposed to be at," he says.

The Metro Council's attempts at settling on regulations for short-term rentals have repeatedly stalled, and the council recently postponed that effort until later this year. Describe the situation as complicated, and O'Connell will stop you right there. He doesn't believe it's really that complicated at all.

"If you throw anywhere from eight to 20 bachelorettes into what was a residential house, I don't think that's a great thing for livability and maybe not even for Nashville being a destination city," he says. "I simply don't think these things belong in residential neighborhoods, period."

For now, whether they belong is a hypothetical question. They're here. But even if short-term rentals aid and abet the bachelorettes, they're not the only thing that's bringing them to Nashville. On that question, the aforementioned host—the one who adjusted her description to target the only customers she was seeing—has a theory.

"My theory has always been Robbie Goldsmith," she says.

Goldsmith, an entrepreneur, launched Bachelorette Nashville in 2013 as a sort of concierge service for bachelorette parties. Since then, the company has grown, changed its name to Bach Weekend, and expanded to three cities.

Says the host, "I just think that when someone goes out and is marketing on the internet, 'Nashville and bachelorettes,' and is putting a ton of effective marketing out there, suddenly when you're Googling or whatever, that's what comes up."

Goldsmith was unable to meet with the *Scene* (due to a recent death in his family), but he responded to an email about "how Nashville became the bachelorette capital of the known universe" like this:

"While Vegas is still no doubt the capital, we definitely seem to be a close second! Although I'm not sure how long that will last."

ON A RECENT TUESDAY afternoon, the Bach Weekend offices on Third Avenue South are busy, with four women working at desks just inside the door, and John Mayer playing in the background. Chief operating officer Rachal Smith apologizes for the chaos—it's an event weekend, she says.

Aren't they all event weekends at a business like Bach Weekend?

Not like this. After trying the concierge model, the company changed its approach to one that was less tedious and more scalable and reproducible in other cities. Modeled after the cruise industry, the company sells package weekends to groups and provides them with an itinerary and private downtown parties with other groups. It's essentially Bachelorette-ageddon.

Bach Weekend books 15 to 20 groups of either bachelors or bachelorettes for the same weekend "that we combine together into one massive group of baches," says Smith.

"I equate it to camp, almost," adds Rosa Castano, director of sales.

Smith and Castano are as enthusiastic about Nashville's burgeoning bach scene as you'd imagine. They speak about it as a positive development, but even so, they seem completely aware of the sillier side of the business. They cite one ongoing serious romantic relationship that began during one of their mega-bach weekends, not to mention many more . . . let's call them *short-term* relationships. A big part of Nashville's rise as a "bach destination," they say, is the casual nature of the NashVegas strip.

Many elements of Las Vegas have become velvet-roped and exclusive, whereas Nashville offers five blocks of bars with live music and no cover (even if the beers are getting a bit more expensive these days).

"Nashville is such a novelty, and a lot of people don't know what to expect," Castano says. "I get people from the Chicago area or even California, and they're like, 'Well, we want to have a place that has bottle service,' and I'm like, 'Cool, here's a beer bottle.'"

Bach Weekend arranged 11 mega-bach weekends last year and 11 this year. Next year, there are 18 on the calendar. A map in the lobby has pins on it showing the far-flung locations that different groups have traveled from, including Toronto and Alaska.

Companies like Bach Weekend have only boosted the market for companies like Pedal Tavern Nashville, which opened in 2010 and now has 10 pedal vehicles on the street, which are booked up for months in advance. General manager Angie Gleason tells the *Scene* that Sundays are now as busy as Saturdays for tavern rides—evidence, she says, that groups are staying in town a little longer.

The bachelorette boom has helped make so-called "transportainment" a growth industry as well. Consider the ever-growing list of transportation options available to ferry parties up and down the downtown streets, plying them with alcohol and Top 40 hits. There are the pedal taverns, of course, which are available from several different companies now but all offer the same basic experience: a group ride on a multi-seat bar/bike, fueled by beer and the opportunity to spend a few hours as a slowly moving public spectacle. There are tractors, massive John Deere ones, that pull wagons with bartenders and DJs on them. There's a thing called the Party Porch, which is half-bus, half-porch. And there's the Party Barge—basically a pickup truck with an extra-long bed retrofitted to look and feel like a boat.

On a weekend night on Lower Broadway, these rolling ragers pass each other like shit-faced ships in the night. One group hooting at the other, the other hollering back, pedestrians on the sidewalk gawking at all of them.

Waiting in line outside a bar, one bachelorette party from Ohio is just starting their weekend. They came to Nashville because they'd heard it's a good place to party, and their goal, says one bridesmaid-to-be, is to get the bride-to-be "to where she doesn't remember her name." As of 10:45 p.m., that name is Emily. Congratulations, Emily.

Much ado has been made over the emergence of New Nashville in recent years—Husk over T.G.I. Fridays, Crema over Starbucks, Jason Isbell over Toby Keith. This is something different, though. If that was an evolution, this seems like a mutation.

This is the new New Nashville.

Wooo

Desegregation and Its Discontents

ANSLEY T. ERICKSON, 2019

FROM THE PERSPECTIVE OF the present day, Nashville's late-20th-century school desegregation story may feel like ancient history. The city was a much smaller place in 1971. Its growth ambitions were just that—ambitions—rather than cranes and convention centers and tall-skinnies and a thing called "The Gulch." It was also a much less diverse place—with black and white residents but few of the global immigrant communities that now call Metro home.

Its schools were much different places, too. They operated then under a court order for desegregation, one that rezoned schools and transported students out of their neighborhoods to achieve statistical targets for each school. As a result, few to none of Nashville's schools were more than 90 percent students of one racial category or another. The order was lifted in 1998, and almost immediately the gains began to slip away.

"Desegregation and Its Discontents" by Ansley T. Erickson, first published in a slightly different form as "History Repeating" in the *Nashville Scene* on August 13, 2015. Reprinted with permission of FW Publishing.

Today, the city is home to stark school segregation. Although Nashville has taken some measures to foster demographic diversity in its schools in the last few years, for much of the last decade approximately 6 percent of the city's children have attended a school that is more than 90 percent black; many of these schools also have more than 90 percent of children living in poverty. Put differently, roughly one in every seven black children in Nashville attend a highly racially and economically segregated school. Both district and charter schools contribute to this figure.

Despite the fact that the participation of middle-class and white families in Nashville's public schools has fallen substantially since 1998—that is, well after the end of desegregation—many Nashvillians will point to desegregation, and particularly the use of busing to transport students out of their neighborhood, as a turning point in the school system's struggles today. That's when public support for schools fell, they say. That's when the school system hit hard times.

Desegregation does illuminate Nashville's current school system and its struggles, but not in the way many Nashvillians think. There are far more continuities in the city's inequalities from past to present, and in the limits of the city's attempts to address them, than are obvious. Perhaps with a fuller understanding of a complex and much-misunderstood element of Nashville's history, its citizens can help cast a new route forward.

THE YEAR WAS 1971, and a mayoral runoff dominated the dog days of another hot summer. Then as now, the city's central concern was much the same: education.

Incumbent Mayor Beverly Briley and insurgent Metro councilmember Casey Jenkins competed to see who could most vociferously oppose a controversial new development in Nashville schools—desegregation through busing. For the first time, most Nashville schools would no longer serve nearly all-white or all-black student populations. Instead, students would ride buses out of their neighborhoods to help achieve court-specified racial ratios.

Reading newspaper accounts in Nashville's two dailies of the period, it's clear that candidates Briley and Jenkins saw busing not as an opportunity, but an intrusion. Desegregation, they felt, threatened cherished realms of family authority and property rights. Like many white Nashvillians opposed to busing, they thought those rights extended beyond the home to the local school.

Jenkins organized rallies that interrupted court proceedings. Once busing for desegregation was ordered, he preached outright defiance. (Neither he nor other desegregation opponents said anything about the system's long use of busing to segregate, when they transported black students and white students by bus to segregated schools). Opposing busing became his campaign's sole issue. Fifteen thousand came to his rally at the State Fairgrounds speedway, roaring their assent as Jenkins decried breaking down the schools' racial separation as "communism" "creeping in to the city." He promised to delay or close school.

That was beyond his authority, but no one minded. "We want Casey!" the huge crowd stomped and chanted.

Briley spoke in more measured tones. Privately, according to *Nashville Banner* reporter Dick Battle, he was uncertain what his stance on busing should be. Publicly, his disdain rang loud and clear. When constituents wrote to him, he replied that Nashville's busing order was the "worst" in the nation. He did "not believe that the school is a social experiment," as if segregation itself were not just such a thing.

Neither Jenkins nor Briley said it directly, but both succeeded in assuring white constituents that the privilege they had long enjoyed in Nashville's schools, often at clear costs to their black peers, would continue. On the topic of what made busing's drastic measures necessary, Briley and Jenkins said nothing, as did many other local opponents.

But Kelly Miller Smith, long-time civil rights leader, Nashville parent, and pastor of First Baptist Church Capitol Hill, presented the case succinctly. In an archived letter, she writes that busing was an effort "at remedying the glaring inequities in public education as far as black young people are concerned. . . . The problem is not busing. . . . Rather, the problem is racism. . . . We see busing as a significant and effective effort at dealing with the real problem."

The "real problem" was not hard to see. In 1970, before busing began, 43 of Nashville's 140 schools operated with 99 percent or more white students; 86 had fewer than 10 percent black students. At the other extreme, 21 schools served 90 percent or more black students. Sixteen years after *Brown v. Board of Education of Topeka*, the 1954 case that deemed segregated schools unconstitutional, the vast majority of Nashville's students, black or white, essentially attended schools sorted by race.

Inequality aligned with segregation. Thousands of black students in Nashville attended schools that were visible threats to their health and safety. These firetraps, described in a 1970 MNPS study as having insufficient plumbing and crumbling ceilings, all but embodied the concept of separate but unequal. Black teachers used their own dollars to cover funding gaps not present in largely white schools.

Gaps in achievement were just as wide. Before busing, 71 percent of black Nashville elementary students scored below the national average in math, as opposed to only 30 percent of white elementary students. Reading scores showed black students dramatically behind as well. If those students could have access to the superior facilities and resources often found in white schools, Nashville desegregation advocates hoped to end their long-standing lags in performance and opportunity.

And long-standing they were, having malingered past an earlier phase of desegregation in Nashville. After the Supreme Court's *Brown* decision in 1954, black community leaders sued for desegregation locally. The board of education designed a token gradual plan. With tremendous courage, 19 black first-graders enrolled at segregated white elementary schools in September 1957.

The 6-year-olds arrived to face white adults brandishing Ku Klux Klan signs and Confederate flags. Bystanders glowered at small children on their way to school. A nighttime bombing rocked Hattie Cotton Elementary School in East Nashville. (Luckily, it was empty at the time of the explosion.) But calm soon returned—and with it the resumption of scholastic racial separatism, for all but a tiny proportion of Nashville's students.

The broader assault on that racial barrier began in 1971. By then, neither Jenkins's nor Briley's rhetoric could stop the buses from rolling. Casey Jenkins lost the election, but kept up a few months of pickets and protests before leaving town. Briley found quieter but more powerful channels of resistance. After winning his second term, he pressed Federal Judge L. Clure Morton off the case, setting in motion years of minimal judicial engagement with busing. Meanwhile, leaders on the Metro Council restricted funds for buses, worsening logistical challenges and thereby bolstering the argument that busing was burdensome by helping make sure it was.

Nashville had a rare set of opportunities in desegregation. Many other metropolitan areas had school district boundaries that separated the majority-black city from the majority-white suburbs. The Metro Nashville system enfolded the entire county. Combining busing with the scale and diversity of the metropolitan population, Nashville became one of the most statistically desegregated school systems in the country.

Busing was neither popular nor perfect. But it had significant, positive educational and social outcomes for Nashville students, as in many other desegregating districts around the country. In terms of test scores, the data is limited. But a 1992 report compiled by then director Charles Frazier indicated that average scores for Nashville's white and black students rose substantially, while reading and math achievement gaps had closed by between 25 and 40 percent, in busing's two decades.

Nonetheless, Nashville lacked a strong voice in elected leadership standing up for desegregation's benefits. Briley and Jenkins competed instead on the strength of their opposition. It didn't have to be this way. Charlotte's leaders embraced busing and desegregation as part of the formula for their city's growth. Later, Raleigh and Louisville created long-standing coalitions in favor of desegregating their schools.

When those cities sustained desegregation efforts in the late 1990s, Nashville's government and business leadership pushed for an end to court-ordered desegregation. The Chamber of Commerce commissioned a study that asserted that more companies would move to town if schools no longer bused children for desegregation. Mayor Phil Bredesen equated an end of desegregation with a reinvestment in public schools by white and middle-class families. New firms did come to town after 1998, of course. But white families over the next decade became even less likely to send their children to Metro public schools. Turning away from desegregation did not make for a return to investment in Nashville's public schools.

IN 1972, DR. SAMMIE Lucas and his wife hoped to buy a new home. They looked near McGavock School, and liked a house for sale a few miles up the road on McGavock Pike in Donelson. It was owned by the Travis family. Upon visiting the home with the seller's real estate agent, the Lucases decided to make an offer.

But the Travises weren't interested in going to contract. They claimed they had a "color clause" on their property—a restrictive covenant on the deed, barring sale to a black family like the Lucases. They said they worried about how their neighbors, white like themselves, would react to a "Negro" family. The Travises didn't want to help further integrate the school, either.

The real estate agent told the sellers, rightly, that whatever "color clause" they had on their deed had been "outlawed." The Supreme Court ruled restrictive covenants unenforceable in 1948. The dispute came to a settlement out of court, and the Lucases found another home nearby.

The Lucases' story hints at the many roots of segregated housing in Nashville. Private actions—like sellers refusing to sell, or real estate agents refusing to show properties—helped keep most Nashville suburbs segregated and white for decades. But as hurtful as these individual actions must have been to families like the Lucases, they were small-bore compared to the federal policies that helped construct the segregated white subdivisions around McGavock in the first place.

White residents could make their postwar exodus to the suburbs, in large part, because of federal home-financing subsidies that excluded most black neighborhoods and black borrowers. Major federal investments in highway construction made the suburbs more accessible; low tax rates on gasoline eased travel costs as well. As the segregated white suburbs boomed, public housing construction targeted city neighborhoods exclusively, helping to make "urban" seem synonymous with "black."

But the Travises' remarks were telling in another way. They wanted to keep their neighborhood white because that would keep their local high school white too. The Travises were far from alone in linking all-white neighborhoods and hopes for an all-white school. Local officials had for decades thought of and built segregated schools and segregated housing together.

In 1959, Irving Hand and his colleagues on the Planning Commission mapped Nashville's neighborhoods into "planning units." That process required them to define what they meant by a neighborhood. For Hand, a neighborhood had key features—"similar ethnic groups," "population in similar income range"—and local elementary schools were central.

Hand wasn't inventing these ideas. He was borrowing them from nationally influential city planners who had started down this path at the turn of the 20th century. If Hand wanted to link neighborhoods of "similar ethnic groups" and schools, federal urban renewal projects led by his colleagues at the Nashville Housing Authority (the predecessor to the MDHA) provided one opportunity.

Inside their Edgehill urban renewal project, NHA officials figured out how to leverage needed expansions at segregated local schools to generate more funding for segregated local public housing. To maximize the funds, schools had to serve only those who lived in an urban renewal area. For private developers, the school board helped in linking new schools and new housing as well. This cemented the links between segregated housing and schooling. In essence, it formed a circle that kept students corralled by race and income.

Segregation in housing and schooling together had many historic allies in Nashville. The power of those forces dwarfed even an ambitious effort like busing. They still leave their mark on the city—not only in visible patterns of residential segregation but in contributing to the wide gap in family wealth between white families (who built equity and saw properties appreciate) and black families locked out of this aspect of generational accumulation.

We might say Nashville has a robust history of exclusionary zoning, broadly construed. Today, the city has the opportunity to move to inclusionary zoning, which incorporates lower-income housing into the development process. There are many arguments in favor: breaking up clusters of poverty; encouraging cultural and economic mobility; bringing all residents out of social and economic isolation into the bloodstream of the city.

But recent research suggests Nashvillians should think about inclusionary housing zoning as school policy as well. Inclusionary zoning that allows poor families in Nashville to access more upwardly mobile areas can also bring children into more economically and racially diverse school zones. Inclusionary housing policies in Montgomery County, Maryland, and in Chicago show marked improvement in students' educational and life chances. After decades of yoking housing and schools together to create ruts of reinforced poverty and racial separation, rapid growth and the opportunity to invest in affordable housing gives Nashville a chance to break its lockstep.

Some observers are hopeful that recent increases in middle-class and white families choosing to live in the city center will mean a gradual desegregation of schools there. Two Nashville neighborhoods show that these links are far from automatic. In the Lockeland Springs neighborhood of East Nashville, the proportion of white residents increased over the last 15 years. White parents increasingly chose to send their children to Lockeland Elementary—gradually displacing their black peers. Lockeland passed through a period of desegregation, when its enrollment reflected the diversity of East Nashville, but without conscious efforts to retain this diversity, it resegregated. Lockeland is now the whitest elementary school in Metro.

Buena Vista Elementary, just north of downtown, tells another story. There, new white residents are buying homes just across the street from the school. But if they have children, these residents are not choosing Buena Vista for their schooling. In an increasingly diverse neighborhood, Buena Vista remains a segregated black school, with the vast majority of its students living in poverty.

After decades of linking schooling, housing, and segregation, any new desegregation will require intentional and varied effort.

THERE WAS NOTHING EASY about busing. It deliberately disrupted neighborhoods and forced students out of their literal comfort zones. At the start of school each year, nervous parents guided cherished young-sters onto school buses to distant and sometimes unfamiliar parts of Nashville. Former school board member Kathy Nevill remembered one child arriving at a suburban school. The child's mother, living miles away, had been unable to introduce him to his new teacher in person. So she sent him on the bus with a note pinned to his shirt. Hoping to convey her love and care, she wrote, "My name is . . . and my mother's name is . . . and I live at . . ."

In other parts of the county, adolescents had grown up wanting to cheer for their local school sports team or to play in the band at Litton High School. They planned to walk school corridors at Joelton where pictures of their grandparents lined the walls. They resisted adjusting to high school in a new setting. To be sure, busing was hard on black students and white students alike.

But it was harder for black Nashville children and families. Statistical desegregation did not mean equal concern for the educational experi-ences of all children. From travel burdens to school closures, local and federal officials designed desegregation to appease white middle-class families as much as they could. It was a black child who wore that note on the first day of school, because the district bused black 6-, 7-, 8-, and 9-year-olds out of their neighborhoods for desegregation. White children that age stayed close to home.

Sometimes, it seemed that black youngsters were nearly invisible. Most of the local press coverage of the start of busing in 1971 obsessed over white resistance, pickets, and boycotts. Equally important—yet less reported—was the story that unfolded beneath the press' notice in the first days of school.

After months of detailed tallying of where Nashville's students lived, and how they would be zoned to meet court-ordered racial ratios at each school, principals, teachers, and central-office officials prepared to greet their newly diverse student bodies. When the day came, they were stunned to discover just how many black students were arriving for school at McCann or Richland elementaries, at Cockrill and Charlotte Park and others. Hundreds more black students arrived than expected.

In retrospect, their arrival shouldn't have been a surprise. Long-running patterns in city planning had systematically failed to take black communities, families, and children into account. Planners mapped Nashville into areas of "growth" or "decline." Black children living in public housing complexes, formally segregated until a few years before busing began, were swept under the label of "decline." Their city couldn't see them.

Once these youngsters were re-discovered, Metro Schools district officials walked the streets of Nashville's housing complexes, trying to make a better count and rezone accordingly. For the children, that meant a shift to another new school, another new route and routine.

Black communities also faced many more school closures than white communities. In the fall of 1971, six schools in or near North and South Nashville neighborhoods closed. Pearl, Elliott, Jones, Clemons, Howard, and Central were either historically segregated black schools or had rapidly growing black populations. One (failed) proposal from federal officials was even more dire: to close all schools in the district's urban areas. These institutions had long been hubs of social networks and employment in black communities.

Facing another proposed school closure in the late 1970s, longtime educator Newton Holiday described North Nashville residents as "a group of people who suddenly find that everything that was once of great importance to them has gradually been eroded." For a leading group of black clergy, another school closing would be the "coup de grace" for the community.

Busing compounded an already established pattern of disinvestment—some might call it an economic knee-capping—in Nashville's black urban spaces. Two previous decades of urban renewal projects and highway construction had sliced through front yards and cut off retail districts, forced residents from their homes or destroyed property value. Added to these harms, school closures sent another message that black communities, black lives, did not matter.

With city schools shuttered, busing put black students in schools far from home for nine or 10 of their 12 years of schooling. Most white students traveled for only two or three years. For all the good achieved by busing in some areas, being far from home diminished students' after-school opportunities and lessened parental access, especially for those dependent on Nashville's meager public transportation.

Among them was McGavock High School star basketball player Charles Davis, who worked hard to catch the school bus each morning from the

J. C. Napier Homes. Not only that, he had to find a way home after practice or games, as the buses didn't run then. Fortunately for Davis and his teammates, McGavock Coach Joe Allen saw these transportation problems as learning opportunities. Coach Allen asked teammates like Steve Flatt, who lived close to McGavock and had a car, to drive home those who didn't.

He also asked his players to host team dinners in their homes, whether they lived in Napier and Sudekum public housing or in suburban Donelson. Both Flatt, a future president of Lipscomb University, and Davis, a future pro basketball player who would notch eight seasons in the NBA, spent time in parts of the city and with communities they hadn't known before. Fellow coach Milton Harris hoped the students took a message from these dinners: "It didn't matter where you lived, but how you lived in the place that you lived."

From that story, it's obvious Coach Allen believed black students and white students had much to learn from each other. Not everyone recognized this. At times in the throes of desegregation, a convoluted and troubling logic prevailed. The school board's attorneys in 1980 named white children the "primary educational resource" for black children.

Some white Nashvillians dismissed critiques of desegregation's unequal burdens. They said black children were desegregation's beneficiaries; that black communities were the ones who needed busing. What white students stood to gain as learners and as citizens—how schooling alongside black students could broaden the too-narrow worldview cultivated in segregated white schools—went missing.

Often, when desegregation treated black students differently than white students, it did so in the name of mitigating white resistance and withdrawal. Certainly, middle-class and elite white families' departures to surrounding school systems or private schools helped produce major shifts in Nashville school demographics. These created political and economic challenges the school district is fighting to this day.

Yet because of the metropolitan scale of Nashville's school district, it saw less white flight than did systems with separate city and suburban districts. When busing for desegregation ended in 1998, the school district's population was roughly half white students, half students of color (the vast majority of whom then were African American). But the idea of "white flight" had captured education policymaking in Nashville. Fear of white flight pushed the school district often to think of white and middle-class students as their most important constituency. Ironically, after local leadership pushed to end desegregation in part to draw more of those students back into the school system, their departures from the public system accelerated in the late 1990s and early 2000s.

How much should a district focus on the students it wants to have, rather than the ones it does? Today, with the return of middle-class and wealthy families to Nashville's city neighborhoods, the district may see the opportunity to regain economically and socially privileged constituencies, and broaden public support for its schools.

Crafting district policy in the hopes of doing so, however, has costs. After studying Philadelphia's efforts to gain and retain middle-class families, Temple professor Maia Cucchiara argues that "policies designed to create diversity . . . particularly those that use market strategies and incentives to attract the middle class, can result in the marginalization of low-income families." If desegregation is to return to the policy conversation, both *Brown* and black lives must matter.

ONE POINT IS CLEAR. After decades of leading the nation in statistical desegregation, Nashville has regressed to the mean. If the district is to re-engage with segregation as a problem, alongside many other cities nationally that are doing so, its accomplishments as well as its failures in the busing years will be crucial. Leaders will have to transcend the shape of the current education debate, too long focused on controversial interventions like charter schools rather than broader efforts to confront underlying, continued, and complex sources of educational inequality. They will have to recognize that even in the period of extensive desegregation in the city, most white parents in Nashville believed that that local and federal government *should* bend in the direction of their felt needs, and that these mattered more than the rights of black students. In the busing years, local leaders did too little to challenge this view, and convey a more just vision of the city. Will they step up now?

The prime question is how frankly, how deeply, how assertively the city will value the schooling of its children, naming equity as a goal and attending directly to the needs of the black and poor children Nashville has historically neglected most. Those students today are most likely to attend sharply segregated schools, farthest from the educational benefits of the city's diversity, and to live in communities most removed from the economic benefits of the city's growth. Over the last sixty years, that neglect has taken on many forms, from the maintenance of racially segregated schools to neglect of black students within the diverse district to chronic underfunding of the district as a whole.

Perhaps busing for desegregation seems a relic of a distant era. But Nashville residents, like all US citizens, must reckon with the ways that inequalities and injustices decades earlier shape lives today. To paraphrase William Faulkner's oft-quoted maxim, Nashville's desegregation story—its accomplishments, its missed opportunities, its inequalities—shows that the past isn't even past.

Author's note: This is a lightly revised version of a piece originally published in the Nashville Scene. *I would like to acknowledge the late Jim Ridley for his role in encouraging, conceptualizing, and editing.*

Next Big Something

ASHLEY SPURGEON, 2019

AT THE DAWN OF the millennium, filmmakers Joel and Ethan Coen inadvertently gave Southern cool an alley-oop when they transposed Homeric epic *The Odyssey* onto a country musical set in rural 1930s Mississippi. Ancient Greece and the South are both big on archetypes, and *O Brother, Where Art Thou?* delivered. (Nashville, for its part, calls itself "the Athens of the South" and has the replica Parthenon to prove it.) *Gone with the Wind* is a nifty bit of Lost Cause propaganda that grows more distasteful by the day, but louche, casual con man Rhett Butler feels somehow necessary to the Southern identity. Likewise George Clooney at his most Gable-esque: the charming, fast-talking prison escapee Ulysses McGill.

The Greeks and traditionalist South also share roughly the same respect for women. In *O Brother*, women are either sirens or wives. Holly Hunter's Penny embodies two types of white Southern femininity. First, there's the picture of rod-straight strength, a woman who will do anything for her family—the Steel Magnolia. And then there's the Horny Idiot, susceptible to the charms of conmen like her husband, or too in awe of her new beau's credentials to know (or care) that he's running a political campaign on behalf of a proud white supremacist.

But by not ignoring the dirty parts of the South and instead weaving them into the greater story—using the templates of the ancients as a guide, however loosely—*O Brother, Where Art Thou?* is a hell of a lot of fun. That's also largely thanks to the fact it's a musical. All our heroes sing casually, beautifully; they befriend a wandering troubadour with a mystic bent; Clooney's little girls sing in a family band. And when the Soggy Bottom Boys hop in a recording booth to cut a record on the fly, they became a bona fide hit.

Ultimately it was the soundtrack that nudged *O Brother* past the cult status of most Coen Brothers films and into the wider waters of popular success. Produced by T Bone Burnett and recorded partially in Nashville, the *O Brother* OST was stuffed with traditional country, bluegrass, gospel, and folk—and presented with a totally straight face. It won the Grammy for Album of the Year. It probably didn't hurt that the film also paid fealty to the power of country radio.

The sudden popularity of *O Brother* and its celebration of "Americana," roots, and gospel reminded music fans that there have always been left-of-center (or hypertraditional) country artists who don't otherwise fit the Music Row mold. There's an old joke in Nashville that "Americana" means whatever Jim Lauderdale says it means. (Use your search engine of choice and look up "godfather of Americana"; he's one of them.) Another joke, or perhaps not, depending on your viewpoint: Americana is what you call "country music for liberals."

Whether it was some latent nostalgia for "simpler times" or the wheel of public interest rolling back around to something that felt familiar and ripe-for-remembering, Americana had a spotlight moment in the early aughts. Slap a dusky filter and angelic voices on Red State America and you've got crossover appeal. *O Brother, Where Art Thou?* and its soundtrack introduced a wider, more mainstream audience to beloved artists like Allison Krauss, Emmylou Harris, and the film's associate music producer, Gillian Welch, who by her own estimation had arrived in Nashville 30 years too late. Or just maybe, right on time.

O Brother's success also presaged a coming boom for a Southern-inflected Americana writ large—not just string music, but barbecue, barnwood, Mason jars as drinkware, and so on. If leaning out to court major league sports and multinational corporations ushered in the New South of the 1980s and '90s, then leaning back to the rootsy, handmade, and artisanal—all of which just happened to elicit a mixture of nostalgia and novelty as its weathered edges rolled past on Instagram—ushered in the next wave after that.

THE DEATH OF IRONY post-9/11 has been greatly over exaggerated, but it is not such a stretch to say there was a yearning in the air for *authenticity*, however defined. Enter Kings of Leon, a band seemingly incapable of self-awareness and whose origin narrative was as weird and pure as any tale spun out of the heartland, the mythical swath of the country where the diners and truck stops are full of straight-talking folk who speak for the Real America. The band's "about" page could have been lifted from the treatment for an *O Brother* sequel. Allow Steven Hyden, writing in the late *Grantland*, to explain:

> KOL's first two albums were accompanied by a mythic backstory that involved the group's trio of brothers—Caleb, Nathan, and Jared Followill—being raised by a traveling Pentecostal preacher who forbade his boys to taste the sinful fruit of rock and roll. Defying the threat of eternal damnation, the brothers recruited their cousin Matthew to play guitar, invested in a closetful of impossibly tight jeans, and formed a hard-drinking and hip-swinging rock group. That's what the PR said, anyway—it was the kind of tale that is used to establish a band's "realness" in the media, and it actually sort of worked for a while. "Kings of Leon are two-door muscle cars and Piggly Wigglies and racist uncles and upholstery that stinks of smoke," the novelist Dave Eggers wrote of the band's musky 2003 debut, *Youth & Young Manhood*, and I'm pretty sure he meant it as a compliment.

Leon's boys, Caleb and Nathan, had moved to Nashville as an a cappella musical duo in 1997, the same year *Billboard* ran a cover story on the music scene in Murfreesboro, a college town 45 minutes southeast of Nashville. Maybe the racist uncles were, if not genetically then at least spiritually, descended from Rhett Butler and Ulysses McGill.

In addition to the proper arrival of the youthful and young men of KOL, 2003 was in some ways a pivotal year for the kind of place Nashville was on its way to becoming. The Civil War sleeper drama *Cold Mountain* starred Nicole Kidman and featured, in a cameo role, the singer and guitarist of the White Stripes, Jack White. *Cold Mountain*'s soundtrack album, featuring five contributions from White, was produced by T Bone Burnett. By decade's end, both Kidman and White would be Nashville residents, and the White Stripes' "Seven Nation Army," also released that year, would be a sports-arena staple.

On September 12, 2003, the great Johnny Cash died at age 71, not long after his beloved June. His rendition of Nine Inch Nails' "Hurt" would win the Country Music Association award for Single of the Year two months later. "Hurt" and its unbearably poignant music video had vaulted Cash into the mainstream again at the end of his career, but every version of him still carried that "rebel" persona—you can buy posters of him flipping the bird and everything.

But the women of country aren't allowed to have bad attitudes, and The Chicks learned that the hard way in March of that same year, when singer Natalie Maines insulted then president George W. Bush in front of a London crowd. The context for her loathing was the imminent and unnecessary war in Iraq, still chugging along 16 years later and adding bodies to the pile. But America is giddy for any excuse to publicly to exercise its God-given right to woman-hatin', and the Chicks' career never truly recovered, in spite of having 14 top 10 country hits and six N°. 1s.

Just two years later, in 2005, the Johnny Cash biopic *Walk the Line* was there to spin the message of country cool once more. On the soundtrack album produced by, wouldn't you know it, T Bone Burnett, stars Joaquin Phoenix and Reese Witherspoon performed songs as Johnny and June. Nashville-raised Witherspoon won an Academy Award for Best Actress for the role. But country cool, even Americana cool, was not what everyone in Nashville was chasing.

IN 2006, A SONG about Tim McGraw, written and performed by a 15-year-old transplant from Pennsylvania, would change Nashville forever. That same year, the city's long-suffering rock boosters, still trying to foster a recognizable mainstream music identity outside of country, made a move. Musician and journalist Jason Moon Wilkins booked a series of interlocking showcases spread across the city featuring pop, rock, and Americana artists, and promoted them under the banner of Next Big Nashville. (The name was taken from a story Wilkins wrote for the *Rage*, a former entertainment publication from the *Tennessean*.) There was a heavy emphasis on local talent, all of it decidedly off the Music Row radar and far from Americana territory. 2006 was also the year Infinity Cat Records, future home of art-thrash band JEFF the Brotherhood and other likeminded acts, released its first album.

Next Big Nashville's hyperlocal ethos, with a lot of the shows organized around a handful of beloved venues, lent the proceedings the feeling of a large neighborhood block party. NBN had grown out of a one-off party Wilkins had thrown in 2000, called NextFest, which he later told the *Nashville Scene* was "an excuse to get all the people together who weren't a part of the Country Music Association or the Gospel Music Association. They didn't really have a club to belong to. So I thought, maybe we can use this as an excuse to see each other."

In ensuing years, in a series of stakes-raising iterations, NBN would cast an ever-wider net for talent, bringing in regional and national talent to anchor its marquee bills. It would add a daytime industry conference, field trips, shuttle buses, and ever-expanding swag bags. Bands like Moon Taxi, Cage the Elephant, and Alabama Shakes all made their Nashville debuts at Next Big Nashville events, or at its follow-up festival Sound-Land, also a Wilkins production. Even so, it was a slog.

"When you say 'Nashville'—regardless of what I think, and regardless of what we're trying to do, and regardless of who's even booked—sponsors, consumers, whoever, would still think 'country,'" Wilkins told the *Nashville Scene* in 2011, after deciding to change the name to SoundLand. "Obviously part of it was always to try and improve that image to the point that it means country plus all these things," he continued. "At some point, you have to realize there's only so much a guy with no budget can do against millions and millions of dollars that brand [Nashville] that way every year." To talk about why a city that was home to one of the ascendant rock bands of the early aughts still struggled to make itself known as a city where such a thing was possible, we must first talk about the Nashville Curse.

In the early '80s, a post-punk band called Jason & the Nashville Scorchers seemed headed for the stratosphere on the strength of their sharp songwriting and insanely energetic live performances. But the major-label gatekeepers saw one thing holding them back: that pesky word "Nashville" in their name, which to their ears denoted rhinestones and islands in the stream. So as to not be confused for artists they sounded nothing like, the band agreed. And though the Scorchers racked up critical acclaim (hello, Pazz & Jop!) and a strong cult following, they never quite hit it big. And so the Nashville Curse was born.

No Nashville band would ever sell a million records, the Curse said, and, well, if something good keeps not happening you might as well call it something? Then emo-punkers Paramore—riding the successes of hit

single "Misery Business" and a placement on the *Twilight* soundtrack—
broke through in 2007 with an album called *Riot!* And so the Curse was
vanquished forever. At least as far as record sales went.

Wilkins had been told early on that he should take "Nashville" out of
the name if he was trying to market something other than a country festi-
val. He ignored that advice, until he felt like he couldn't. Eventually Wilkins
would be dealt a hand at the table for a new enterprise: the Nashville Music
Council, a partnership between the Nashville Mayor's Office, the Nashville
Area Chamber of Commerce, and the Nashville Convention and Visitors
Bureau. Its members included Jack White (by now a Nashville resident),
Emmylou Harris, Mary Ann McCready (partner at management firm
Flood, Bumstead, McCarthy & McCready, whose clients include Pearl Jam,
Danger Mouse, and My Chemical Romance), Tim DuBois (vice president
at ASCAP), Ken Levitan (then manager for Kings of Leon), and so on.

The idea was basically: What if the message Next Big Nashville had
been selling—not just *country* capital, but Music City in a broad, inclusive, genre-agnostic sense—became the one true meaning of Nashville?
And what if that was the official position of the city? Mayor Karl Dean
was in, and before long the heavy hitters in the city were, too. Soon, they'd
land their first big win.

ARGUABLY THE BIGGEST BOON for Nashville's rising status was the
ABC soap *Nashville*. Created by Callie Khouri, who won an Academy
Award for her iconic screenplay *Thelma and Louise*, the series featured
multiple female leads, all in the music biz: '90s country superstar Rayna
(Connie Britton), mainstream country-pop firecracker Juliette Barnes
(Hayden Pannetiere), and delicate singer-songwriter-poet Scarlett (Clare
Bowen). Finally—some progress in the archetypes.

If you're measuring *Nashville*'s success in terms of piquing interest in
the city, it more than capably did its job. "People want to go [to] the places
that have been on the show," former mayor Karl Dean told *Billboard* in
2014. "A survey by the Nashville Convention and Visitors Corporation
found that of [tourists] who had seen the show, nearly one in five said
it was the motivating factor for them to visit." Exciting! That's what they
call ROI in the *business*. "It's seen by 8 million to 10 million people on a
given night," Dean said. "The attention the city gets, we could never pay
for." Never mind that the city was giving millions of dollars in incentives.

As a creative enterprise, however, the show was all over the place. And
while it was always going to be impossible to make everyone happy, it

always felt like there was a reluctance to make even the explicit "Music Row" storylines explicitly "Music Row." The music always skewed toward rock and pop, with the best country songs adjacent to Roy Orbison (like Season One's "No One Will Ever Love You Like I Do.")

This felt odd, because *Nashville* began its run on ABC, which never shied away from synergy. The network has been broadcasting the CMA Awards since 2006, and was happy to cross-promote with actual country stars and *Good Morning America*'s Robin Roberts. But even though many of its storylines revolved around the Music Row machinery, none of the music on *Nashville* ever sounded particularly Luke Bryan-ish, ostensibly the exact kind of star country music fans want to see. (The show moved from ABC to CMT after its fourth season.)

That said, the production really tried to make the city their own, with in-world verisimilitude and frequent references to people, places, and things around town. "East Nashville hipsters" were explicitly called out on primetime television, but the show developed a devoted fan base who were given a lovely view of the city via soaring establishing shots—a modern, gleaming metropolis amidst green hills, populated by pretty waitresses and superstars, all of whom have a song in their heart. For a city that didn't fully shed its *Hee-Haw* persona until the 2000s, popular conception of Nashville nevertheless changed swiftly.

And ultimately it was the soundtrack that turned out to be the most worthwhile aspect of the show. As Jon Caramanica put it in the *New York Times*: "The soundtrack goes out of its way to ground the show in the city's un-flashy side." The musical director for the first season of *Nashville*? Who else: T Bone Burnett, who, oddly enough, was just a few years away from becoming involved in a Nashville real estate development deal that would eventually get halted because of the possibility of human remains on the proposed building site. Truth is almost stranger than fiction. (*Nashville* featured a *lot* of car wrecks.) Anyway, speaking of Americana, there was Jim Lauderdale, first of his name, keeper of the genre, wearer of embroidered Western wear, in a supporting role as himself.

"It was a town of characters for a long time," Don Cusic, a country-music historian and professor at Belmont University, told *Time* in 2014. "They haven't disappeared, but it's so corporate now." Or rather, the characters *are* corporate now. Down on Lower Broadway, you can find life-size cardboard cut-outs of Charles Esten, the actor who played Deacon on *Nashville*, just as readily as pictures of Johnny Cash. Deacon won't flip you the bird, though.

Tomato Toss

RICHARD LLOYD, 2019

IT WAS STILL MORNING when, on a Saturday in August 2005, a bois-
terous ensemble shambled down 11th Street. The group comprised tat-
tooed hipsters—emblematic of the neighborhood's emerging bohemian
ethos, less flamboyant local residents, and a few laughing children. They
set out from the Five Points intersection and its constellation of trendy
small businesses: three bars, a bistro, an art gallery, and a café. On the
tables at 3 Crow bar, ice was still melting in the abandoned glasses of
recently drained Bloody Marys.

Their destination was only a couple of blocks away, where on the
corner of 11th and Fatherland a large lot, mostly taken up by cracked
concrete, awaited. That morning there were crates of spoiled tomatoes
stacked up on the edge, which was unusual. Also unusually, bulldozers
idled nearby. And, as had been the case for what seemed like forever, at
least to the group, there was sitting in its center a little market, fashioned
from concrete, bathed in white paint and grime, and festooned with plac-
ards advertising cigarettes and beer.

Upon arrival, the festive crew proceeded to empty out the crates,
one tomato at a time. A little gingerly at first, then with rising enthusiasm, they started winging the tomatoes at the market. As their arms

warmed up and their inhibitions cooled, especially good shots caused the over-ripened fruit to explode on impact, delighting the young ones.

Despite their best efforts, the market still stood after the payload was spent, insulted but essentially unharmed. Not for long. Now the bull-dozers moved in, making quick work of the job. A cheer went up from the tomato tossers, who of course had waited around for the climax. Only when the homely structure was thoroughly pulverized did they head back toward Five Points and a full day of further revelry. Noon approached, with the Southern sun beating down on the pile of smashed concrete and spoiled tomatoes.

And that was that.

BEFORE NASHVILLE'S METRO DEVELOPMENT and Housing Au-thority seized the property in 2005, setting the stage for that morning's bizarre festivities, the East End Market was an unsavory fixture in a fast-changing neighborhood. Stacked cases of domestic beer crowded the claustrophobic interior. The cashier worked behind bulletproof glass. Steel wool and glass tubes filled with ersatz flowers were conveniently placed at the checkout—a detail that might perplex someone unaware that these items (sans flowers) are easily combined to fashion a DIY crack pipe.

Placed as it was in the lot's dead center, the market offered nowhere to hide. Somehow, this exposure did not deter routine quality-of-life in-fractions outside, including public drunkenness, open-air drug dealing, and the occasional quick and dirty act of prostitution.

In sharp contrast, neighboring blocks teemed with a robust stock of vintage homes, though many had fallen into disrepair during decades of local economic decline. Starting in the late 1990s, a new local population of artists and early career professionals was spearheading their still un-even rehabilitation. The "revitalization" of East Nashville had also gotten a boost from an unlikely source: On April 16, 1998, a tornado ripped through the East Side, tearing off roofs, downing trees, and damaging some houses beyond repair. The insurance money that came pouring into the neighborhood soon thereafter would both quicken the pace—and raise the value—of the renovations.

But the funnel cloud didn't have a silver lining for everyone. In the East End Market's backyard sat the local Head Start, serving the children of less advantaged East Siders, including some from the nearby pub-lic housing project less than a mile south. The playground offered the children a clear view of the market and its tawdry goings-on. Vacant lots pocked the area, along with still more grab-and-go, low-end beer markets. Of these, none were more obnoxious to changing local sensibilities than the East End Market. Unlovely and unloved, it was a poke in the eye to both new and old residents, with their various upward aspirations.

SEVERAL YEARS AFTER THE infamous Tomato Toss, I sat with Meg MacFadyen at the Bongo Java East cafe, about a hundred yards up 11th Street from where the East Market once stood. Over coffee, she explained the origins of the Tomato Art Festival, now a signature annual event in an East Nashville reshaped by more than a decade of rapid gentrification. Along with her husband Bret, Meg owned and operated the Art and Invention Gallery, just around the corner on Woodland Avenue, and the festival originated with her burst of inspiration in 2004.

"We would have a show about every six weeks" she explained, "and I knew in the middle of August I needed to do a show and I knew that our sheet metal building, no matter how much air conditioning is going, is going to be hot. And I thought, well, what can we do that people will want to come out and be really miserable and uncomfortable?" The Gallery occupied a converted mechanic's garage, sheathed in corrugated steel, a structure that is indeed bound to swelter in the summer months. Meg decided that rather than just sit out the high summer, she would lean into the situation instead.

"We came up with the decision that tomatoes were probably one of the better parts of August anyway. And so just kind of tongue-in-cheek we did this Tomato Art Show. And all these people did tomatoes and stuff like that, and for reasons unbeknownst to me, about 1,000 people showed up. I mean, it was kind of a thing out of the gate."

The voluble Meg presided over the gallery's retail operation, while the more taciturn Bret, an artist and craftsman, sweated away in a rear studio, dubbed the Garage Mahal. The modest enterprise sat just off the Five Points intersection. Art and Invention was an early entry in a bundle of new amenities signaling a very different local identity, including Bongo Java and an assortment of bars, bistros, boutiques, yoga studios, and fitness centers.

When Art and Invention held the first Tomato Art Show in 2004, this process was still in its incipient stages. Its surprising popularity provided an early indicator that a new neighborhood population was coalescing, composed of artists and musicians, members of the LGBTQ community, and early-stage young professionals. These "pioneers" quickly became notorious for their East Nashville chauvinism, enthusiastically propping up local business, even as other Nashville residents remained reluctant to "cross the river" from downtown and then more-prosperous west side districts.

From the jump, the locals proved much more than passive consumers, as Meg noted. "For some reason unknown to me, folks started walking through the door in [tomato-themed] costumes," adding their own creativity to a markedly jocular event. The enterprising gallerist quickly grasped the potential in this spontaneous enthusiasm. The next year the Tomato Art Show anchored the first Tomato Art Festival, enlisting other local businesses to host events such as Bloody Mary and tomato-centric food contests.

Meg MacFadyen's burst of inspiration in 2004 and 2005, abetted by the ingenuity of East Nashville residents and entrepreneurs, planted the seeds of an event that has grown far beyond what anyone could have imagined, drawing a staggering 60,000 visitors in 2018. Every year, Five Points and surrounding blocks are closed to traffic and lined with small vendors selling arts and crafts, vintage goods, and refreshments. Strategically placed stages sample the considerable local musical talent, with other forms of street performance interspersed on the intersections. The Hip Zipper, a Five Points purveyor of vintage clothing, stages a fashion show; the Tomato King and Queen march at the head of the Tomato Parade; runners compete in the Tomato 5K; children bounce on inflatable houses in the "kiddie playland," and adults seek respite from the heat drinking Bloody Marys or craft beers in one of the several bars clustered in the zone.

Meg continued to effuse that "the people of East Nashville are what make this festival unique and fun and colorful," doggedly favoring neighborhood contributions to the panoply of attractions. At the same time, the residential composition is dynamic, as surging housing costs price out many of the arty sorts so instrumental to creating the East Nashville "vibe" of the mid-2000s. Moreover, while neighborhood residents propped up the early attendance, tomato enthusiasts are now clearly magnetized from all over the city. The erstwhile perception of East Nashville as a dicey destination spot in 2005 has long since been retired. The first incarnation of the festival was a largely ramshackle, DIY accomplishment, complete with the "tomato toss" targeting the East End Market. Today the city provides logistical support, while corporate logos interspersed among the homey entertainments signal big money sponsorship. There is much fun to be had, but no tomatoes are thrown at anything anymore.

The turbo-charged expansion of the East Nashville festival mirrors the gentrification of the neighborhood as well as the explosive growth of the city as a whole. And as with those developments, those present at the creation feel both pride and a measure of regret.

If we view the Tomato Art Festival as a symbol of larger urban processes, it is worth going to its roots for clues to just how all of this happened. The story is emblematic of trends evident in cities throughout the United States, including the elevated role of the arts in new development strategies. At the same time, it is also a distinctly Nashville story.

Meg envisioned the Tomato Art Show as a creative solution to a local dilemma—the dripping August heat and poorly insulated gallery space. Meanwhile, the redevelopment of East Nashville faced standard challenges wrought by a long cycle of disinvestment and concentrated poverty, as well as the peculiarity of the local built environment, which made gentrification on the Northern model especially hard to implement. The garage cum gallery perched on East Nashville's trendiest intersection also occupies the nexus of the global and the local, of city culture and urban design, and of the past and the future of Music City.

IT MIGHT BE EASY to interpret the transformation of East Nashville, like the gestation of the Tomato Art Festival, as an organic process. In this version, visionary entrepreneurs and intrepid new residents contributed both imagination and sweat equity to the rehabilitation of a neighborhood long in decline. Indeed, the website of Art and Invention tells just this story: "Before the Five Points District of East Nashville became a hip, fun destination, they saw its potential. With that vision in mind, Bret and Meg converted an old garage at 1106 Woodland Street into an artist's studio. . . . Three years later the Art and Invention Gallery was born."

The foresight is indeed impressive, at least based on Meg's description of what they initially bought into. Local foot traffic was comparatively minimal, and illicit commerce vied with the handful of fledgling new businesses opening around the same time. "When I first started putting in my gardens out front, you had to be really careful because you would find used things that you really did not want to touch or get stuck with. So the people on the street were either vagabonds or prostitutes or stuff like that—and you kind of kept your weather eye out." Still, as early as the late '90s the proximate residential population was already growing more affluent and educated. This was a sharp contrast with much of the East Side and especially the area just to the south of the Shelby Avenue thoroughfare, where the James Cayce Homes, the city's largest public housing project, anchored concentrated poverty.

Once provided with places to go, the new residents quickly made themselves known. "So in a short amount of time it really has turned around, and I would say, when we first got this building, you could just sort of feel that it was turning. We figured, like, five years. But within a year, it was really different."

In this shift, the city government played a quiet but crucial support-ing role. The Metro Development and Housing Authority had already created the Five Points Redevelopment Area, a "design overlay" gerry-mandered to capture the local stock of historic housing and, especially, "the commercial corners." The overlay contained both Five Points and Martin's Corner, where the East End Market stood as garish obstacle to the city's plan.

Within the overlay boundaries, MDHA encouraged adaptive reuse of existing structures, while subsidizing infill for a neighborhood rich in vacant lots. New developments were subject to design guidelines meant to encourage density and pedestrian life. These include mixed commer-cial and residential uses, structures abutting the sidewalk, and surface parking lots either absent or concealed. In this, the agency follows now dominant principles of "enlightened" urban design, even if auto-centric Nashville's preponderance of strip mall-style boulevards makes for rocky terrain.

"We follow trends," I was informed when visiting MDHA's offices in 2006. "Adaptive reuse. Density. Lofts. Bricks. Everyone wants a ware-house district." But the industrial revolution in the United States mostly skipped Southern cities, leading the official to concede: "We don't really have the building stock." He added, a little ruefully, "They want it anyway."

The "they," it seems, referred to the city planning hive mind, which had settled on a design ideal called the New Urbanism. Despite its forward-looking name, this agenda is actually about turning back the clock, advocating for the dense, mixed-use neighborhoods sometimes found in older cities, built before cars changed everything. The model is Greenwich Village, the much-loved Manhattan district that is also not exactly a typical American environment. Enthusiasts for the New Urban-ist agenda go beyond just extolling its aesthetic or practical advantages, ascribing to it almost mystical powers, to foster community, deter crime, and unleash artistic energies.

Unhappily for planners charged with this mandate, Nashville came of age after the Second World War, when old neighborhoods were routinely being blasted to make way for elevated expressways and the suburbs were draining downtowns. In fact, Music City entered the 2000s as one of the lowest density cities in America, with strip mall oases nestled among still undeveloped pasture and woodland within the city limits.

In this case, resorting to a garage in lieu of conventional "warehouse district" loft conversions is poignant. MDHA in fact already owned the building; the mechanic had gone under as the neighborhood hit the skids. For a few years, it was provisionally occupied by the District Attorney's special police task force in East Nashville. Enhanced local law enforcement was Phase One in the city's efforts to redevelop the depressed neighborhood; Phase Two involved the deliberate transfer of local city-owned structures to the hands of select private entrepreneurs—that is, to duly designated "visionaries." Partnered with the local nonprofit Rediscover East, MDHA leaked news of the garage's availability selectively.

"It was kind of word on the street that it was available," Meg said. "And so we bought the building from MDHA. It was affordable and suited our needs."

Other elements of the agenda were less easily managed. East Nashville illustrates the rather unusual and contradictory mandate of MDHA, both managing subsidized and public housing in the city and incentivizing private development. In a surely admirable nod to the former role, the agency is headquartered on the expansive grounds of the James Cayce Homes, working both sides of Shelby Avenue and the divide between East Nashville's past and future. A product of the postwar injection of federal dollars into cities—called "urban renewal"—the project's "super-block" design violates every principle of the New Urbanist agenda. So does another federally subsidized renewal project, the tangle of interstate highways circling downtown. These elevated conveyances repel pedestrians, restrict local automotive access points, and rob East Nashville of its most valuable natural amenity: the riverfront.

When major events are held at the East Bank sports stadium, traffic essentially pins East Siders in their neighborhood. These mid-20th century public works are regularly indicted for the economic collapse of East Nashville. But more had gone wrong than that. The heavy footprint of urban renewal juxtaposes, in the space of a few short blocks, to subsequent fruits of malign neglect—seedy strip malls, abandoned structures, rubble-filled lots, and low-end vice emporiums.

Five Points inherited an unusual oasis of densely built, sidewalk abutting commercial property along with the old garage—hence its vanguard role in the new MDHA agenda. Martin's Corner, conversely, had vacant lots, the run-down Bill Martin's Supermarket, and, most egregiously, the tiny East End Market. Its proximity to the Head Start is a flagrant violation of citywide zoning regulations that had nonetheless been ignored for years. A local attorney, who was rehabbing a nearby Victorian, pressed that point, while providing photo-documentation of the lot's NSFW activities.

THE TOMATO TOSS WAS listed on the makeshift schedule of the inaugural Tomato Art Festival.

"It was all meant in the spirit of this festival that they have in Spain, where the streets run red," Meg said, referring to La Tomatina, annually held in the Valencian town of Buñol. "The whole town shows up and it's littered with rotten tomatoes. They throw them at each other." Also staged in August, La Tomatina is billed as "the world's largest food fight," and draws some 40,000 participants, more than four times the town's permanent population. Although the Tomato Toss in East Nashville did not quite follow the Tomatina blueprint, it does signal the mix of local and cosmopolitan inspiration that shape local art scenes in cities throughout the US.

A tomato battle royale faces logistical impediments, as photographs of La Tomatina illustrate. In Spain, participants fully commit to being plastered in tomato goo, something that would undercut all of the other events at the Art Festival. So, Meg says, "there were all these old buildings that were going to be torn down, and we chose one." Indeed, abandoned, unloved, and obsolete structures abound in the early stages of gentrification. The one they chose, though, was especially freighted with symbolism, planted obdurately at the crossroads of a neighborhood on the move.

Those who participated remember the unruly and frivolous event as spontaneous—something that, Meg says, "captured people's imaginations and sense of play and none of that was intentional." Of course, the tomatoes did not magically appear, even if the organizers did not quite foresee either the intensity of unleashed energy in the tomato bombing or the subsequent fallout. The enthusiasm was stoked during the spirited march of the tomato mob. I talked in the subsequent weeks to several participants, who recapped the event a little sheepishly. They variously recalled feeling "swept up in the moment," describing the event as something that "just sort of happened," and even conceding "maybe we got carried away."

These protestations of (believably) innocent intention come as a result of ensuing criticism, largely conducted on the highly active East Nashville listserv, a pre-Twitter forum for aggressive virtue signaling. "It was kinda fun for people to watch—little kids and everything," Meg said, clearly weary of the topic when I raised it five years later. "So it was all in that sort of spirit. But then people, I don't know, got up in arms about different things that I would have never considered. Like, they thought we were throwing perfectly good food and wasting food. Some people thought we were being racist because we were throwing tomatoes at a building where minorities shopped and then we tore it down. Some people thought we should have collected the tomatoes after, for compost."

Architectural critic and design activist Christine Kreyling lived just up the street at the time, dead center between Five Points and Martin's Corner. As a consultant for the Nashville Civic Design Center, she co-authored *The Plan of Nashville*, wrestling a New Urbanist vision for the city's future from its problematic present layout. Predictably, she endorsed MDHA's design guidelines in 2007, noting wryly of the market: "It did not represent the most elevated use of the lot."

When I asked about the Tomato Toss, she hedged. "I did not like the market, I did not shop there. I would not have felt comfortable walking my dogs by there at 11 o'clock at night," she said. "But it sent the wrong message to throw tomatoes at it."

The problem with the message was unanticipated by the participants, but clearer in retrospect. In La Tomatina, everyone throwing tomatoes gets reciprocally pelted; it is a social leveler and a democratizing event. Throwing tomatoes at the market, conversely, expressed hierarchy. It is likely that most East Nashville residents were happy to see the market go, but only some residents threw tomatoes at it. Those that did perhaps also animated fear in others of their own ultimate local displacement, and did so in what appeared an unduly callous manner. But the listserv was a bastion of the more affluent, educated, and white newer arrivals, noisily progressive in their views while also trapped in the contradictions they inevitably inhabit.

On my visit to MDHA, an agency official brushed off my questions about the market, tersely claiming that "the yuppies decided to throw tomatoes at it," as if there was no way to see that coming. His tone implied exasperated disapproval, exonerating the agency of complicity via semantic sleight-of-hand. In fact, the timing of the demolition, as one might expect, was not dumb luck. "It was all planned out," Meg affirmed.

MDHA transferred the lot to private developers, adding a subsidy through the technique of tax increment financing, in which the increase in local property taxes services the city bond. A red brick complex, appropriately abutting the sidewalk, was erected on the lot, with upstairs condominiums and commercial storefronts at the ground level. These were filled in by a hair salon, yoga studio, art gallery, and a quirky gift boutique.

As the building went up, a temporary structure was placed on the vacant lot across the street, housing the office of the site manager. In 2006, the second and last Tomato Toss was held. This one got less attention, but its target—the prefab office—was also symbolic. By then, some locals already were beginning to rue new developments in which they were, inevitably, also complicit. So after attacking the ghost of East Nashville past the year before, they turned their sights on its future.

NASHVILLE IS WIDELY RECOGNIZED as Music City, although its signature music did not exactly imbue it with hipness for much of the 20th century. Its mid-South address, sprawling built environment, and conservative cultural legacy should all be viewed as impediments to 21st-century models of urban aspiration. And yet, despite all this, the erstwhile "Hillbilly Music Capital of the World" has managed to catch fire, celebrated in national media outlets for being, of all things, cool. Well before the "It City" label adhered, *GQ* trotted out a new nickname for a city long premised on musical traditionalism: "Nowville."

East Nashville, today identified with the city's "alternative" music scenes and progressive sensibilities, has played a key supporting role in the Nashville makeover. The city boom is largely dependent on its new appeal to young and highly educated residents, including workers in a growing tech sector. This is the case for all the "winners" in the cutthroat interurban competition for "new economy" market share, from Austin, Texas, to Columbus, Ohio. The new amenities cultivated on the East Side, and showcased in the Tomato Art Festival, correspond to the lifestyle demands of this highly coveted demographic. In this case, city leaders no longer view the arts as peripheral luxuries, but instead as crucial catalysts for economic development.

East Nashville illustrates new metrics of place value, in both cultural and design terms. Compared to building a stadium, convention center, or arena—things Nashville has also done in recent decades—the city investment in East Side transformation is both low-cost and under-the-radar. It has also paid impressive dividends. This approach, sometimes called "neoliberal" urban planning, aims to ignite the private market while piggybacking on the entrepreneurial instincts of creative sorts like Bret and Meg.

They "make the scene," though the big profits typically end up in someone else's pockets. And who can complain about such an innocuous and genuinely cool thing as the Tomato Art Festival? After all, as one later festival banner put it, the tomato is a "uniter, not a divider."

Despite the routine expression of such optimistic and sincerely felt bromides in a very liberal neighborhood, the new East Nashville in fact illustrates the growing divide between the educated professionals so assiduously courted by city boosters and the increasingly isolated local residents not similarly advantaged or valued. The neighborhood is no longer affordable, even for the type of young professionals who ignited gentrification and argued over the tomato toss back in 2005. For the poor, lack of affordable housing has become a citywide crisis.

To see the East End Market, with its apparent clientele of vagrants and prostitutes, as emblematic of the "old" East Nashville is a gross disservice to the more mundane reality of its longer tenured residents. More telling is the indifferent placement of the Head Start adjacent to it, something the city felt compelled to address only after more affluent residents moved in.

Today, folks talk about how "family-friendly" the area has become, now that its grosser elements have been uprooted. This commonplace observation ignores the fact that Cayce's median age is well below that of the city as a whole. Public housing projects—and low-income, racially segregated communities in general—are disproportionately home to young children, and whether these will ultimately benefit from a newfound interest in local schools and safety remains to be seen. The East End Market is of course long gone, and so is the Head Start that once operated behind it, replaced by a charter school.

In 2013, plans were announced to demolish the Cayce Homes and construct mixed-income housing. Both moves further represent the impulse to encourage market mechanisms in the service of public goals. Given the manifest past failures of public housing and public education, perhaps we have nothing to lose with this approach. Still, despite the earnest rationalizations of free market enthusiasts, it appears likely that far more innocent remnants of the "old" East Nashville will end up bull-dozed by all the local improvement.

Also in 2019, the Art and Invention Gallery's long run at the center of East Nashville's spectacular boom reached its end. In April, a press release announced that the MacFadyens were selling the property to real estate investor Christian Paro and retiring to Woodbury, Tennessee. Their early prescience regarding East Nashville's potential had been spec-tacularly vindicated, thanks in no small part to their own contributions. Now, that vision, along with the sweetheart deal from MDHA, bore its last fruit. As William Williams reported in the *Nashville Scene*:

> The couple paid $165,000 for the two-parcel site (the other parcel is home to the little buildings comprising The Idea Hatchery). The release does not disclose the price Paro will pay for the properties, which span a col-lective approximately 0.5 acres. For comparison, and sitting on 0.35 acres, a nearby commercial building home to a Pilates studio and a real estate office (at 966 Main St.) recently was listed for sale for $2.5 million.

Already, older conflicts have receded from memory as prams and shoppers traverse the increasingly spiffy local sidewalks. So it is worth recalling that morning in August 2005, when the lurking atavism of the march to progress was made briefly manifest, in a hail of rotten tomatoes.

The End of the Beginning

CARRIE FERGUSON WEIR, 2019

WHEN CASA AZAFRÁN OPENED on Nolensville Road in December of 2012, Executive Director Renata Soto proclaimed the $5 million community center, with its tall Moorish arches and brilliant mosaic mural facade, the "Gateway to Immigrant Nashville."

Indeed, given its location just south of I-440, near the Tennessee State Fairgrounds and with a view of the ever-expanding skyline, the center immediately became a landmark and a symbol for the growth and change that had been under way along Nolensville Road for decades. And just as its location stood at a midpoint between the city's immigrant neighborhoods and its traditional downtown power centers, its name—a combination of the Spanish word for house, and the Arabic-derived word for saffron—intentionally linked the city's Latinx and Middle Eastern cultures.

When Casa Azafrán opened, Nolensville Road was already dotted with Mexican bakeries, Kurdish groceries, Asian markets, African restaurants, a thriving Muslim community center. Many a used car lot and tire repair shop had long displayed "se habla español" signs, and inexpensive furniture stores and pawn shops yielded to Spanish-language churches and gyro restaurants. And taco trucks. Lots of taco trucks.

Along Nolensville Road—in the area of neighborhoods named Woodbine, Glencliff, and Radnor—and all the way down south, straight up against the Brentwood city limits, live a brilliant collection of men and women with roots in lands torn by unspeakable strife and economic hardships. Some found ground on Nolensville Road and its surrounds because refugee resettlement agencies sought both affordability and community when they procured an apartment for a recent arrival. Others are there because, well, la familia or el amigo was already there. Whole apartment complexes have been known for hosting heavy populations of Burmese, Somalis, Mexicans, among other relative newcomers. Little starter casitas have been within reach and small businesses have thrived.

All these people have been mixing together like in no other part of Nashville, in a slice of the city known for its hard-working ethic, post–World War II growth, and scrappy vibe. No doubt, when Nashville began its current boom, Nolensville Road already was doing what Nolensville Road has always done: providing both comfortable familiarity and opportunity for regular folks.

"One of the secrets of Nolensville Road is that it always feels like home," says Lokman Rashid, a Kurdish entrepreneur and long-time Nolensville Road local. "No matter where you are from. You can find your butcher, small grocery, fresh bread. You find the things here that you can't find in other parts of Nashville. But it always has changed. It hasn't stayed the same in the years I have been here."

What wasn't there yet in 2012 when Casa Azafrán opened to house nonprofits that serve immigrants, refugees, and the local community were the brand-new condos in the back lot. And what wasn't there yet either was the hipster coffee house across the street. That arrived in 2016, moving into a vacant building that had once housed a liquidation business called El Baratillo. And in 2012, there hadn't yet been any real steep property value hike or proliferation of tall-skinny houses. Past tense. What also wasn't yet in the plans: A $250 million pro soccer stadium just up the street, at the Fairgrounds.

Rashid arrived in 1993, at the age of 24, from a refugee camp in Turkey. He was alone and knew no one in Nashville. But there were already many other Kurds here, and many more to follow. Nashville is home to the largest Kurdish population outside of Kurdistan.

Rashid went from custodian, to Overton High School's campus director, to Woodbine-area house flipper, real estate agent, and Nolensville Road commercial property owner. Last summer, he and his nurse practitioner wife, Faiza, signed a lease to open a primary care and urgent care clinic, Amed Family Clinic, near the former Lowe's store off Nolensville. She will work there with her two nurse practitioner brothers, her Kurdish cardiologist brother-in-law, and a Somali nurse practitioner.

"I am living the American dream," Rashid says. "The Kurds, we came from nowhere. No identity. Persecution. But we came here and engaged and have built a successful community in Nashville. We own 300 to 350 small businesses."

And, he says, the evidence is that others are taking chances and doing well along Nolensville, too. The commercial building he owns, for example, provides retail space for a Mexican botanica, a Cuban grocery and bakery, a sign shop owned by an Egyptian, an African American owned barbershop, and a tax preparer he describes simply as "American." Rashid chuckles with some glee when he describes the mix of tenants. But when he considers the future of his community, he offers an asterisk.

"Nobody knows what is going to happen," he says.

Every apartment or house he and Faiza have lived in since they married in 1995 has been off of Nolensville Road. The first home Faiza's parents purchased, when they moved out of their resettlement apartment—the since-demolished Colonial Village near Belmont University—was on Hewlett Drive in the Glencliff neighborhood. The area has been affordable and profitable for someone, like Rashid, who flips real estate.

"I used to be able to buy houses under $100,000 and I used to have many to choose from. Sometimes, I think I have to give up that kind of business. The market is slowing down," he says. "The concern is big developers coming into the area and that Nolensville Road will turn into East Nashville, or Germantown, or Eighth Avenue South. We don't know what is going to happen."

The rent in the area is now $1,100 to $1,400 a month, up from around $800 for a place that could house a family. Little cottages around 1,000 square feet, which a decade ago were under $100,000, are going for more than twice that, if not more. And yet, this is all still less expensive than East Nashville or Germantown, or any neighborhood in the city's urban core, for that matter. As new people move into these more expensive dwellings, and the tall-skinnies move their way south down Nolensville, residents and businesses alike echo Rashid's uncertainty.

ORAL HISTORY INTERVIEWS, CONDUCTED in 2016 for a report called *Envision Nolensville* and later archived at the Nashville Public Library, capture the history of a place once known more commonly by the name Flatrock. It was mostly working class, and mostly white, until Nashville finally began desegregating its schools in the 1970s. It was tight-knit—a place where kids cruised the Shoney's and hung out at the bowling alley.

In 1992, when Carlos and Lillian Yepez came to Nashville from California and opened a little taco stand inside a modestly stocked Mexican grocery called La Hacienda at 2615 Nolensville Road (while simultaneously trying to set up a tortilla factory in the back), the neighborhood was increasingly popular with Kurdish families and Central American and Mexican construction workers who had come to build Middle Tennessee's fast-growing suburbs. (La Hacienda would make headlines in 2014 when President Barack Obama made a stop there after delivering remarks about his executive actions on immigration at Casa Azafrán.)

In the late 1990s, some of the Latinx guys got work building the downtown arena and the East Bank football stadium, and so they brought their wives and children to Nashville, too. At the same time, more Kurds arrived, both through direct refugee resettlement and by way of Dallas, the other city that saw a lot of newly arrived Kurds.

This era also marked the arrival of refugees from Vietnam, Ethiopia, Somalia, Bhutan, Burma, Iraq, Cuba, Eritrea, and Sudan, among other nations. There are now more than 140 languages spoken in the Metro Nashville public schools, with a concentration of students who speak languages other than English living in the county's southeast quadrant.

The tensions have been there, for sure. When the "English Only" referendum was on the ballot in 2009—it would have required Metro government be conducted only in English—then Councilwoman Anna Page said many of her constituents wanted badly for her to support it. She didn't.

But Page, in the *Envision* report, says that while the "demographics of the neighborhood have changed dramatically over her lifetime, the aspirations of its residents have not. 'We all want a safe neighborhood. Good investment. Good schools.'" And that commonality has apparently been the gift Flatrock has offered to so many for so long—regardless of where they came from to get here.

Maybe it's also why the looming and unavoidable change feels so daunting. Of course, this part of town is not unlike other rapidly changing parts of the city like North Nashville, the Nations, and Edgehill, for example. All have their own rich histories, and yet longtime residents are now subject to displacement at the worst, and a change of flavor at the least.

"It is a special place that is not going through a unique experience," Soto says. "It is now like other gentrified areas."

All this change is happening in a section of the city that has a higher percentage of renters, a high percentage of businesses that rent, and more families living in poverty when compared to Davidson County as a whole.

Leon Berrios, a Nashville attorney and bandleader of the popular band Revolfusion, lives in an apartment complex off Edmondson Pike, where several families from Sudan and Burma once lived. He often saw the kids outside playing soccer. But then the complex owners put in a pool and installed new high-end kitchen counters. They also raised the rent to $1,200 a month. The immigrant families moved out. Now the neighbors are mostly white.

Berrios, who has lived and worked on or around Nolensville Road for more than a decade, says, "The new ones who arrive will go directly to Murfreesboro."

Leah Hashinger, the development director of the Tennessee Immigrant and Refugee Rights Coalition, came to Nashville in 2010. She taught in a mobile English language teaching program, which meant she drove to her students. Many lived in the Tusculum area, in apartments called the Highlands, Stonebrook, and the Vistas. Her students were from places like Congo, Burma, Bhutan, Iraq.

"I was really blown away," she says. "But now, the Burmese families are gone. The Nepali families are gone. They were established, but they just couldn't afford to buy homes when the rents went up."

Conexión Américas and TIRRC, whose offices are both housed at Casa Azafrán, say they see the change reflected in their clientele: They're increasingly living further way in Antioch, LaVergne, and yes, Murfreesboro, as Berrios notes.

In the 2017 follow-up report to *Envision Nolensville*, the writers said Metro Nashville government and other agencies had created plans to address a variety of issues, citing reports such as NashvilleNext, nMotion, WalknBike, and Middle Tennessee Connected. But the plans didn't address looming business displacement and the diluting of the very thing that makes Nolensville Road unique—its delicious diversity.

The *Envision II* report got specific and offered recommendations to city leaders—backed up with statistics and case studies from other US cities. It urged a coordinated effort at community engagement and data collection on business displacement risk. It also promoted transportation improvements such as traffic calming. On the subject of affordable housing and business support, they offered two main directives. First, build and preserve more affordable housing and offer tax abatements to low-income owners. Second, create ways for small business owners to buy commercial property, both preserve and expand affordable commercial space, and help business owners access capital to grow their businesses.

"Displacement of businesses is real. If left to market forces, many of them are soon not going to be able to be there," Soto says. "It has already happened. Some have closed because they could no longer afford the rent."

Soto points to the popular Flatrock Coffee, Tea & More at 2640C Nolensville Pike, which closed in early 2019 after nearly five years in business. It was the only coffee shop of its kind for a long time and a popular community meeting space. The owners posted a goodbye on the shop's Facebook page saying the new property owners wanted to more than double their rent. "We are just another casualty of the growth explosion in Nashville," they wrote.

Workers' Dignity, or Dignidad Obrera, whose storefront office is at 335 Whitsett Road, a two-minute walk from the former coffee shop, often challenges Nashville lawmakers on affordability. Their members—many of whom are Latinx construction and hospitality workers—are living in crowded apartments just to afford the rent, and they're getting displaced from their community.

Andrés Martínez, director of policy and communications at Conexión Américas, says the right people are connected and talking about these issues since the *Envision II* report came out, but there is no action—not from government or from any private or nonprofit entity—to make any of the recommendations happen.

It's like everyone is just watching and waiting for the inevitable. As Berrios puts it, there's only one thing for sure about Nolensville Road anymore: "It is no longer a place to start out."

Tech of the Town

STEVE HARUCH, 2013

IN SOME WAYS, MARCUS Whitney has the perfect Nashville tech founder story. It starts in a Mexican restaurant.

The day he arrived, Labor Day 2000, he was still wearing his uniform from Atlanta's Rio Bravo Cantina. He was visiting the Nashville location, and as it happened, the Music City outpost was slammed. The manager pulled up Whitney's information in the corporate system—checked out, looked good—and told him to get out on the floor.

He went home with $140 that day. Soon he was splitting his time between Nashville's Rio Bravo and Le Peep, where his attitude impressed the well-heeled Belle Meade clientele. "You seem like a smart guy," Whitney remembers a customer saying to him. "Why are you waiting tables?"

"See that over there?" he replied, pointing to a book about the Web language HTML. "I'm studying to become a programmer."

As fate would have it, the customer's last name was Frist.

Whitney started attending user group meetings, networking, and sharpening his programming skills. Eventually following a lead from one

"Tech of the Town" by Steve Haruch, first published in the *Nashville Scene* on February 21, 2013. Reprinted with permission of FW Publishing.

of his best tables, he applied for a job as a developer at HealthStream—a company run by Bobby Frist. He got the job in April 2001, a day after his son was born.

He worked there for a year—it was "a confusing time in the company," Whitney says—before leaving for an agency called Anode where he would meet formative challenges.

"The guy I replaced, I think, literally would choose another technology set for every single project," Whitney remembers. "So I walked in and inherited ColdFusion technology, this weird database called 4th Dimension, Microsoft ASP, PHP, Java—like, if there was a technology you could build a Web app on, he had done it. The server room had Windows, and it also had Linux, and it had—I mean, it was unbelievably exotic. . . . I spent a lot of late nights when everyone else was gone, with the lights dim, trying to read all these books and understand all this technology that I did not understand. But I ended up learning it."

Flash forward to October 23, 2012, a gala event at the downtown Schermerhorn Symphony Center. The occasion is the Nashville Technology Awards, and one of the night's biggest honors is Chief Technology Officer of the Year. Standing at the podium, facing the concert hall's grand tiers and sonically exacting fixtures, is this year's winner, Marcus Whitney. Within months, he'll have an even bigger prize—$5 million in Series B financing for his Nashville-based company Moontoast.

As remarkable as Whitney's rise, though, is the number of peers now present to applaud him. Among the night's other winners will be Kate O'Neill. Her company [meta]marketer works with clients ranging from the Grand Ole Opry to Ingram Content Group to optimize the way customers interact with their websites. Even the dazzling 20-foot video display that frames Whitney was created just blocks away, near the Entrepreneur Center on Broadway, in the offices of LMG Design Studio. Months before, LMG's Ken Gay had worked there perfecting Madonna's Super Bowl halftime show.

There too is Clint Smith, CEO of online email marketing company Emma. Maybe the most dramatic local tech success of recent years, Emma has gone national, with satellite offices in Portland, OR, Denver, Austin, and New York City. And yet Smith describes being at a neighborhood supper party a few years ago and having to explain what he does for a living.

"Oh, you mean like a Constant Contact or an Emma?" his neighbor asked—assuming Smith's office must be some lesser local version.

"It's funny," Smith says, "the assumption that [we] were in San Francisco or somewhere like that."

But he's not. He's in Nashville, where a close-knit—some might say incestuous—community of local tech pioneers has risen through the ranks. A new generation of small, nimble companies is bubbling up across the city, staffed by skeleton crews of obsessive coders and CEOs crazy enough to believe they can build the next big thing. They talk in a patois of acronymic geek-speak, venture capitalist jargon, and affirmational sloganeering. The names may be unfamiliar to many Nashvillians—Cardagin, Evermind, Kiwi, Waffle, Zeumo—but their ethos is not.

They believe Nashville has what it takes to be a great technology city—and moreover, it's a point of pride. Scroll to the bottom of Populr.me, and you'll find a tagline more likely to be inlaid on a guitar or stitched on a bespoke tie than displayed on a website specializing in HTML5-based micropublishing: "Proudly made in Nashville, Tennessee, USA." And as more break through to a national stage, they want to see others join them, and extend what they've done.

For that to happen, though, the city will have to figure out how to keep and attract tech talents who, at the moment, are more eagerly courted (and more richly compensated) in established development hubs. And as Nashville shows an aggressive new focus on tech cultivation and recruitment, its tech community must decide whether it's worth trading some of the city's sense of mutual supportiveness for a sharper competitive edge.

THE RISE OF MOONTOAST says much about the tortuous development of Nashville's tech culture. In the early aughts, once he'd signed on with Anode, Whitney found himself on a small team that was basically a startup operating within the company. They developed a digital signage platform called FireSign and made their first installation at the Frist Center.

"I didn't realize it, but it really kind of determined what my professional path was going to be," Whitney says, "into products and startup." After leaving Anode to start what he calls an "ill-fated" consulting firm, Whitney landed as one of the first employees at Emma. The company, whose name is a portmanteau of "email" and "marketing," had been successfully launched by dot-com-crash survivors Clint Smith and Will Weaver, and it was ready to grow.

"But the platform they had was built by an intern at Vanderbilt," Whitney says, "who, the legend says, they paid in beer." After Whitney helped completely rewrite Emma's system, Smith and Weaver offered better than a few cases of Natty Light: They made him a partner. He went on to help hire out the remaining technical team, and stayed on for three years.

Then came the tweets heard 'round the world.

Whitney was at South by Southwest in 2007 when Twitter debuted. "It was unbelievable," he says. "It was the first time that I got to experience mobile devices literally determining where dollars were going to go locally." That got him thinking in new ways.

"I believed that social was going to change the way that marketers worked completely," Whitney says. At the time, though, Emma was not in a position to capitalize. "The right thing for them to do was to solidify the business," he explains, and they did—only without their new partner. Over a tumultuous 60-day period in 2007, Whitney left Emma, which was now serving 10,000 clients; started his own technology company, Remarkable Wit; and separated from his wife.

"A very, very intense period in my life," he deadpans.

As Remarkable Wit was developing its client base, Whitney met two key figures, Joe Glaser and Bucky Baxter. Though known mostly for music—Glaser for his world-class guitar shop, Baxter as a first-call pedal steel player and former Bob Dylan sideman—they had an idea for a company that aligned exactly with Whitney's innovation thesis: Social media would continue to grow; e-commerce would continue to grow; online marketing would continue to grow; and "somewhere in there, in that intersection, there was a great technology opportunity."

Glaser and Baxter collected angel funding, and Whitney began operating what was basically a startup within his own startup. In March 2009, Baxter and Whitney launched Moontoast at South by Southwest, the event that had, in a sense, inspired its invention. By summer 2010, the company would have $6 million in Series A financing secured.

What Moontoast does for a client roster that includes Big Machine Records and Lexus is create direct-to-consumer campaigns and in-newsfeed apps. That second part seems obvious enough—everything, including email signups and purchases, happens seamlessly inside the Facebook newsfeed, without requiring consumers to jump to an external site.

"It's very 'duh,'" Whitney says, "but still nobody's doing it but us." In fact, the "duh" aspect is the secret to a killer app, and the hardest to accomplish. The goal is something easy to use that masks its true complexity, thus making it difficult to copy or steal.

Later in 2010, Moontoast would open an office in Boston, with Whitney spending an average of 175 days a year traveling back and forth. The expansion led to speculation that Whitney was moving the company, a rumor he has worked hard to dispel.

"I've always been working for Nashville," he says adamantly. He has never forgotten that he landed a job his first day here, or that user groups at Cummins Station helped him learn and grow.

"I have a debt of gratitude to this city," he says. "My life is here. I moved my parents here. I've got two children here. I've got a fiancée here. My best friends are here.

"The other thing," he adds, "is that in order for me to have a great professional career, Nashville has to evolve as a startup city."

In a city notoriously resistant to change, that will be no small feat. But at least Whitney and his fellow Music City tech pioneers know what obstacles they face—and maybe how to overcome them.

BY THE TIME HE sold it in 2007, Mark Montgomery's Echo Music had offices in Nashville, London, New York, and Los Angeles, with clients ranging from Kanye West to Keith Urban. But in the aughts, when he was pitching the monied classes of Nashville his fairly novel idea—targeted online music sales—he got mostly cold stares, or blank ones. He laughs remembering one incredulous response from a potential investor: "You wanna sell *what* on the *where*?"

To be sure, Nashville has come a long way since Montgomery started selling "what" on the "where" more than a decade ago. Even so, three key problems persist in the wider startup ecosystem.

First, there is not enough technical talent in Nashville, especially at the senior level—the level of experience needed to produce the simplicity Marcus Whitney cites as the grail.

"So you're better off trying to do something that's pretty damn difficult to pull off, but you make it feel simple," Whitney explains. "Well, guess what? That doesn't require junior and midlevel developers. That requires software architects and great, experienced engineers who've been there and done that and been through fires."

The Nashville Technology Council publishes a quarterly Tech Jobs Report, which typically lists anywhere from 800 to 1,200 unfilled positions in Middle Tennessee. "It's huge, and it's a challenge right now," says Liza Massey, the council's president and CEO. "What we have got to get really good at now is not just creating our own tech graduates and employees, but bringing them in."

Montgomery is more blunt: "I think we lack the technical co-founder and pure tech talent to really bring the market into a sort of nationally competitive realm." And as Nashville's profile has risen, senior talent has been recruited away.

"Corey Watson, who used to be head engineer at Magazines.com, works for Twitter," Whitney says. "Rick Bradley, he works for GitHub. . . . I know that Facebook has approached developers in this market."

Second, not enough investment capital is going to small, risk-taking startups in Nashville.

"The deals are way better than they were, but they're still not there," Montgomery says. Part of that has to do with an old-money mindset. At meetings for Partnership 2010—the Chamber of Commerce's economic development initiative, now Partnership 2020—Montgomery says he told the "85 old white guys in suits" this: "Look, Nashville doesn't fund what it doesn't understand, and all it understands is health care services. And if you really want to be a national player, you've really got to start thinking outside of what your comfort zone is."

There's a reason that comfort zone is the shape and size it is. Landon Gibbs of the venture capital firm Clayton Associates explains it simply: "Historically, Nashville has been a health care community—people have seen a lot of success." And investors are in the business of succeeding. Part of the hesitance has to do with the kind of in-between area tech startups represent. Venture capitalists typically don't want to invest below $1 million because the math doesn't make sense for them: It's too much risk for too little reward.

Third, Nashville isn't generating enough big ideas.

Relative to other markets, Montgomery writes in a recent Tumblr post, Nashville is still producing "C-plus/B-minus ideas." And as the story of Clint Smith's neighbor demonstrates, even the really good, really successful ideas that originate here don't necessarily get associated with Nashville.

Whitney acknowledges all these challenges. But he says quality of ideas is not his biggest concern.

"The ecosystem is more important than the idea," he says. "When you launch a venture, you're starting with 5 percent true, true awareness of the reality of what this business could be, and 95 percent is uncertain. And over time, as you go to market, and you create, and you get the proprietary knowledge from sales interactions, you close in on something close to, I would say, 80 percent, at a max. . . . In a strong ecosystem, you close that gap faster. You can adjust, and you're not so dependent on the strength of that initial idea."

Michael Burcham, president and CEO of the Entrepreneur Center, phrases it more tersely: "Good ideas are worth about 20 bucks. It's all about execution." Taken together, the obstacles are daunting, Montgomery believes, but not insurmountable.

"I think those things are all being worked on," he says, "and quite frankly, I think we're on year three of a 20-year continuum."

OR IS THAT YEAR six? Many, like Kate O'Neill, believe the spark really ignited over the course of 12 hours in August 2007, when Nashville's isolated tech community first saw the strength of its numbers. The setting was a crowded, bustling, "miserably hot" Exit/In; the occasion, the very first BarCamp Nashville.

The BarCamp concept of bringing tech-minded people together for an "unconference" was born in the Bay Area. While the first Nashville iteration didn't follow the rules exactly—against form, the event featured scheduled speakers, including serial entrepreneur and Brazen Careerist founder Penelope Trunk—it laid an important section of the tech scene foundation.

"The whole idea was to bring the community together," says Dave Delaney, a social media marketer who helped organize the first Bar-Camp Nashville along with Whitney (his recruiter to work at Emma) and O'Neill. "Many of them met for the first time in person."

That physical connection proved crucial. In that pre-Facebook, pre-LinkedIn version of Nashville, the bloggers, coders, entrepreneurs, and marketers in attendance mostly knew each other only digitally through a network of blogs. Many were aggregated by the WKRN-hosted hub Nashville Is Talking, spearheaded by Brittney Gilbert and later run by Christian Grantham, who now works in the aboveground moonshine business. But meeting in person, at BarCamp Nashville, brought needed new levels of networking.

"That was a pretty key moment," O'Neill says. "It was such a great connecting point for the Web and digital thinkers in town who didn't have a physical venue." At the time, she worked as a Web developer at Magazines.com, sharpening the analytics skills she would use to start her own company, [meta]marketer. (O'Neill took the award for Social Media Strategist of the Year at the 2012 Nashville Technology Awards Gala.)

"Within a few years," O'Neill says, "there's a slew of geek-related opportunities—Firefly Logic Geek Social, the Nashville Geek Calendar." Add to that mix Podcamp (a content-side version of the BarCamp concept) and well-attended meet-ups around Ruby on Rails and other programming languages, and serious momentum began to build.

Opportunities for meat-space networking spread. Delaney's Geek Breakfast template—coffee and computers, basically—has been exported as far away as London and Johannesburg, and he continues to host the events in Nashville monthly. That a schism would develop, albeit briefly, in 2010 between social media- and marketing-focused BarCampers and those more interested in hard coding only showed how much the community had grown.

But if any company proved what benefit real-life social networking could bring to the city's nascent tech scene, it was CentreSource. An early (and ongoing) BarCamp sponsor, CentreSource helped modernize Nashville's technology infrastructure and vocabulary.

As founder Nicholas Holland puts it, "The open-source movement had not found a home yet in Nashville; on the flipside, it was roaring in tech centers like Silicon Valley, New York, Boston, Austin. We had early on decided to use the open-source stack." CentreSource was one of the first companies in Nashville to provide digital strategy for companies that, in many cases, didn't think they needed it.

"Our competitors laughed and said no one would pay for strategy," Holland recalls. "I don't know a single firm in town that doesn't charge for strategy now."

In 2010, *net* magazine named CentreSource one of the top three design agencies in the world at a London ceremony. Here, it is just as well known for hosting Yazoo-fueled monthly events that draw upwards of 250 tech-minded Nashvillians—a forum where peers can blow off steam and toss around ideas. Yet even when beer isn't flowing, CentreSource has served as an important connecting point, thanks to Holland's allowing anyone to rent a desk in the company's collaborative workspace.

When relocated New Yorker Brian Daily, Jason Moore, and former Nashville Technology Council president Tod Fetherling all started working on separate projects at the CentreSource offices, something interesting happened: They got to talking and realized their interests overlapped in important ways. With CentreSource as essentially their creative lab, they decided to start a company together. Stratasan, a cloud-based health care analytics company, launched in September 2010.

But if BarCamp provided what O'Neill calls a "gelling of sorts," the gel only spread so far. For Nashville's tech scene to take off, it needed more institutional backbone. That need ushered in the next major development on the city's tech front.

JUST AS MONTGOMERY HAD found himself frustrated with the investment community, Holland encountered a similar disconnect at the enterprise business level. He remembers going to a Nashville Technology Council board meeting and asking how many were going to BarCamp. "Crickets," he says. "They had zero idea about this occurring right under their nose. And it highlights the maturity process that Nashville has had to go through to understand this kind of entrepreneurial stuff."

Around 2008, when Holland was developing one of the first location-based iPhone games—GPS Assassins, which eventually sold to Seattle-based WorldBlender with around 24,000 active players—he pitched Vic Gatto of the venture capital firm Solidus Co. on the idea of investing. That's when Holland learned about the $1 million threshold for traditional venture capitalists. (Full disclosure: Solidus is an investor in SouthComm, parent company of the *Nashville Scene*, and Gatto serves on its board of directors.)

Gatto knew Solidus couldn't get in the tech startup game playing by the old rulebook. But he was also sympathetic to the plight of Holland and other tech startup founders. "Vic was really the only VC that was going to BarCamp, showing up on panels and like, really starting to venture out into the space and connect the dots with us," Whitney says.

So Gatto led the way in establishing a microfund called JumpStart Foundry, which launched in March 2010 to help back new technology-based companies early in their development.

"It was such a ragtag group of people—ridiculously wealthy guys next to guys with three failed startups," Holland says. "We had no idea what we were doing." But for taking that chance with JumpStart, Holland calls Gatto "one of the unsung heroes of Nashville."

JumpStart Foundry was built on a fairly simple, if unconventional, premise: A group of companies still in concept (or "seed") stage would pitch their ideas to the Foundry members. Then they'd leave the team while the Foundry debated.

"We'd argue, and we'd yell, and somebody would have to say, 'I'm going to be the champion for X company,'" Whitney explains. "And then they'd walk back into the room and we'd say, 'OK, here's $15,000, here's your team from the Foundry, go make something great.'"

JumpStart was testing uncharted waters—uncharted in Nashville, at least. (It was modeled partly on programs like TechStars, started in Boulder, Colo., and Y Combinator, started in Silicon Valley.) "None of the state regulators understood it," Holland says. "Hell, half the start-ups in town were suspicious of it." But it was mixing things up, and the tech-funding gears, frozen for so long, slowly began to turn.

Meanwhile, a new venue and connecting point was finally taking shape. In August, the Entrepreneur Center, a project more than three years in the making, opened its doors on Lower Broad.

"I don't think the public really saw it happening, but if you were in the know, it was really starting to come together," Whitney says. If 2007 was pivotal for the grassroots Nashville tech community, 2010 marked a similar turning point for the city's larger tech-hub aspirations.

"You're starting to realize who has money, and you're starting to see angel deals getting done," Whitney says. "And you're starting to kind of understand what this EC thing was really going to be about."

Sitting above street level at 105 Broadway, next door to Joey and Gavin DeGraw's bar/nightclub The National Underground, the Entrepreneur Center doesn't look like much from the outside. But every day, people are fighting for their professional lives inside.

President and CEO Michael Burcham is happy to rattle off the vital stats: more than 5,000 visitors in its first 24 months; 1,500 business concepts screened; 50 companies incubated and launched through the EC; total seed and angel money raised by EC startups approaching $20 million. He delivered these to a meeting of StartupAmerica leaders in Washington, DC, on Feb. 5, where he says the name Nashville was on everyone's lips. (Perhaps Burcham couldn't help but "break into the goofy grin of the newly popular," as the *New York Times* put "it.")

Of the 50 businesses that have come through the EC, "well over half of them have already reached a break-even point and are now self-sustaining," Burcham reports. Jamplify, a social media platform that rewards users with tickets or other merchandise for creating buzz around bands, took home top honors at Midem, one of the world's largest music industry conferences, after going through JumpStart last summer.

Later this year, the Entrepreneur Center will reopen in Rolling Mill Hill, where it will join Emma, Hands On Nashville, and the Center for Nonprofit Management. The new EC will be three times the size of the Lower Broad location and include dedicated space for corporate employees to work away from their offices on new ideas.

"There's a lot of cross-pollination we'll be doing on that hill," Burcham says, "and our goal is to make Rolling Mill Hill, when we all get there together, sort of the creative campus of Nashville."

IF THERE IS BROAD agreement about the three main obstacles facing the tech community, there has certainly been internal disagreement about how best to address them. Montgomery says the Nashville Chamber of Commerce approached him looking for a recommendation on the workforce front. "So we put together a pretty substantial thought process for them," he says with a shrug, "and they're building a fucking website."

That website, WorkITNashville.com, launched officially on Feb. 5 with an event at the Frist, and packages Nashville as a vibrant hub bubbling over with music, arts, great neighborhoods, and, most importantly, good tech jobs. Smith, Whitney, and O'Neill are among the smiling faces beckoning prospective tech workers to town, along with a searchable database of open jobs.

Thinking he could help "home-grow some talent," John Wark, a long-time programmer and part-time Belmont instructor, took matters into his own hands: He founded the Nashville Software School in January 2012 after talking with local entrepreneurs about the talent shortage. He runs an intensive vocational program specifically tailored to the needs of Nashville tech companies.

"John's a doer," Montgomery says. "Everyone else sat around and whined about it, and he figured it out."

The NSS focuses on practical skills. "We're training people to get entry-level software developer or Web developer jobs," he says. "There are no gen-ed requirements. We're teaching people how to program."

The first class started in June and consisted of 15 people. Most had never done any programming or even taken a Web design class. Several were musicians. Of the 14 students who graduated in November, however, eight had full-time jobs before Christmas. Two more have landed positions since the New Year, and all the remaining graduates are either doing contract work or actively interviewing.

A point of pride for Wark is that the NSS is, as far as he knows, the only program of its kind in the country operated as a nonprofit. That helps keep the cost relatively low for students. Partnering with local companies also helps offset those costs, though Holland says he'd like to "cast a cone of shame on the large companies" for not taking the lead.

On the financial side, JumpStart has helped, as has a similar micro-fund called Bullpen Ventures, which Holland used to incubate his new business, Populr—a platform that allows users to create drag-and-drop single-page websites called POPs, short for "Published One-Pagers."

Wark admits the NSS is only "one piece of the solution." Even if they bear a decent number of successes, a few well-run microfunds can only close the gap so much. But Burcham says there's another force that's already applying noticeable pressure on local investors: outside investors. He cites Jamplify as an example of a Nashville startup that quickly drew interest in New York—which in turn sparked interest in Nashville.

"And while it takes a little time," Burcham says, "nothing begins to move a market [like] seeing this sort of traction of things coming in and out of the market—other eyes looking in, saying 'We want that.'"

That's a lesson Mike Butera is learning, as he introduces a product that's already turning heads across the country.

"SO THIS IS MADE in Nashville," Butera says, running his hands along the sleek mahogany-stained body of the Artiphon Instrument 1. "The wood's cut right across the river. Cumberland Architectural Millwork is one of our partners and investors. And it's all designed here, by people who've worked for and designed some of the top audio consoles and consumer electronics."

The Instrument 1 is about the size of a ukulele, but instead of a sound hole it has a dock for an iPhone 5. Instead of strings, it has two touch- and velocity-sensitive pads: a narrow one for strumming, fingerpicking or bowing; the other, about the width of a fretboard, for forming chords or playing individual notes on raised ridges that mimic strings but don't move.

The iPhone, rather than the playing surface, provides the sound processing, through two speakers that can handle up to 30 watts. A player can hold it like a guitar or under the chin like a violin, and through an almost endless variety of apps can make it sound like anything from an acoustic guitar to a squelchy, arpeggiated synthesizer. As evidenced by numerous videos posted to sites like TechCrunch—which brought Butera onstage during the Consumer Electronics Show in Las Vegas— the Instrument 1 largely elicits wide-eyed, slack-jawed delight. A gaggle of *Scene* staffers reacted much the same way, giggling in amazement.

Butera says he continues to be amazed by the response wherever he shows off the Instrument 1, which will sell for $800 and precede a less expensive consumer-grade version. Artiphon attracted so much attention at CES that the annual National Association of Music Merchants invited them to its Los Angeles trade show.

"We think that you're ahead of the curve," Butera says NAMM organizers told him, "and it's likely that you are pushing us out into a new category that in the next couple years is gonna be so obvious."

Still, despite all the glowing press, Butera says, "it has been really difficult to figure out where to go for money in town. And part of that is, we have certain values about how we want to do it. We want to maintain . . . our principles of environmental sustainability, domestic production, things like that." He likens Artiphon's position to that of local clothiers like Imogene + Willie or Otis James—companies whose signature is handcrafted quality, and who must reconcile rising demand with their principles.

"We have the same struggle," Butera says. "We can make these by hand. They're very expensive. . . . If we could make it in Nashville, and it [only] cost $5 more, would we do it? Yes. But is anyone stepping up to provide those services to us? Would the investors support that? Do people care about that enough? It's just an ongoing question."

Pre-orders for the Instrument 1 begin later this quarter, and while bringing the project to life has brought its share of frustrations, Butera remains committed to Nashville even with the lure of outside money.

"I have not yet gone to Silicon Valley with this for a reason," he says. "I think it's better done here."

HERE IS THE LAST American city dedicated to music, trying to become the next American city dedicated to technology. An unlikely progression? Perhaps not.

"Musicians and coders are the same animal." Mark Montgomery says. "When you look at it, they're both math equations. They have a very similar mind. And they have very similar quirks. Coders are wacky as hell, right? Musicians are wacky as hell."

If not wackiness, then maybe it's some combination of creativity, attention to detail and mastery of patterns that draws similar minds to music and programming. Which makes sense. After all, "three chords and the truth" just might be the purest line of code ever written in Nashville.

Singer-songwriter Matt Urmy started his own tech startup after becoming frustrated with the many apps he was using to manage his music career. The all-in-one solution he helped develop, Artist Growth, just launched its second version, which includes a deeper set of tools for management companies to also access and organize data for their artists—including booking dates, merchandise sales and inventory, even live performance royalties that can be reported as soon as the band walks offstage.

"On the creative side in software design, it's very much like writing a song," Urmy says. "After days and weeks and months of struggling with a line of code . . . [getting the finished product ready is] like the final days of mastering." And there's another important similarity he sees: "a strong sense of the tech community supporting and helping people to really grow this sector of Nashville."

Kate O'Neill agrees. "My late husband and I were songwriters together," she says. "I do feel like the songwriting and music community has played a massively significant role—the style of interaction, the collaboration tendencies within it. I don't think it's one to be downplayed."

"It's a total parallel," Butera says. "And the Nashville music industry was put on the map because people started to realize they could get a lot more done through those network effects, rather than just the lone songwriter."

"I've worked in the Bay Area, Portland, Chicago . . . but it has not felt like a truly supportive networked community like it does here," O'Neill says. "It's noticeable in the songwriting community here, and it has carried over—the collaborative songwriting culture here. Inevitably what happens is we tell our respective stories, but the upshot always seems to be, 'How can we work together?'"

In April 2012, Bridgette Sexton opened a post on the official Google blog with this observation: "Nashville and Silicon Valley have a lot in common. They're both filled with smart, creative people building businesses together. Nashville's start-up scene may be less well known, but it's bursting with energy and creativity like the rest of the city." Sexton had just been here for a Google for Entrepreneurs event at aVenue that sold out in four minutes.

It's a sign, among many, that the momentum felt in the startup scene is real. Nashvillians who once were surprised to read Alex Ross columns about their hometown orchestra in the *New Yorker* can now read about Nashville startups in TechCrunch, Venture Beat, and *Forbes*. Recently, Apple featured the real-time multi-angle video-compiling app Streamweaver, designed and based in Nashville, at the top of iTunes' App Store.

The wins are starting to pile up, too. "Rivals[.com] sold for $100 million to Yahoo," Montgomery says. "My company sold for 25. StudioNow for 37.5. You know, every time that happens, the boats go up a little bit." In January, Moontoast secured $5 million in Series B funding. That same month, Streamweaver raised $1.3 million in Series A funding, which was led by former Facebook privacy officer Chris Kelly. Franklin-based recipe app Just a Pinch recently raised more than $1.5 million. Populr has already raised $475,000.

"As investors are getting more comfortable and seeing that risk profile getting lowered," says Clayton Associates' Gibbs, "you're going to see more dollars flowing into the technology community."

"We have to not get complacent and not start patting ourselves on the back," Montgomery says. "Fuck that. Now is the time to push the pedal to the metal."

Whitney's optimism is similarly cautious. "We all know each other, we know each other's families—it's a cool, cool community," he says. "I'll tell you what the con is: We're not aware of how competitive, how aggressive these other markets are. And so we don't really execute, generally speaking, with the same type of precision and aggression. We're a little more relaxed. There are benefits to that! But I think sometimes we're just not really aware of what it takes to compete at that level. And that's a little concerning."

O'Neill doesn't quite see it that way. "As much as there may be more maturity and sophistication in other markets," she says, "the greatest advantage we have here is connectedness."

That connectedness, along with a lot of hard work, has 2013 primed to be a big year for tech in Nashville. Where that could lead is anyone's guess. But if Nashville has proven anything over time, it's an ability to become something new without losing itself along the way.

"There's never going to be another Silicon Valley, and we don't want to be Silicon Valley," Montgomery says. "We want to be us. And us is a quirkier, wackier, a little more Southern, a little nicer version—but with an incredible amount of creativity woven into it. We're a good place to be, and we have good people."

Author's note: By the end of 2018, Cardagin, Evermind, Jamplify, Kiwi, Waffle, and Zeumo were no more. Streamweaver had either gone under or undergone a serious transformation into an IT services company. The Nashville Scene *was no longer owned by SouthComm. Artiphon went to market with a less expensive consumer-grade version and racked up endorsements by musicians, including T-Pain. In 2014, Kate O'Neill shut down [meta]marketer and later decamped to New York to become a consultant and speaker. Emma sold to New York-based Insight Venture Partners in 2017 for an undisclosed amount, and Clint Smith stepped down as CEO. In 2015, Nicholas Holland sold Populr to Nashville-based Kindful, for an undisclosed amount.*

That same year, Marcus Whitney left Moontoast to become president of JumpStart Foundry, which had recently been named the N°. 13 accelerator in the country. But after Y Combinator and TechStars dramatically altered the landscape by upping their investments from $15,000 for 7 percent equity to $125,000 for the same stake, JumpStart pivoted to acting as a seed stage investor in health-care tech startups. "HCA is a 50-year-old company," Whitney tells me via Google Hangout. "There's no guarantee it will be this successful for another 50 years." Pointing to the disruption that befell the music industry and sensing, as others have, that the real reason Jeff Bezos chose Nashville for its operations center is its concentration of health care infrastructure, he says: "Amazon is going to gobble up talent left and right."

The Promise

MERIBAH KNIGHT, 2017

WHEN I FIRST VISITED the James Cayce Homes on the East Side of Nashville, I discovered a different city entirely. A city of crumbling apartments, generational poverty, segregation, violence, waning social programs. A community buckling under the weight of historic neglect.

I wondered how Nashville, the so-called "It City," could claim such good fortune, such boom times, while all of this was happening right in the shadow of downtown. Less than a mile from Nissan Stadium, and within walking distance of glittering, newly built skyscrapers. The tension was thick. So much to reconcile. It's a community that feels like it's splintering, cleaving apart right before our very eyes. With wealth on one side of the street, and poverty on the other. I figured there must be stories there, important stories. Stories this city and maybe even this country needed to hear.

Built in the late 1930s, James Cayce is Nashville's largest public housing complex. Today it's smack in the middle of the city's fastest gentrifying neighborhood. And it's a place going through a metamorphosis of sorts.

Excerpts from The Promise © 2017 Nashville Public Radio. Reprinted with permission.

The city has an ambitious, almost billion dollar plan to tear Cayce down and rebuild the project as a mixture of low income, middle income, and market rate apartments. It wasn't always that a public housing development sat on such valuable land. But now it is. And now the city says it's time to change things. To break up the concentrated poverty that officials say has crippled Cayce for far too long.

The plan is called Envision Cayce, and Nashville has never attempted anything like this, on such a large scale. But Cayce, in particular, is a challenging case—because for years it's been ignored, tossed aside, and in many ways purposely cast aside by the powers that be. Because it tells a story Nashville's boosters would rather forget: one of inequality, of disregard, of strife, of violence, of poverty.

As a reporter, I set out to reconcile what I saw before me—the vast inequality, the broken promises. To gather the stories of those who lived it and let them tell it for themselves. The work that came out of my time in Cayce is a podcast titled *The Promise*. And it's about this tension. About a community divided over race and economics. Where many residents feel pushed out by their new, more-affluent neighbors. Left behind by the city that claims to be on the up.

The Promise is about Nashville; it's about housing policy and gentrification. But at its heart, *The Promise* is about widening inequality in this city and in this country. A wealth gap that hasn't been bigger since the Great Depression. Today, the average annual income for a family living in Cayce is $7,968. But walk across the street and the average income shoots up tenfold. One Vanderbilt study drilled into these numbers. It showed that between 2000 and 2011, those who lived two blocks outside Cayce saw their median income almost double. Meanwhile, residents in Cayce saw their income decrease, by up to 20 percent. America's growing inequality, all realized in a few city blocks. Inside Cayce incomes plummet, asthma rates soar, and the murder rate is exponentially higher than the rest of the city. It's a narrative the city may prefer to ignore, but Cayce's residents have stories to tell.

What follows are excerpted, edited interviews, with residents featured in *The Promise*.

MS. VERNELL

Vernell McHenry has lived in Cayce for almost two decades. She moved while grappling with a drug addiction and after being homeless, sleeping at the city's mission. But as she settled in to Cayce, things started to shift. She got active in the neighborhood, made friends, got sober. And when the housing authority announced its plans to overhaul Cayce, about six years ago, she's advocated for its residents, trying to making sure the city's housing authority didn't ignore their concerns. On any given afternoon you can find Vernell sitting on a metal folding beach chair, usually on her stoop, or one of her neighbors'. She looks out onto a dusty courtyard. Watches the kids play. She smokes a cigarette. Maybe two. She's there. But in her mind she's taking in the sunset at her imaginary beach house.

It's an old Victorian house. And it is purple. Because that's my favorite color. So it's kind of bright. But you can see it. And when the sun sets down behind the horizon it is so beautiful. The beach is the sandy beach. The water is blue. We got my palm trees sitting out there. And I am sitting and sipping on a pineapple spritzer. With the little umbreller. I do travel away from here. I don't just sit here. I travel away from here. My mind be traveling honey, they be like Ms. Vernell you all right honey? I done left scene, honey.

As children and neighbors pass by:

Good evening, young man. You have a good day today? Alrighty.

Hey, Tay. Gonna be a heartbreaker, boy.

Well, hello. How you doing today? How you been doing? You have a good day in school today? Hello, Marcel.

Well, hello, Yana-poo!

I've never been where I couldn't come outside like a pretty day today. Enjoy my weather. Enjoy watching the children play, you know. And I do have a certain amount of claustrophobia. Because I was abused. And my step-mama used to put us in closets.

I'm a runaway. I was a runaway. I ran away when I was 13. The abuse in my mind. . . . It couldn't be no worser in the streets to me than it was right here in this home. I mean, I'm getting three squares and a cot. Don't get me wrong. But, being where you can't hug nobody. Or when the parent comes you get like this [*she ducks*]. I made my own choice.

When I ran away I met this young lady. She was a stripper. She had an 8-month-old baby. So we made a deal. I go to school in the day when you sleep, and when she went to work at night I took care of the baby. I was very smart as far as survival, you understand where I'm coming from?

On the change coming to Cayce and her advocacy for the neighborhood.

I wanted something better for me and better for the neighborhood. Because the way I look at it, this neighborhood, it's a good neighborhood. When I first moved in it was quiet. Everybody looked out for each other. You understand what I'm saying? As the years changed the people changed.

The song is "A Change Is Going to Come." My goal is to let them know [Envision Cayce] is coming. It's going to happen. You need to prepare yourself. I don't consider myself as poor. I consider myself as low income. What I mean by that when I go to the meetings I ask questions so I can prepare myself. And that's how I look at it and Envision Cayce. I think it's going to be a good thing.

In early June Ms. Vernell visited the first new building for Envision Cayce. She had hoped to move in, but after seeing the apartments and realizing they had no outdoor spaces she worried that it would feel too confining. She was so used to greeting her neighborhood from her front stoop, it was her social life.

I'm going to just still pray about it . . . that being closed in . . . I hope I'm downstairs. I'd rather have a downstairs [apartment].

Three months later, Ms. Vernell is sitting on her stoop one Friday afternoon. Around her a gaggle of kids play. She has some news about that new apartment she'd been waiting for.

They called me but I turned it down. My furniture is not going to fit in there.

Changed my mind. It's too small. It was no balconies. Nowhere to sit outside. You know. Nowhere you can . . . like we doing now. It's sun. We can sit outside and mingle with our neighbors and talk. You can't do that. You know. They say they're going to try and put an area outside, but I drove through there the other day, me and my cousin. And it's really nowhere for anybody to sit. Not in a shady spot. I've seen all the cameras they got. But, it's just it's too small. It's just the main thing: It's too small.

BIG MAN

Big Man, whose real name is Dexter Turner, lives in Cayce with his wife and their two children, Roderick and Valencia. On any given day Big Man is usually holding court from his back stoop on South Eighth Street. A pair of dingy cement steps surrounded by a couple decrepit wire clotheslines.

I guess I'm like everybody daddy. Everybody therapist.

What you want to know? I mean I'm just a person, a human being, I mean you know a person that still respect and appreciate his hood even though it's always going the wrong path but. . . . We try to make it better. It's going be better.

I was born in let's see, Louisville, Kentucky. Moved to Nashville like in '69, '68. I was young then, like three or four. We moved to Nashville. We lived on Woodland then. Lived on Woodland Street. From there we moved to what they call Sam Levy (public housing), it was Sam Levy, but we used to call it Settle Court. We lived over there when I was growing up. I guess from that we moved to University Court (public housing). Well I moved the University Court, which is the projects out south. And then I moved here.

Sitting on his stoop talking about Cayce's struggles with gun violence.

It ain't the people. It's not. Because, see, like this right here. . . . It's a good day. But you can't say nothing going to happen. You can't say nothing stupid won't happen. I wish it wouldn't but it might be a good day today.

But I mean, I done learned how to adapt to this. It's like a cactus. You can throw me out in the sand and I am going to grow.

A few weeks later, a Friday in late May.

Today Friday. Today a good day to barbecue. . . . Chicken. Couple pieces of ribs, some pork chops, and some good ol' hamburgers. But ain't nothing like a barbecue burnt hot dog. It's the best. Gotta have a little burn on it. Gotta have a little burn.

1:15 p.m.

All I heard was some shots. Came out the door. They said that somebody was shot. Dude ran down the sidewalk. I looked at him. He fell on the ground. The other one, I don't know which way he went. And they said there was a dude up there in the car dead. I didn't go all the way up there. I came right back in my house. I mean, this shit right here is just ridiculous. I'm through. I can't even do this. I can't even do it. It's not making no sense. See, now I got to worry about what I'm going to tell my kids happened in front of the house. I try to protect them from stuff like this.

I don't know what else to say about shit around here. I got tired. While Big Man sits on his stoop, Detective Cole Womack walks up to question him about the shooting.

DETECTIVE: OK, can you tell me what you saw?

BIG MAN: Hmm, that's basically what it is. Heard it, came out the door. That's all I can tell you. Seen one guy laying on the ground. Walked up the sidewalk they said there was a guy in the car.

DETECTIVE: What's your name? I'm sorry.

BIG MAN: Big Man, that's what they call me. I'm just being honest.

DETECTIVE: I'm just taking notes.

BIG MAN: I'm just giving you my notes. You understand what I'm saying. You ask me what I heard. I told you what I heard.

DETECTIVE: So then after you heard the gunshots you came out from upstairs. Or you're downstairs aren't you?

BIG MAN: I'm downstairs.

DETECTIVE: So you came outside?

BIG MAN: Yup, came outside. Guy laying on the ground.

DETECTIVE: Do you know. . .

BIG MAN: I don't know, because I don't know nobody around here. I just come outside. For real.

DETECTIVE: I didn't finish the question, so I was going to ask you what you saw he was wearing. I didn't ask you if you knew who he was.

BIG MAN: I think it was a red shirt. He was right there on the ground.

DETECTIVE: Could you tell where he was shot at?

BIG MAN: I didn't, I just told him "Be still, calm down," and walked off. I said, "Don't cry."

DETECTIVE: Did you see a gun anywhere? Between the houses.

BIG MAN: Well, I don't know. I didn't see that much. The only thing I can tell you is when I came out the door he was there. When I walked up the sidewalk everybody was right at a grey car out there. So I left it at that because the thing about it is. The reason why I left is because I got to get my kids off the school bus.

DETECTIVE: Gotcha. Do you have a phone number so maybe I can reach you later on and put it in my notes?

BIG MAN: What you want?

DETECTIVE: Nothing, you all have a good day. Be careful.

Detective Womack walks away.

I wasn't expecting to come home and get ready to go out and get the stuff and first thing you hear is gunshots. That's not part of my plan. That's not part of nobody's plan. It's not part of my plan to come out the house and see somebody laying in the front yard. That's not part of my plan. It's not part of my plan to hear somebody done got murdered.

Big Man's friend Chico comes over, sits down next to him and hands him a warm Bud Ice.

You know what, that's not bad. It's quite refreshing.

OFFICER MATTHEW CAMMARN

Metropolitan Nashville Police Officer Matthew Cammarn. On April 12, 2016, a little after 6 p.m., Officer Cammarn, who'd been on the force for only three years, was sitting in his cruiser on South Seventh Street near the James Cayce homes.

When a call came in for a shots fired call. So I am cruising down South Seventh. And I get toward Sylvan. And there's people running toward one area. So I rolled down. I see the large group and I chirp my siren. And I heard people, when I got out of the car. "Police are here. Police are here."

So I was standing there, and I observed the individual pushed the female and then start walking away.

He walks past me. And I say, "Stop, dude. Talk to me." And he says, "F you, I didn't do nothing." So at that point I can't let him walk away. I grabbed him, because he was still continuing to walk past me, and that's when he took a swing on me. At that point I wrapped up with him and I took him to the ground and he continued to attempt to assault me.

A bystander, a man named Andrew Hunter, pulled out his smartphone and began filming. The video, which is grainy and crude and a little under 90 seconds, was uploaded to Facebook and viewed more than 3 million times. It quickly went viral, getting picked up by news outlets here and abroad.

As I was on top of him, telling him to stop resisting and giving me his hands, I got kicked in the head. At first, when I felt it, I thought I got hit in the head with a piece of metal or something like that. Like a baseball bat.

I thought they would probably be helping me, but I guess not, and very quickly I realized they weren't helping me they were trying to pull me off him to free him.

And I was like, "Well, this is it. I am going to pass out. I'm going to die." At that point I was like, OK, this is going too far. I was about to draw down [my pistol].

A single neighbor called 911.

That was uplifting to know that somebody called out of the whole crowd of probably about 50, 60 people that are all too busy videotaping and just being bystanders.

Following the incident, Officer Cammarn was sent to the hospital and diagnosed with a concussion. In the aftermath of the assault the city cracked down; the mayor and the police chief visited Cayce the following day to say things were about to change. MNPD sent officers from various precincts to patrol Cayce, on foot, on bike, by car and even mounted patrol. Meanwhile, the housing authority installed 150 new cameras in Cayce.

I mean, you had motors officers down there. You had people coming over there from different precincts to work. Just to sit there. And to clean it out. To make sure the people there were supposed to be doing what they were supposed to be doing.

Officer Cammarn's condition didn't improve. After weeks of pain and dizziness, he was diagnosed with Post-Concussion Syndrome, a mild traumatic brain injury. He didn't work for months.

It was killing me. To be cooped up in the house and not be able to do anything. It was very hard on me. I started to fall into, like, depression, and I was having anxiety about not being able to do stuff and go out. Because I was in pain, constant pain, and it wouldn't go away. I couldn't go play volleyball. I couldn't wrestle with my kids. I couldn't play soccer with my son. Because I couldn't run. So it was hurting me, emotionally and mentally. It caused me to be very angry and temperamental with my family. Which was not fun. Which is kinda why I am in the situation that I'm in now.

So July Fourth was my wedding anniversary. Two days later after the anniversary, while I was at work, she texted me and said, "I'm packing some stuff at my parents for a little bit." I couldn't understand why. I was destroyed. Um, I was with her for nine total years. We had two kids. So, it's been a year now. But it was really rough. It's something that I got to live with. But I am alive. My kids love me. I love my kids. That's my main focus. My kids.

Brian Shannon, the 22-year-old who fought with Officer Cammarn that day, was convicted of aggravated assault, a felony. The first on his record. He served 30 days in jail, on weekends between his shifts at a fast food restaurant. Shannon's cousin, Michael Mays, the guy who kicked Cammarn in the head, he had prior convictions and as a result was sentenced to 4 years in prison. For Officer Cammarn, his divorce is settled. Recently other departments started showing the video at police trainings—as an example of good instinct and tactics, because he didn't stop fighting and he didn't pull his weapon. Cammarn's brother, who was going through the Denver Police Academy, watched it in his training. When Cammarn went to his graduation, he was greeted by the cadets.

They were like meeting like somebody famous. It was so funny. And then their instructors came to shake my hand and you know, said, you know, "Good job out there," and stuff like that.

Today, Cammarn's back to work in the same precinct. Patrolling the same streets. He admits he avoided Cayce for months, only going if he had to. He had PTSD from the incident, he said. And it caused him to be more on edge.

After my incident happened, I just felt like nobody cared about police. I said, you know, them people down there. They want to be like that, they don't need police down there then. Well, obviously I've changed my mind about things. Because you have time to reflect.

I don't know if the kids are an icebreaker. But they do help, you know, because kids are innocent and you see the joy and the cheer inside their little minds. They just have no recollection about what's going on in life. They're just happy. They're making the best out of everything. They could be sitting there playing in the dirt, in their little minds they're creating something in the dirt.

TONYA SHANNON

Tonya Shannon grew up in Cayce with her mom and her two brothers. But as soon as she was able to leave, she left. She was determined not to raise her own kids in Cayce. But as Tonya learned, leaving Cayce is rarely a clean break.

My earliest memory, I can say, I remember going to kindergarten and we would walk to school. I went to Kirkpatrick Elementary school but we lived on South Seventh so we had to cross two streets before we got there. But we would go in groups like my next-door neighbor. He would walk with me. And then another young lady that I met she would walk and then as we were walking everyone else would join in and we would just walk to her Patrick. I remember the first day I was crying because my aunt dropped me off. My mom didn't.

I mean, it's like it was a fun time. We would have bubble gum hunts instead of Easter Egg hunts. It just seemed like fun. I loved to go to school. I would cry when I was sick and I couldn't go to school.

You know, the ice cream truck would come around. We called it a popsicle truck. But the ice cream truck would come around and you could buy everything off of there: pickles, candy apples, chips. Any kind of ice cream. I can say I had a good, you know, a good first couple of years. And then, you know, I can say when I turned about 10, I seen someone shot. And you know my life just kind of changed after that. I wasn't a very happy kid after seeing that.

We were walking to East Park and as we were walking there was a guy one of my friends knew and she was asking him for a dollar or something. And I didn't know if it was her uncle or whatnot. She asked him for some money and he gave all of us a dollar. I was so excited because as we walk to the park you go by this store, Johnny's Eats Shop. And you could go in there and they had penny candy. But as we were walking he told us to "get down, get down." And I am like, "What's going on?"

So we duck down behind trees, and then there was a car over there so we ducked down behind that. And he got killed. Right in front of us. They shot his brains out. I cried and cried. I was like, I wanna go home. I don't want to go swimming anymore. I want to go home. And, I remember, my mom wasn't there yet. And I just sat at home and you know, my friends came over, we were sitting on the porch and we talking about it. And I was like, "Did he die? I know you can get shot in the head and . . . did he die?" I just kept saying that. And they was like, "Yeah, he died." And it was just eerie to me. I just couldn't, I didn't feel safe anymore.

I just realized we were in the hood. We were in the projects. But after that, it was like, I wanted to either be in someone's house playing with Barbie dolls or something. Or be in my own house playing with Barbie dolls. I just didn't feel safe. I didn't feel safe.

All of my friends they, I mean, they were having kids young. They were having children at—one of my friends, we were in like 6th grade. And she was pregnant and we were riding the school bus to 6th grade. But the next thing was when we got to high school she dropped out. Didn't finish. And then she having another one and another one. It was just like a cycle. And I just knew that I didn't want that.

At 16 years old, Tonya discovered she was pregnant. She was so afraid to tell her mother she waited three months.

And I came and said, "Mama, I got to tell you something." And I just set the pregnancy test on the table, and she was like, "What is this?" I was like, "You never seen one before? Did they not have pregnancy tests when you . . ."

"What this mean, you're pregnant? I'll be damned. I thought you were going to be somebody."

I said, "Mama. I can still be somebody."

I was downstairs packing some things in a bag. She was like, "Where are you going? What's all this stuff for? You throwing it away? What you doing?" I said, "No, Mama, I'm moving out. I got my own place." And when she told me, it was like a stab in the heart. She said, "You doing what? You ain't gonna make it out there. You just 18 years old. What, you getting you a project?" That's what they called living in public housing, a project.

"What, you got you a project?"

And I was like, "No, Mama, I don't have a project. I have an apartment. I don't want to live over here. I don't want to be in this environment. I don't want my son, I want him to be able to be able to go outside and play on the playground and, you know. No, no I don't have a project." Just her saying that just motivated me more to prove to her that I am gonna make it. I'm gonna make it.

I knew what I was doing in my life, I wanted the opposite of what I had. I wanted the opposite.

But Tonya's life, despite being away from Cayce, was in chaos. Her husband was abusive, physically and emotionally. And despite her pleas to her mother—who had been in an abusive relationship of her own in the past—Tonya was not encouraged to leave him.

I stayed with him for years, and he was abusing me and my children. And my mom telling me, "Stay with him." It just stuck in my head. OK, I'm going to stick it out. It's going to get better. It's going to get better. It never got better. I think I stayed in the abusive relationship with my husband because of my mom.

When her husband lashed out at her and her son one night, something shifted.

It just something popped in my head like, this is the last straw. I got to go. You done started hitting my children now. No.

When she thinks about her mom, who still lives in Cayce, Tonya gets emotional. And she knows her determination to leave for good, wasn't the obvious choice.

It's like she's stuck in a rut. She stays in the house, and that's just gonna be her life. Staying in Cayce. And I think that's how some of the families there are. It's generational. Your grandmother stays there. Your mom stays there. So you're going to stay there. And you lead by example. So if that's what you learned, your mama stay here and she's been fine, "OK, I'm going to do it." And I just decided to do the opposite. I do not want to stay in Cayce. This is not where I want to raise my children. I don't know if it makes people depressed and stuck in a rut, I don't want to get it, whatever, the Cayce-itis. I don't want it. No, no, I don't want it.

BIG MAN & WOLFGANG

Sitting on his stoop, looking across the street to the new fancy homes on the block, Big Man wonders aloud what might happen if he goes to visit his new wealthier neighbors. And in an effort to answer his question, a meeting is brokered and a friendship blossoms.

They don't look at us as being people over here. They look at us as being a nuisance. I mean, you can go out this door. I can walk out my door right now, and if walked to any one of my neighbor's house and say, "Hey, can I have a cup of sugar?" If they got it, they gonna give it to you. But if you walk up there, and knock on one of them doors and say, "Can I have a cup of sugar?" there gonna be around 8 polices, SWAT team, and they gonna tell you was doing a burglary.

We are a community within a community. This is what this is. This is the part of the community that they don't want to hear. They don't want to see.

Stephanie Jackson and Wolfgang Blair are the owners of a sleek modern house Big Man can see from his back door, the one he says would call the cops if he went asking for a cup of sugar. Stephanie works for a Fortune 50 company and Wolfgang is an investor and lawyer.

WOLFGANG: I get his position. I would have the same position, too. But you know, it's gotta happen organically. He needs a cup of sugar. Walk up the hill, the door's open. We'll have a drink at the same time and get to know each other.

We believe in regeneration of neighborhoods. Not gentrification. And I think the distinction has to do with your own personal values. So we believe that going into an area that people have forgotten about. And we choose to live there. We bring everybody up. And so our value system is to bring hope, to bring it up, to regenerate it and to bring back the values that we're all in the 21st century.

I grew up in the deserts of Arizona. My father was a traveling salesman. My parents never went to college. You know I put myself through college and graduate school. So I don't consider myself a person of privilege. So I don't really look at it like I am saving anybody. Now granted, because I'm white, I probably have had some advantages. But I took advantage of those advantages and now it's time to give back to other people. So.

STEPHANIE: And we had people tell us, you know it's dangerous to get off on Shelby [Avenue]. You know, don't do that at night, blah blah blah. And so we came over here, and we didn't feel that.

Big Man walks up the hill to Wolfgang and Stephanie's house to meet them for the first time and see the inside of the house he's looked at from a distance for so long.

BIG MAN: Woooowwww

WOLFGANG: Yeah, it's different, isn't it?

Big Man steps out to the porch to show Wolfgang and Stephanie where he lives in Cayce.

BIG MAN: OK, let's see. If you look out your door. I live, well, I guess what some people call a rig. That big green van right there. That's my van.

WOLFGANG: It's always parked there.

BIG MAN: Yeah, that's my van. It's either there or a little bit down in front of that Jeep. But I live down that sidewalk right there.

STEPHANIE: Oh wow

BIG MAN: Well, I mean, what some people say is it's two different cities. You know. This a city, but that's a city within a city.

WOLFGANG: Kind of, yeah.

BIG MAN: It's people over there, they really—I ain't even going to lie to you—they scared to walk up through here because the first thing they think is the people up here going to call the police on them.

WOLFGANG: Nawww. No.

BIG MAN: I mean, I'm being serious.

WOLFGANG: I mean, I'll be out watering stuff. And I know what you're saying, because I was raised out west, so race means like nothing to me. So, I see, black person walking they won't look at me. But I'll say, "Hey, how you doing?" and then we'll start talking to each other. But they will never . . . they're afraid. I know they're afraid.

BIG MAN: I mean, it's the point. That. It's some misconceptions. I mean, it's a lot of people over here where you'll probably go down through and say, "I might get robbed." I mean, you got to think about it. It's generations of families that's over there.

WOLFGANG: Yeah.

BIG MAN: And you gotta lot of them people that, only thing they know is them projects.

WOLFGANG: Yeah.

BIG MAN: I mean, you got a couple of them that's fortunate to take their kids probably a little bit past Shelby and, say, they gone downtown or they done gone to the football game.

WOLFGANG: Yeah.

BIG MAN: You got a couple of them that might be that fortunate. But you got a lot of them that's not. So you got a lot of kids, and a lot of people that's over there. They don't know about this, they don't know about the people up here. They don't meet people up here.

WOLFGANG: We tell people where we live and they're kind of nervous.

BIG MAN: Yeah, I know they're nervous.

STEPHANIE: I hear [gunshots] and I sometimes don't know if it's firecrackers or gunshots. You know. But I do hear them. And, um, do I worry? No, it's like, cuz I can't worry. Because I can be walking downtown Nashville and I get hit by a car, I can get shot. I mean. You just can't.

BIG MAN: I mean, that's the whole point. You can get done anywhere.

WOLFGANG: So, we believe in what's called regeneration. Regeneration is going to a neighborhood like this and giving people hope. Hey, we're like you. Let's get to know each other. Let's help each other. And let's regenerate the community.

BIG MAN: Instead of tearing it down.

WOLFGANG: Exactly.

BIG MAN: At the rate that things are going. The price of living. I mean, yeah, you struggle just to keep a roof over your head now. Let alone keeping food on your table. And I mean, you got some people that's two-family households down here that's barely making it.

WOLFGANG: I hear exactly what you're saying. That's why I am here. That's why I believe in regeneration. Cuz if I can say, "Hey, I'll help you. I can give you some hope." That's how we're going to change the system together. See what I'm saying? See, I have no problem going to the mayor and saying, "Hey this guy told me Section 3, he's got kids in jobs." I'll snap and do that. But you don't think about doing that because that's not where you're coming from. You know?

BIG MAN: The people over here. Say you, see now, you walk over here now and you ask them what do they want. What do they need? They going to tell you remodeling, tearing them down, that's not going to help nothing.

WOLFGANG: Yeah, I hear ya. I hear ya.

BIG MAN: But what these people really have to say. It don't mean nothing.

WOLFGANG: No, but that's why I'm here. To give a voice to the community and guys like you.

BIG MAN: The only thing you have to do is give them people some jobs that's already living here to help remodeling them. Help, you know, spruce 'em up. Put in some porches out there where we can sit out on the patio stoop or something. We ain't got to run through no gates and things like that. Where our kids got a better basketball court.

Over the next month or so, Big Man and Wolfgang start hanging out. They watch sports together, talk about life and work. They even start trying to launch a small business to employ residents in Cayce during the big renovation.

BIG MAN: Yeah, yeah, he aight. He aight. He a man of his word. I give it to him. He aight. Yeah, yeah. He doing what he said he was going to do.

Metro Police Press Release: November 16, 2017. East Precinct detectives are investigating an apparent murder-suicide involving suspected shooter Wolfgang Blair, 61, and Stephanie Jackson, 56, inside the couple's 601 S Ninth St. residence.

BIG MAN: Maaannnnn. All I know is I talked to him, what, Sunday? I mean, it was like, everything with him was peachy keen. And I mean, when I talked to him, when he called me he was talking about when he was coming back. He said, Tuesday, no later than Wednesday morning. And it was like, OK, I'll see you then.

It's like for me to get to know this person. I got to know this man. I actually been up there. After that I been up there again, though. I mean, me and him have actually sit down and talked, whatever. You would never think that this what they had capable on they mind. I mean serious. I mean I've known some people that took their lives. But I mean, they really had problems. I mean, but this? To see what you got. To see the things that you have. I don't see it. I don't see it. Man, they had a hideaway TV in the living room. C'mon! This motherfucker actually goes up the motherfucking wall. But what I'm saying is the perception of what you see from this person. Naw, you wouldn't expect this shit. I mean, you couldn't see it.

For Big Man, whose problems seemed mostly to revolve around money, the idea that someone like Wolfgang would murder his girlfriend and kill himself confounded him. Wolfgang seemed to have everything—the fanciest house in the neighborhood, a nice car, a good job. In some ways, the deaths of Wolfgang and Stephanie made Big Man realize they had more in common than he imagined. Clearly, Wolfgang was living with these secrets, these demons. And Big Man thought, "That's me."

Wow, I thought I had problems. I mean, for real—in perspective, I thought I had problems.

I mean, we all got it in us. . . . It's there. It's there.

All I know is I met two, I can kinda say, wonderful people. They was cool. They was actually somebody you could actually talk to. There wasn't no ifs, ands, buts, nothing like that. He was actually, you actually tell he cared about what he was doing. . . . What else could you learn? Shoot, he got money. He happy. Look at his house. Look at everything he got, shoot. I ain't got none of that. Shoot. I don't know.

But I guess everybody just the same.

A Monument the Old South Would Like to Ignore

MARGARET RENKL, 2018

IN 1978, THE CITY of Nashville leased 18 acres of a Civil War monument to a local businessman who wanted to start a new baseball franchise—the Nashville Sounds, then a Double A expansion team for the Southern League—and needed a place for his team to play. It was a ludicrous arrangement from the start: a privately owned ball field built on public land.

And not just any public land. Greer Stadium was built at the base of St. Cloud Hill, where the Union Army erected a stronghold after taking control of the city in 1862. Fort Negley was an investment designed to protect the Union's hold on Nashville and its strategic access to roads, railroad lines, and the Cumberland River.

Fort Negley Park is not a Civil War monument in the South that celebrates the heroism of the Confederacy, in other words. Fort Negley Park is a Civil War monument in the South that celebrates the preservation of the United States of America. The question of what will happen to it has roiled Nashville for more than a year.

In part, that's because it's a crucial site for African American history as well. During the war, the grounds surrounding Fort Negley served as a de facto refugee camp for escaped slaves. In an irony lost on no one today, the Union Army immediately forced those refugees into service; under brutal conditions, some 2,700 of them built Fort Negley itself. Many lost their lives and are believed to be buried at Fort Negley Park. When the South surrendered, the survivors—joined by other freed slaves—settled there. Today the area is gentrifying, home to new art galleries and coffee shops, but it is still populated largely by low-income African Americans.

In their midst now lies one badly overgrown and dilapidated minor-league ball field. Greer Stadium has sat empty since the Nashville Sounds departed at the end of the 2014 season. As part of a preserved Civil War site, the stadium's location has long been designated as public parkland, going back to 1928, when the city bought it from the descendants of John Overton, a longtime crony of President Andrew Jackson. That parcel was always meant to revert to parkland once the Sounds decamped.

The actual fort at Fort Negley Park was dismantled after the Union Army withdrew in 1867, but history set its hand on the site a second time during the Depression, when a facsimile of the fort was rebuilt there by 800 laborers funded by the Works Progress Administration. That reproduction ultimately fell into ruin and for decades was closed to the public, but 1996 brought a plan to restore the site again. Fort Negley reopened in 2004, on the 140th anniversary of the Battle of Nashville. The next year it was designated a National Historic Landmark District.

Three years after the Sounds left, Mayor Megan Barry released a request for proposals related to the site of the old stadium. The request was not for Metro Parks to create a plan for desperately needed green space in an already overpaved urban core. The request was not for the Metro Historical Commission to create a plan to preserve the legacy of African Americans who gave their lives to preserve the Union. It was not a request for the Friends of Fort Negley, an advocacy group, to create a plan to expand the educational reach of the site.

The plans the mayor requested were for private development under a land-lease arrangement much like the one that allowed Greer Stadium to be built there in the first place.

Let's call what happened next the second Battle of Nashville.

For years this city has been undergoing rapid, unchecked growth, and it desperately needs affordable housing and subsidized work spaces for artists and innovators. That much everyone agrees on. When the mayor's office approved a plan by the Cloud Hill partnership, headed by the developer Bert Mathews and the music producer T Bone Burnett, for a mixed-use private development that would include music and art studios, retail space, and housing at three price points—affordable, work force, and market rate—it made a kind of sense.

But an army of green-space advocates and historic preservationists quickly mobilized to point out what would seem to be obvious: Nashville owns a lot of land, and there is no good reason to allow for-profit development in a park with huge historic significance.

For an entire year, Betsy Phillips, a local historian, published article after article in the *Nashville Scene*, looking at every possible angle for understanding the importance of Fort Negley, particularly its significance to African American history. The bottom line, she wrote in December, is that we preserve historic sites for future generations because "we don't know what the future might need from the past."

The best-selling historical novelist Robert Hicks, an advocate for preserving Civil War historic sites, entered the fray. A Nashville council member sued Metro government, arguing that the mayor's office didn't follow city rules in granting the development contract. The country music legend Kix Brooks took to Facebook to plead for preserving the integrity of the park. Historic Nashville Inc., a nonprofit that each year releases a list of the nine most endangered historical sites in the city, took the unprecedented step in 2017 of naming only one: Fort Negley.

The Friends of Fort Negley, led by the historian Clay Bailey, took a multipronged approach to raising the site's national profile. It petitioned the Tennessee Historical Commission to designate Fort Negley Park a "historical memorial," a label that under state law means a site cannot be altered without a waiver from the commission itself. With help from Nashville's NAACP chapter, it submitted a proposal for Fort Negley to be included in Unesco's slave route registry—the first United States site to be nominated for this international recognition.

The group produced a website and a video summarizing the issues for a public that was finally tuning in: In its annual Open Season on Open Spaces report, the Cultural Landscape Foundation in Washington recognized Fort Negley as one of 13 nationally significant landscapes in need of protection.

And all this was happening against the backdrop of a national debate about Civil War monuments. Defenders of monuments to Robert E. Lee and Nathan Bedford Forrest, the Confederate generals most often at the heart of these contentions, are fond of pointing out that such statues weren't erected to celebrate the institution of slavery; they were erected to celebrate Southern history. The anti-monument contingent rolls its eyes at this argument: If not for antislavery sentiment in the North, the South would never have seceded.

It's important to note that Southern attitudes to Civil War monuments are not uniform, though the pro-con divide typically follows the rural-urban divide.

In 2015, Nashville's Metro Council voted to petition the Tennessee Department of Transportation to plant obscuring vegetation in front of a truly hideous statue of Nathan Bedford Forrest on I-65. The giant statue is visible from the highway to anyone entering the city from the south, but it stands on private land, and for that reason the department declined to intervene. Never mind that the TDOT itself *removed* the obscuring vegetation back in 1998, when the statue was first erected.

Last month activists took matters into their own hands and painted the statue pussy-hat pink.

The Tennessee Heritage Protection Act was passed in 2013 and updated in 2016 with what seemed to be an express intent to prevent municipalities in Tennessee from taking down Confederate memorials. (Yes, this is the same act currently being invoked to protect Fort Negley.) Last month city leaders in Memphis found a novel way around the state's intrusion into municipal decisions: They sold two city parks to a nonprofit. Within hours of the sale, statues of Nathan Bedford Forrest and Jefferson Davis had been removed.

On January 12, back in Nashville, the development controversy finally came to a close when an archaeological survey commissioned by the city found it "highly likely" that the former slaves who built Fort Negley are still buried there. Cloud Hill formally withdrew its development proposal, and it's not clear what will happen to the Greer parcel now. Nashville's 2018 parks budget does not include funding for bulldozing Greer Stadium and returning it to parkland, but Mayor Barry recently acknowledged that the presence of slave graves changes the way the old baseball stadium should be approached.

"The likelihood of graves means that we should reassess plans for this site so as to better honor and preserve the history of the men and women who died in the construction of a fort that helped save the Union," she wrote in a statement. "As we move forward, I want to see that whatever happens with the Greer Stadium site will honor that history, while bringing the community together around a shared vision. I have faith in the ability of all stakeholders to work together to identify and coalesce around this vision."

It's fair to assume that the supporters of other Civil War monuments around the state of Tennessee will not be coalescing around this vision to preserve a site that celebrates a different kind of history, but the Friends of Fort Negley is moving ahead with plans of its own. Last Thursday it announced that Kix Brooks will serve on a new committee. Its goal: to unite Nashville around a plan—and funding—for a reunified Fort Negley Park.

Who Will Hold the Police Accountable?

TED ALCORN, 2019

ON AN UNSEASONABLY WARM February afternoon in 2017, Jocques Clemmons was driving through the James A. Cayce Homes, the largest public-housing complex in Nashville, when he rolled through a stop sign and into the parking lot of the building where his girlfriend and younger son lived. A big, affable father of two, he was 31 years old and, like most of the neighborhood's residents, black.

Officer Joshua Lippert of the Metro Nashville Police Department had been watching the stop sign from his Chevy Impala, where he sat alone. The car was unmarked, but easily recognized as belonging to the department's "flex" team. Unlike patrol officers, who respond to calls for service in a fixed geographic territory, flex officers primarily move between neighborhoods that have high crime rates, looking for misconduct and engaging on their own initiative. People in Cayce call them the "jump-out boys" for their proclivity to drive up abruptly on suspicious activity and make arrests. Like most Nashville cops, Lippert is white. He turned on his lights and followed Clemmons into the parking lot.

Clemmons's mother, Sheila Clemmons Lee, a caregiver for the elderly and disabled, was feeding her charges lunch when her phone rang. It was Clemmons's girlfriend, and she was screaming. At first, Lee could make out only a few words—*police, shot.* When she and her husband arrived at Vanderbilt University Medical Center, Clemmons was in surgery. A detective approached and asked whether her son had an arrest record. Then a doctor came out and told her Clemmons had died.

"I need to see my son," Lee recalls saying, but the detective barred the family from viewing the body, explaining that it had to be protected as evidence. By then, the police had tweeted notice that an officer had shot a "gunman" at Cayce Homes, accompanied by an image of a revolver. "This is his weapon," the tweet read. Lee wouldn't see her son's body until a week later, at the funeral home.

In his first interview with an investigator the afternoon of the shooting, Lippert said that when he pulled up, Clemmons exited the car he had been driving and fled on foot, dropping a handgun as he tried to escape. Lippert said he tried to kick the gun away, but Clemmons managed to pick it up, and raised it in his direction. Lippert then shot him from about 10 feet away, hitting him once in the hip and twice in the back.

But there were ambiguities: The first officer to arrive after the shooting didn't see a handgun on the scene—Lippert said he'd put it in his pocket to secure the area—and a subsequent lab analysis of the weapon found no identifiable prints or DNA linked to Clemmons.

Unlike the police departments of many neighboring cities, Nashville's didn't have dashboard or body cameras for most of its officers. Later that night, based on footage pulled from distant security cameras, the police announced that during the chase, Clemmons had "rushed and rammed Lippert"—though they would retract that account the following week, when footage from another camera came to light showing that the two had never collided. In their investigative files, the police referred to Clemmons as the "suspect" and Lippert as the "victim," and they obtained a warrant to search Clemmons's cellphone and social-media accounts. Lippert's attorneys declined to comment on behalf of their client for this article. (Later, the district attorney announced that state law enforcement would take over this investigation and those of all future cases in which officer-involved use of force results in death.)

No one doubted that police face unique risks, but the apparent one-sidedness of the department's account of the shooting felt to many like a provocation. Lee recalls thinking the police were "dehumanizing my son and painting a picture of him that's not true." A police spokesman said, by email, "In critical incidents, the MNPD works to disseminate accurate information to the community as expediently as possible to inform and negate any rumor or false information."

Lee had raised Clemmons and his three younger sisters as a single mother, and even as a child, he was protective of her and the girls. Beginning when he was 7 or 8 years old, he worked at his grandparents' fruit stand at the old Nashville Farmers' Market, where his outgoing personality made him a natural salesman. "The whole city knew him from the farmers' market, especially the older folks," his sister Aja Tate recalls.

In high school, he fell in with what Lee thought of as the wrong crowd, and ended up with a record in the juvenile-justice system. Upon graduating from high school, he moved to Knoxville to try to get a fresh start and married the mother of his first son, but later he returned to Nashville. Every few years, he got in trouble with the law again, convicted of drug possession, misdemeanor assault, and driving without a license. For the past few months, he'd been staying with Lee. A Dallas Cowboys fan, he would often watch games with her. Now Lee picked out a casket for him decorated with the team's logo.

Two days after Clemmons's death, on a Sunday afternoon, Lee and her family walked to a pedestrian bridge overlooking downtown. The children held hand-lettered signs. "Fly high, Joc," read one. At the bridge's apex, the group released 31 balloons, one for each year of his life.

As they turned back toward the base of the bridge, a clutch of young people approached. Introducing themselves as community organizers, they asked Lee for permission to coordinate a response to the shooting, and she gave them her blessing. "We're going to get justice for your son," one of them said—though they were only beginning to understand what justice might mean in this case, and what would be required to attain it.

BY OUTWARD MEASURES, IT has been a great few years in Nashville. With a rate of job growth since the Great Recession that is among the highest in the country, the metro area attracts throngs of new residents, and in 2013, the *New York Times* declared Nashville "the nation's 'it' city." For some, part of its appeal is its reputation as a progressive oasis in a conservative region: Nashville was among the first major Southern cities to desegregate all public facilities, and in 2016, its voters favored Hillary Clinton over Donald Trump by nearly two to one. But yawning inequalities, with a strong racial dimension, persist. In 1968, planners ran Interstate 40 through a thriving cultural district in the predominantly African American area of North Nashville, weakening property values and ruining local businesses. Since the late 1990s, the city's public schools have grown more segregated. The city has reliably elected Democratic mayors, but never a black one, even though more than a quarter of the population is African American.

Perhaps nowhere is this unequal treatment more striking than in the criminal-justice system. According to a recent analysis by the Brookings Institution, the North Nashville zip code 37208, whose population was 82 percent black in 2010, has a higher rate of incarceration than any other area of the country: Of the people born there from 1980 to 1986, roughly one in seven was incarcerated in 2012. (Cayce Homes sits in the rapidly gentrifying 37206, where the incarceration rate was about half that of 37208, but still nearly four times the national average.)

For many Nashvillians entangled in the criminal-justice system, the trouble begins with a traffic stop, which makes those interactions a potent symbol of the mistrust between officers and some citizens. Months before the traffic stop that ended in Clemmons's death, a grassroots group called Gideon's Army had analyzed police traffic-stop data and published a 213-page report, "Driving While Black," showing that black drivers were stopped more frequently than white ones. It also found disparities in how drivers were treated during stops; for instance, police were far more likely to cite probable cause to search a vehicle if the driver was black.

While it is rare for a traffic stop to escalate to a shooting, the group connected traffic stops to their potential for more catastrophic harm. In a presentation to the city's leaders in January 2017, just a month before Clemmons's death, Gideon's Army's founder, Rasheedat Fetuga, demanded that the city drastically reduce its use of traffic stops to forestall future tragedies. "We all want to avoid a Ferguson-type situation," she said.

Police Chief Steve Anderson, a 71-year-old white man, later responded to the report with a letter, published online, in which he denied that the department's policing strategies had any explicit bias. Police are deployed to areas that have high crime rates, he wrote, where a larger share of the population is black. The "real disparities," he argued, weren't biased police stops, but the elevated rates at which blacks were killed and victimized in crimes. He didn't address the disparate ways in which stops of black and white motorists were conducted.

Broader research suggests that how police are deployed only partly explains these disparities. A recent analysis of nearly 100 million traffic stops around the United States found that black drivers were more likely to be both stopped and searched, and higher crime rates in neighborhoods where black people tend to live explained only part of this difference.

Within days of the balloon release, several dozen activists gathered in the home of a veteran organizer, Clemmie Greenlee, who had converted her garage into a community room. They sat in a circle as D. J. Hudson, a librarian and founding member of Nashville's chapter of Black Lives Matter, pushed the group to develop a concrete set of demands. They'd watched as police violence roiled other cities, such as Ferguson, Baltimore, Chicago, and Oakland, and residents in those cities tried to secure indictments of officers—with mixed results. Now that it was happening in Nashville, they agreed that the highest priority was holding Lippert accountable for the shooting, but they also wanted to overhaul how their police department was governed. One of them raised an unaddressed demand from the "Driving While Black" report: The city needed a civilian oversight board for the police department.

Compared with other institutions of municipal government, police departments are unusually insulated from scrutiny. Whereas other agencies give the public an opportunity to comment on policy changes before they go into effect, the decisions of law enforcement may be shared only after the fact, if at all. While the police chief usually answers to the mayor, city councillors, or members of a police commission, those officials can be reticent about second-guessing their public-safety officials. Barry Friedman, a professor of law and the director of the Policing Project at NYU School of Law, writes, "When it comes to policing, the ordinary rules of democratic governance seem to evaporate."

Beginning decades ago, some cities have sought to address this deficit by involving citizens more in police decision making. In 1948, Washington, DC, created the country's first civilian review board to investigate complaints about police. Spurred by the civil-rights movement, demands for civilian oversight increased during the 1960s, but went largely unmet. Only in the 1980s and '90s, as minorities gained more political representation and the idea became more accepted by officials, did oversight boards proliferate.

The strongest oversight boards can investigate misconduct, discipline officers, and recommend changes to policing strategies. Peter Hammer, a law professor at Wayne State University Law School, argues that by demonstrating transparency and accountability, civilian review boards can help rebuild trust between police and the communities they serve. "If we are trying to find pathways out of the racialized policing we're seeing, community oversight is the sort of thing we have to embrace," he says. But creating them has proved contentious, even as police-involved violence has gotten more mainstream attention.

By 2016, about half of the 50 largest police departments in the US had an independent civilian-run board to investigate complaints, and just six had some ability to discipline officers. That same year in Newark, New Jersey, the local chapter of the Fraternal Order of Police (FOP)—a national membership organization that advocates for police officers—filed a lawsuit against the city's new civilian complaint-review board seeking to substantially weaken it. (Last month, an appeals court ruled that the board could largely function as planned. The FOP has petitioned for the Supreme Court of New Jersey to take this case on appeal.) And in March, Utah's legislature passed a bill to preemptively bar cities in the state from establishing independent boards with certain oversight powers over the police. "Giving civilians oversight of policing—that shouldn't be radical, but it is," Hammer says.

Eleven days after Clemmons's death, as a few raindrops began to fall, dozens of people marched to the courthouse for a regularly scheduled meeting of Nashville's Metro Council, which represents its consolidated city and county government. As they filled the wooden benches of the public viewing area, a protester raised her hand and was ignored; she stepped to a mic anyway and began to speak. When the vice mayor chided her for interrupting and suggested she return for a public hearing on policing practices scheduled for the following month, the crowd behind her erupted into chants of "Justice for Jocques!"

Eventually, the council members broke with protocol and granted the protesters 20 minutes to speak. After Clemmons's sister Aja Tate described the trauma of her brother's death and the seeming impunity of the officer who had killed him, Greenlee approached the lectern, bent the microphone down so it would reach her diminutive frame, and asked the city to establish a community oversight board for the police.

THEY WERE NOT THE first Nashvillians to call for civilian oversight. According to Davie Tucker Jr., a longtime Nashville resident and the pastor at Beech Creek Missionary Baptist Church, the city's modern era of advocacy for police reform began when he was just a teenager. He recalled the Friday night in 1973 when officers responding to a report of a burglary surprised a group of young people playing dice in a vacant house and opened fire on them as they fled, killing 19-year-old Ronald Lee Joyce, a black student at Tennessee State University.

Days later, hundreds of students and other community members marched from Joyce's home to the courthouse in the rain. In a pamphlet prepared around the same time, a coalition of activists made holding the officers accountable their first demand, but their second was for a civilian committee to amend policing practices. The police chief, who had also struggled to address a wave of murders, resigned, but a grand jury did not indict any officers, and no civilian oversight board was created. Joyce's family filed a lawsuit against Nashville, and the city settled for a reported $50,000.

After other instances of police violence against black Nashvillians in the early '90s, community members pressed city leaders to create a civilian review board. Instead, the mayor asked the city council to revamp the Metro Human Relations Commission, which provides diversity training to police cadets and makes recommendations to the mayor's office about what it perceives as discrimination. Later, the police department created its own Office of Professional Accountability, but data from 2005 to 2015 show that of complaints initiated by civilians, the office finds against the officer less than one-sixth of the time. (In Lippert's case, the office recommended he be exonerated for violating departmental policy, even before the state completed its investigation.)

During the '90s, as violence crested in many major American cities, policing was undergoing a major change. Departments that had long been primarily reactive—responding to calls for service as they came in—began trying to proactively prevent crime. In what came to be known as "the new policing," they drew on geospatial analyses of crime data to concentrate officers in areas with the highest crime rates (a practice using this technique was developed in New York City, under the name CompStat), where they employed proactive tactics such as pedestrian and traffic stops.

Nashville embraced these strategies under Ronal Serpas, a self-described "CompStat champion" who headed the police department from 2004 to 2010. He launched a program called Mission One, in which detectives and other officers not already assigned to patrol spent one night a month in areas with high crime rates, supplementing the policing already going on there, in part by doing investigatory traffic stops. "I used to say all the time: Criminals don't ride horses—they drive in cars," Serpas told me. "That's where you find guns, that's where you find dope, that's where you find people with warrants, that's where you find people leaving the scene of crimes."

Traffic stops more than doubled under Serpas, and rose another 42 percent under his successor, Anderson, to a high of 445,000 stops in 2012. At that point, drivers in the city were being stopped nearly eight times as frequently as the national average. In the years that followed, the frequency of stops gradually declined, but remained far higher than in comparable cities.

The practice didn't bother Officer Keiara Ward, who joined the department in 2015. Born and raised in North Nashville, she happily enlisted in the precinct that covered that area. About 12 percent of Nashville police are black, like Ward, compared with 28 percent of the population. On many occasions, she responded to a call and encountered someone she'd grown up with. "The people felt good that a familiar face was out there," she told me.

Like other officers, she was trained to scrutinize vehicles for nonmoving violations—a broken taillight, an expired registration—and use that pretext to make a stop, where in conversation the driver might give cause for a search. She estimated that she conducted seven or eight stops a day—high even among Nashville officers. There were no quotas, but each officer filled out paperwork listing the day's activities. "Say that I turn in an activity sheet, and I only have one or two things on there," she says. "It's like, 'What were you doing in the other hours?'"

Proactive policing techniques can contribute to public safety: A report by the National Academies of Sciences, Engineering, and Medicine concluded that, when focused on hot spots with consistently elevated rates of crime, certain proactive strategies can reduce the incidence of crime in the short term. (There hasn't been enough research to gauge the long-term effects of those strategies.) And the Supreme Court has unanimously ruled that any traffic violation is legitimate grounds to make a stop.

But the report also concluded that subjecting people to certain proactive strategies—particularly stop-and-frisk of pedestrians and pretextual traffic stops—can deeply harm their attitudes toward police. David Weisburd, a professor at George Mason University and one of the report's editors, explained that the key to successful proactive policing is maximizing its impact on crime while minimizing the harm it inflicts on people and improving community trust. "Nobody wants to be stopped by the police," Weisburd told me. "When police use stops or intrusive strategies, they need to be extraordinarily focused."

"DRIVING WHILE BLACK" HAD caused only a brief stir in the local media, but the activists who had usurped the council meeting now had their representatives' attention. "We're ready to listen and to take action to address the problems of our community," the vice mayor told them.

But Nashville's Metro Council is unusually large, with 40 members, which makes it fractious and, in the eyes of keen political observers, more susceptible to the influence of mayors. Megan Barry, Nashville's mayor at the time, was seen by some as deferential to the police department. (Barry declined to comment.)

The department also wields considerable influence in its own right. Chief Anderson has spent nearly all his career in the department, joining the force in 1975 and succeeding Serpas as its leader in 2010, and his long tenure there reflects his political savvy. When the deaths of Michael Brown, Tamir Rice, Eric Garner, and others sparked a national outcry for police reform, he navigated the politics skillfully: In November 2014, when Black Lives Matters protesters converged on police headquarters for a demonstration, his officers were covered widely in the local press for meeting them with coffee and hot cocoa.

But when it came to establishing a civilian oversight board, a police spokesman told reporters such a board was unnecessary, since the department already met with residents thousands of times annually and there were other institutions in place for reviewing police misconduct. A spokesman for the mayor equivocated, saying, "It is not something Mayor Barry is pursuing at this time."

For Lee, the period following her son's death was one of deep anguish. She had taken a leave from work, and often found herself lying awake late at night thinking about him. On her Facebook profile, she alternately poured out her sorrow, surrendered herself to God, and lashed out at Lippert, as well as the mayor and police chief, whom she saw as protecting him. On March 30, which would have been her son's 32nd birthday, she posted, "I don't think I'm going to make it through this day please pray for me please." A police-department spokesman emailed, "We understand Ms. Lee's grief and, as we have communicated, are sorry for her loss, as we would be with any mother who lost a child."

Six weeks later, state law enforcement completed the investigation of Clemmons's death, and at the invitation of District Attorney Glenn Funk, Lee and her family met with him in his office. The family began by sharing some memories of Clemmons, but when Funk started to speak, Lee's spirit fell. An eyewitness had corroborated that Clemmons had dropped a gun and retrieved it, so Funk felt Lippert had a reasonable claim of self-defense and wouldn't prosecute the officer.

For Lee, the decision was devastating. "How many others will have to be murdered by the hands of the ppl that's supposed to protect and serve us before somebody be held accountable," she posted that night. At dusk the next day, Clemmons's children and sisters joined with activists and silently marched east through the city, toward the mayor's house, carrying a coffin. By the time they arrived at Barry's home, they were trailed by police cars. One officer commanded them through his loudspeaker to clear the road. The group leaned the coffin against the mayor's gate and said a prayer before dispersing.

The most experienced activists had always felt that truly reforming policing practices would require fundamental changes in the department's governance. A small group of them, including several members of Gideon's Army, had already begun meeting—in the offices of the NAACP and the local Black Lives Matter chapter, at restaurants, and in churches— with the mission of formulating a proposal for a community oversight board that they could bring to the Metro Council.

Recently they had learned that one of the city's best-known social-justice organizations, Nashville Organized for Action and Hope (NOAH), was developing its own proposal, and the groups joined forces in a coalition that would eventually be called Community Oversight Now. Founded by local faith leaders, NOAH had broad reach, representing more than 50 organizations that together included more than 10,000 members. They tended to be older, wealthier, and whiter than the members of Gideon's Army, and had access to the city's top politicians; once a quarter, the organization's leaders met with Mayor Barry.

It was a somewhat awkward alliance, but Kyle Mothershead, a member of NOAH's criminal-justice task force, had worked with several of the activists before. A white man raised in Madison, Wisconsin, he had spent eight years as a Nashville public defender, then started his own practice focused on criminal defense and civil rights. It was he who obtained the traffic-stop data analyzed in the "Driving While Black" report, while requesting records from the police department about how it handled misconduct. An adept lawyer, he now took the lead in drafting a bill to create a civilian review board.

That summer, the activists met with progressive council members and the council's Minority Caucus to discuss their proposal. With funding from the Tennessee NAACP, they ran ads on one of the city's premier black radio stations. But in July, while still not taking a position on their efforts, Barry announced that she was in talks with NYU School of Law's Policing Project to undertake a new study of the city's use of traffic stops. (Within months, she would commission it.) One of the mayor's senior aides, Lonnell Matthews Jr., recalls that the mayor wasn't opposed to an oversight board, but preferred it be a collaboration between the police and the community, rather than developed independently by the department's critics. "She wanted it to be an inclusive process," Matthews says.

Mothershead thought the Policing Project might validate the findings of "Driving While Black"—but many activists felt the mayor wanted to undermine them. The coalition decided against discussing the issue with institutional players such as the mayor's staff or the police department before first building more grassroots power. Mothershead protested; he wanted to start discussions right away.

The difference of opinion created tension in the coalition. As an alliance between committed black activists and well-heeled liberal whites, who differed in their views of the city's abiding institutions and the best strategies for reforming them, Community Oversight Now was split by the same divisions that ran through Nashville as a whole. "Even within the coalition, it was precarious at best," says Tucker, who participated in some meetings. "I was often worried it would fall apart."

As the summer of 2017 passed, the coalition was also struggling to keep the issue of police oversight in the public eye. Clemmons's death had begun to fade from public memory, but his mother, who'd returned to work, wasn't moving on. On a Monday in late September, she left work and gathered with her family and other activists on the sidewalk outside the East Precinct, where Lippert was stationed, for what they called a "sit-in." They wore T-shirts that said "Fire Officer Lippert" and brought signs and lawn chairs.

Lee and other activists returned the next day, and the next. They weathered the rain and the cold. By November, it was nearing dark each day when they arrived. Although Lee still wore her Fire Officer Lippert T-shirt, at some point it dawned on her that nothing she could do would help her son. But a community oversight board might help someone else.

"The next time this happens here, if anything is worth doing that will help the next family that comes along, that helps them get justice a little easier," she says, "then Jocques's death is not in vain."

But inside the halls of power, Mothershead felt the campaign sputtering. In meetings, city officials asked whether he'd spoken with the police department about the bill, but the coalition had barred him from doing so. Admitting that he had not yet consulted with them "felt like amateur hour," he recalls. Some council members balked at the bill's language, including a provision authorizing the board to order officers to participate in mediation and other "remedies" if accused of misconduct, regardless of guilt. One council member, Brett Withers, told me, "There were some aspects of the ordinance that no doubt arose out of folks' frustration with trying to get accountability from the police department itself, but we thought went too far."

"How can one expect to change an institution without including it in the process?" Mothershead wrote to me in an email. Hoping a more conciliatory approach might save the bill, he gave the other activists an ultimatum: Let NOAH discuss the bill with the mayor's office and other city institutions, or it would pull out. The others said no—they felt the campaign belonged to the community, not the politicians or police—and NOAH withdrew. Unable to present a unified front, let alone win over the police or the mayor, the activists couldn't round up the votes they needed. In January 2018, the Metro Council soundly rejected the bill, and after a final pilgrimage to the East Precinct a day shy of the first anniversary of Clemmons's death, Lee ended her sit-in.

THAT COULD HAVE BEEN the end of it. But less than a month after the Metro Council's vote, the mayor's coziness with the police department spilled into public view when Barry acknowledged having an extramarital affair with an officer on her security detail, who had improperly claimed pay for personal time he had spent with Barry. She resigned shortly thereafter, pleading guilty to a felony, and was replaced by the vice mayor, David Briley. (Because Barry had no prior criminal record, prosecutors agreed to deferred adjudication of her case, meaning that if she successfully serves an ongoing three-year probation sentence, the charges against her will be dismissed. Nashville's Board of Ethical Conduct ultimately concluded that Barry had violated Metro Nashville's standards of conduct, but didn't find that the relationship had influenced her judgments about the police department.)

In this atmosphere of renewed scrutiny of the city's leaders, Community Oversight Now decided to try another path to an oversight board. It would bring the proposition directly to voters, by gathering signatures to put it on the ballot in the fall.

This approach was more ambitious than the first. The coalition had just a few months to collect a number of names equal to 10 percent of the votes cast in the preceding local general election—about 4,700. With new legal help, they drafted referendum language calling for a well-funded board that would draw four of its 11 members from "economically distressed" neighborhoods and would be empowered to issue subpoenas to compel witness testimony.

The organizers fanned out across the city, soliciting signatures at supportive businesses, a weekly jazz series, and a Janelle Monáe concert. Tucker and other pastors shared word of the effort with their congregations, whose members got involved.

By July 2018, as the deadline approached, the activists had just over 4,000 signatures. In a delicate rapprochement, NOAH had offered to enlist its vast membership in collecting names. But reluctant to reengage after the damaging split, Community Oversight Now rejected the help, even if doing so kept it from reaching the threshold.

That decision might well have spelled its defeat. But then, less than a week before the deadline, Officer Andrew Delke of the Metro Nashville Police shot and killed Daniel Hambrick.

It began with an attempted traffic stop. While driving through the city that evening looking for stolen vehicles, Delke started to follow a suspicious car, lost track of it, and then spotted a white sedan in the parking lot of a public-housing complex, with Hambrick nearby. When Delke drove up abruptly, Hambrick fled the scene on foot, holding a handgun, and the officer gave chase, with no idea whom he was pursuing. Nor had he been issued a body or dashboard camera, so only when footage from a surveillance camera was released did it become clear that as Hambrick outran him, the slowing officer stopped to plant his feet in a firing stance and took aim. He squeezed off four shots, hitting Hambrick three times.

Hambrick was 25 years old when he died. Two days before the shooting, he had posted an update on Facebook about a job he'd taken in an up-and-coming part of town. His mother, Vickie Hambrick, who is legally blind, depended on him as few parents do. "He was my only child," she says. "He was my eyes and my everything."

The activists began to realize something profound had shifted in the city's residents. In the final week of July, the activists collected as many signatures as they had since their campaign began that spring. On the submission deadline of August 1, Lee carried a box of 8,269 signatures into the county clerk's office to have the measure certified and put on the ballot.

Journalists connected the shooting to the campaign for police oversight. Public officials who had stayed on the sidelines after Clemmons's death were more outspoken in questioning Anderson's leadership; NOAH issued a statement asking Mayor Briley to fire him. "Most people could not rationalize how that tape looked," says Tucker. "It upset their sensibilities."

In late September, after examining the evidence, District Attorney Funk sought and obtained an arrest warrant for Delke for criminal homicide— the first time in the city's history an officer had been charged in an on-duty shooting. (A grand jury later indicted Delke for first-degree murder, and he entered a not-guilty plea, claiming he acted in self-defense and with a justified use of force. Through his attorney, Delke declined to comment for this article.)

Still, opponents of civilian oversight dug in. The local chapter of the FOP filed a lawsuit attempting to halt the referendum, arguing the number of collected signatures was insufficient, but a court tossed that out. The organization launched a half-million-dollar public-relations campaign to defeat it, with highly produced television ads, one of them warning that civilian oversight was a ruse that would allow politicians to "appoint big-money donors to new unelected government posts." Briley announced that he supported civilian oversight of the police in general, but not the language of the ballot referendum.

The activists had few resources for paid advertisements, but they had shoe leather. The coalition presented at events held by ministerial groups, neighborhood associations, and the local chapters of the NAACP and the League of Women Voters. They sent 15,000 texts, phone-banked thousands of homes, and knocked on hundreds of doors. Gicola Lane, an organizer, says the coalition reached out to black citizens whether or not they were active voters. "People in my neighborhood don't vote," she explains, but the effort to create a community oversight board motivated them to register. "It's just a different kind of feeling when you have people you grew up with on the news or leading campaigns."

On Election Night, the activists congregated in the multipurpose room of an apartment building on Rosa L. Parks Boulevard to watch the returns. At 9 p.m., a ripple began coursing through the crowd as those closest to the television reacted to the news. The amendment had passed overwhelmingly, with a final tally of 134,371 votes in support and 94,129 against.

The activists poured onto the dance floor as "Ain't No Stoppin' Us Now" began to play. Lee and Hambrick, who had both lost their sons, stood holding each other and swaying to the music. Their cheeks were stained with tears, but they were smiling. Tucker was overwhelmed, not only because Nashville would have its long-sought-after community oversight board, but also because a plurality of the city had affirmed a request from its most disadvantaged residents. "The black vote couldn't do this; the immigrant vote couldn't do this," he explains. "There had to be a significant number of white people who voted, who believe that policing is unfair."

The organizers were still giving speeches of gratitude and congratulations when Clemmons's younger son walked to the front of the room. Only 10 years old, he was nevertheless well aware of the meaning of the campaign, having participated in the first rally held in the days following his dad's death. Wordlessly, he slipped up next to Lane, wrapped his arms around her, and began to cry.

MOTHERSHEAD WAS AT HOME and had just put his kids to bed when he learned of the victory. He was in total disbelief, and humbled by the achievement. He'd advocated for a community oversight board in the hope that it would reform police practices, reducing the number of unnecessary traffic stops and arrests. But following the vote, he felt the coalition had accomplished something categorically different: providing true representation for the city's most marginalized residents. "That wasn't where my head was. That's where their heads were. And I see it now," he says.

Civilian review boards vary widely in their powers; the board that Nashville enacted would be strong. It would have an annual budget of at least $1.5 million, sufficient to hire a staff of investigators and analysts, and although the mayor and council each selected two of its 11 members, the remaining seven were reserved for the community's nominees. Of the individuals ultimately appointed, seven are black and one is Latino. The group includes three former police officers, as well as a community organizer nominated by Gideon's Army.

But less than two weeks after their appointment, a Republican law-maker in the state legislature introduced a bill to greatly reduce the authority of civilian review boards statewide, barring them from issuing subpoenas to compel witness testimony and precluding them from tailoring their membership by socioeconomic status, demographics, or employment history. The bill passed, though the activists succeeded in amending it to allow the board to issue subpoenas if it first gained the Metro Council's approval.

In April 2019, the board hired as its full-time director William Weeden, a criminal-defense and civil-rights attorney who had worked for eight years on Chicago's oversight board. He hopes to build a team capable of investigating misconduct, evaluating policing practices, and recommending changes. Traffic stops are "definitely on the radar," he says. The legislature's recent bill would make his work more difficult, he explains, but "we'll find other ways of accomplishing our goals—hopefully we can."

Despite calls for his ouster in the wake of Hambrick's death, Anderson still helms the police department, with the support of Mayor Briley. While Anderson has agreed to work with the community oversight board, he holds authority over whether its recommendations are implemented. "They have to make their own success," he says. "I think that when they look at how we handle our own oversight, they're going to find very little to do." As to whether the campaign for community oversight or the nascent board itself had affected police-department practices, a spokesman had a one-word answer: "No." After years of delays, the department still hasn't provided all officers with dashboard and body cameras.

Of course, the community oversight board was never the ultimate end itself. The goal was always to reset the relationship between the police and the policed, which is made not in Nashville's municipal offices, but in its streets. Police shootings had been the focal point of the campaign, with surviving family members its leading champions, but the activists envision more profound changes in the culture of the police department. Some of the grievances seem like nuances, but are no less important for it: the way Clemmons's death was investigated as an assault against Lippert; the department's inability to see how the disparate harm of traffic stops was poisoning its relationship with the black community; the department's persistent failure to increase the representation of minorities among its officers. "It's like changing a religion," says Sekou Franklin, an associate professor of political science at Middle Tennessee State University and a longtime organizer who was deeply involved with the campaign. "You can change the time of service from 9 o'clock to 10 o'clock, but the beliefs and the culture and traditions—that larger shift—is going to require an all-hands-on-deck approach."

The police department is evolving, nevertheless, in ways that may validate the more inclusive approach to reforms that Barry had championed. In particular, the analysis of Nashville's traffic stops that she commissioned corroborated the findings of "Driving While Black." It also found that traffic stops "had no discernible effect on serious crime rates," a conclusion with implications for cities elsewhere. After reviewing the report, Serpas, the former chief who led the department as traffic stops were ramping up, told me, "Using 'traffic' as a blunt instrument to fight violent crime probably is not as effective today as we thought it was 15 years ago."

Anderson is still skeptical of the findings—"I think the Policing Project picked their data points," he told me—but he acknowledged that the groundswell against traffic stops took the matter out of his hands. "The public discussion was too much of a distraction to what we do," he says. So, shortly after the report's release, the department began to change its practices. Patrol officers discontinued the use of the detailed sections of their activity sheets that many say encouraged proactivity, and the impact was immediate. From October 2018 to February 2019, officers recorded 60 percent fewer traffic stops than they did during the same period the year prior.

In its place, the department has put more emphasis on "neighborhood policing" that prioritizes relationship building over enforcement. In Cayce Homes, an entire flex team was shifted to this approach, with a sergeant and nine officers, including Officer Ward. She still drives the same unmarked black car, but now spends most of her time bicycling or walking through the complex, falling into conversation with passersby. "We're not approaching to investigate you or to arrest you," she says. "We're approaching to actually get to know you." Officers doing rotations in the Mission One program have shifted to community engagement as well.

The work of the community-engagement team runs counter to some officers' views about their profession and personal identity. At first, Ward was worried by the comments she overheard from other officers—"They made a lot of jokes about us being a social worker and not a police"—but her concerns have been allayed as some of that grumbling has subsided. Still, the new approach requires a change in mind-set. One morning, while walking by a parked car, two of Ward's colleagues caught an unmistakable whiff of marijuana. As former flex officers, they were inclined to approach the vehicle and investigate—but they settled for flagging the car over radio in case a nearby patrol officer might opt to respond, and then moved on.

On some matters, common ground is elusive. While Cayce residents reliably call Jocques's death the "Clemmons" shooting, officers who patrol the area still refer to it as the "Lippert" shooting.

Many of the pressing concerns of Cayce's residents and the disadvantaged people of Nashville are beyond the reach of police. One-tenth of the city's population is living below the poverty line, including one in five black Nashvillians. And gentrification, compounded by an affordable-housing crisis, is displacing tens of thousands of longtime residents: The black share of some historically African American neighborhoods has plummeted by as much as 20 percent, according to an analysis by the *Tennessean*. The city's future may well depend on how citizens organize around those challenges.

On what would have been Clemmons's 34th birthday, Lee and a few activists returned to the pedestrian bridge with a handful of balloons. They chatted cheerfully about the upcoming mayoral election on August 1; that morning, Lee had met with a Democratic state legislator who was challenging Briley. Lane was musing about running for office herself. (A month later, she officially announced her candidacy for Metro Council.) It was remarkable to think that just a little over two years earlier, they had all been living in the same city, unknown to one another. At the apex of the bridge, Lee turned to say a few words about her son. Then she turned again and let the wind catch her balloon and take it away.

Editor's note: This story is part of the project "The Presence of Justice," which is supported by a grant from the John D. and Catherine T. MacArthur Foundation's Safety and Justice Challenge. On June 18, 2020, Mayor John Cooper, David Briley's successor, announced that MNPD chief Steve Anderson would be retiring in the coming months, staying on the job in the interim and consulting on his replacement.

Florida Nashville Line

STEVE HARUCH, 2019

"THERE'S A SOCIOLOGIST, RICHARD Florida, who is known for the concept of the Creative Class."

That's former Nashville mayor Karl Dean, speaking to *Focus Magazine* in 2017, when he was running for governor of Tennessee.

"He talks a lot about how cities that will do well in the future—and I think this applies to states—are the places," Dean continues, "that are successful in promoting talent, technology and tolerance." Oddly enough, this came as part of Dean's answer to the question: "What do you see as the biggest state-level issues facing the LGBTQ community of Tennessee and how will your administration confront them?"

Dean clearly believed that Nashville was one of the cities that will do well in the future. In fact, it had already done well, rising considerably in stature under his watch. It was during his tenure as mayor that Nashville was dubbed "It City" in the pages of the *New York Times*. Implicit in Dean's discussion of creative-class recruitment was that he understood the mechanisms underlying Nashville's jump from relatively sleepy Southern city to red-hot destination, and therefore he knew how to re-create it on a grander scale.

To call Dean a student of Richard Florida's 2002 book *The Rise of the Creative Class* would seem an understatement. The three Ts Dean ticks off—talent, technology, and tolerance—come directly from *TROTCC*. Clearly, he had done the reading.

"The economic need for creativity has registered itself in the rise of a new class, which I call the Creative Class," Florida writes in his internationally bestselling book. This new class, he says, encompasses 30 percent of the workforce, or about 38 million people. "I define the core of the Creative Class to include people in science and engineering, architecture and design, education, arts, music, and entertainment, whose economic function is to create new ideas, new technology, and/or new creative content," Florida continues. "Around the core, the Creative Class also includes a broader group of *creative professionals* in business and finance, law, health care, and related fields" (emphasis Florida's). That is a lot of workers.

"The book's thesis—that urban fortunes increasingly turn on the capacity to attract, retain and even pamper a mobile and finicky class of 'creatives,' whose aggregate efforts have become the primary drivers of economic development—has proved to be a hugely seductive one for civic leaders around the world," Jamie Peck writes in a lengthy analysis, noting that competition amongst cities for access to the creative-class playbook "subsequently worked to inflate Florida's speaking fees well into the five-figure range."

The gist of Florida's book is that "we have entered an age of creativity, comprehended as a new and distinctive phase of capitalist development, in which the driving forces of economic development are not simply technological and organizational, but *human*," Peck writes. "In essence, the book seeks to describe a *new* new economy, in which human creativity has become the 'defining feature of economic life.'" Put more crudely, the world is the creative class's oyster, and cities who want to get ahead had better get to shucking themselves.

"I think one of the strongest things we have in Nashville is that we are constantly bringing in—as capital—creative people," Dean told the *Nashville Scene* in 2010. This time, he was talking up his music business council, which functioned as a kind of multilevel marketing operation for the city itself, part of an intentional rebrand of Nashville as more-than-just-country Music City. "Whether it's songwriters or musicians or performers or technicians, we're bringing in people whose talent is their ability to be creative," Dean said. "They revitalize the city."

It's not just sociologists and politicians who say these sorts of things. "The greatest thing about Nashville is that it's welcoming," the late songwriter and poet David Berman told the *Tennessean*'s Dave Paulson in 2018. "Nashville only thrives when talented people from out of town move here from somewhere else." And that influx of talented people—who go on to find a niche in the local economy and, in some cases, help expand it—has a long and storied history. In his snappy and still-relevant 1970 book *The Nashville Sound*, Paul Hemphill explains:

> Ever since 1925 Nashville had hosted WSM radio's Grand Ole Opry: the oldest continuing radio show in America, a five-hour procession of fiddlers and country comedians and yodelers and cloggers that every Saturday night drew a few thousand visitors to a hulking old downtown tabernacle called Ryman Auditorium and was broadcast all the way to Canada. . . . [A]fter World War II, small recording studios began popping up here and there to accommodate the colony of country musicians and writers living in or around Nashville to be near the Opry. Then somebody else opened up a sheet-music publishing house. Finally, by the early Fifties, all of the makings of a recording complex were there: publishing houses, competing record-pressing plants, talent agencies, clothiers specializing in show costumes, shops selling guitars and other musical instruments, and even boardinghouses catering to hungry young men fresh in from the country to try their luck at writing and singing country songs. The Opry was getting so big, they added a shortened Friday-night version and started thinking about split sessions on Saturday nights. And the recording business had blossomed into a full-blown industry, adding first $30 million, then $50 million and finally $60 million a year to the Nashville economy. Like it or not, the business-minded Founding Fathers had to agree to still another subtitle: "Music City, USA."

Note the order in Hemphill's account. First, the Opry succeeds. Then its success attracts musicians hoping to also succeed. Businesses crop up to cater to those who are succeeding enough to afford their services. Once—and not until—the success passes some kind of threshold, the city's aristocracy, which for so long had looked down on country music and its trappings, has to grudgingly accept that, welp, there is money to be made in them there hillbilly songs. Hemphill describes a typical sentiment: "It isn't every day you can pick up an industry like that." (The late

Jim Ridley once described Nashville as "a city that's ruthlessly unsenti-
mental when the past butts up against money.")

For his part, Florida loves to hold up Nashville's status as a statistical
outlier in terms of music industry concentration. "In 1970, Nashville was
a minor center focused on country music. By 2004, only New York and
L.A. boasted more musicians," he wrote for the *Atlantic* in 2009. "The
extent of its growth was so significant that when my research team and
I charted the geographic centers of the music industry from 1970 and
2004 using a metric called a location quotient, Nashville was the only
city that registered positive growth. In effect, it sucked up all the growth
in the music industry."

Never mind that in 1970 Columbia Records was recording 10 percent
of its pop records in Nashville, it's not exactly clear what Florida is holding up Nashville as an example *of*. A place where industry infrastructure attracts more of that industry? (In this case, the specific example he
begins with is Jack White moving to Nashville from Detroit.) Whether
there is a discernible "Nashville Effect" beyond that is not up for debate
here. In any event, Florida is fond of calling Nashville "the Silicon Valley
of the music business," which he did in 2009, 2011, and 2013.

It is also unclear whether Nashville ever joined London, Singapore,
Dublin, Auckland, Memphis, Providence, Green Bay, Cleveland, Toledo,
Baltimore, Greensboro, Des Moines, Hartford, Roanoke, Rochester, and
numerous other locales in paying upwards of $35,000 for one of Florida's
speeches, or ordering one of the lightly customized $250,000 workups
available from his consulting partner Catalytix Institute. The manner by
which Dean became a Florida man may be as simple as his having read
the book. But there is such a consistent trail of these kinds of remarks—
creative people are key!—that it's clear he was an acolyte.

Here's Dean again, in an interview with the *Nashville Scene* in April
2011: "I think more and more people are beginning to understand that
the future is gonna be with those cities that attract the creative folks—
like, even in health care—people who are entrepreneurs, who create new
businesses; and in music, and in technology."

Keeping in mind that Florida's Creative Class includes more or less the
top-earning third of the workforce, it's worth revisiting Jon Meacham's
observations in his 2014 *Time* piece "The South's Red Hot Town." There,
the historian and author of *Thomas Jefferson: The Art of Power* muses:
"In some ways the current boom can be traced to a conversation at the

Masters Golf Tournament that took place nearly half a century ago with legendary Nashville banker Sam Fleming." Merle Haggard seeing Johnny Cash perform at San Quentin this is not. "There," Meacham continues, "Drs. Thomas Frist Sr. and Jr., and Jack Massey, who was part of the deal to buy Kentucky Fried Chicken from Harland Sanders, talked over the economic virtues of privatized hospitals built to accommodate the growing Sunbelt. They saw an opportunity to professionalize the management of, and attract capital to, a heretofore cottage industry. They were right, and HCA"—Hospital Corporation of America—"was soon born."

"More than 250 health care companies remain in the city," Meacham continues, "including 13 publicly traded companies directly employing over one-eighth of the city's workers and putting $30 billion into the local economy annually. . . . [T]he sector has experienced overall growth of over 63 percent since 2000 and employment growth of nearly 20 percent over the past decade."

Well, "Hospital Corporation of America is extremely rich" certainly doesn't sound as sexy as hip professionals in designer eyewear tapping on their MacBooks and sipping single-origin espresso. And Meacham doesn't once use "creative" as a noun. But as Janet Miller, CEO of commercial real estate firm Colliers Nashville, told *Worth* in 2018, health care is the city's "wealth creator." It's the money behind the money, and little of significance gets done in Nashville without its largess. Even the city's art museum, after all, is known in the local shorthand as simply "the Frist."

The health care industry, at least as constituted in Nashville, is not only powerful and tremendously wealthy, but particularly resilient as well. Garrett Harper, vice president for research with the Nashville Chamber of Commerce, told Kim Severson of the *New York Times* in 2013: "Health care is countercyclical. . . . It inoculates the city against a lot of the winds that blow." It's also colossal. "By some estimates," Severson wrote, "half of the nation's health care plans are run by companies in the Nashville area."

While it may be true that health care is countercyclical, that didn't stop the Great Recession from wreaking havoc on other pockets of the industry. Still, while other companies struggled, some to the point of near-bankruptcy, HCA managed to do much better than survive.

"In fact, profits at the health care industry giant HCA, which controls 163 hospitals from New Hampshire to California, have soared, far outpacing those of most of its competitors," Julie Creswell and Reed Abelson wrote in the *New York Times* in 2012. "The big winners have been three private equity firms—including Bain Capital, co-founded by Mitt Romney, the Republican presidential candidate—that bought HCA in late 2006." HCA's growing profits helped raise the value of Bain's holdings to "nearly three and a half times their initial investment in the $33 billion deal."

Companies trying to replicate HCA's runaway success didn't strategize how to attract more creative people to their ranks. "Its success inspired 35 buyouts of hospitals or chains of facilities in the last two and a half years by private equity firms eager to repeat that windfall," Creswell and Abelson write. Furthermore:

> Among the secrets to HCA's success: It figured out how to get more reve-
> nue from private insurance companies, patients and Medicare by billing
> much more aggressively for its services than ever before; it found ways
> to reduce emergency room overcrowding and expenses; and it experi-
> mented with new ways to reduce the cost of its medical staff, a move that
> sometimes led to conflicts with doctors and nurses over concerns about
> patient care.
>
> In late 2008, for instance, HCA changed the billing codes it assigned
> to sick and injured patients who came into the emergency rooms. Al-
> most overnight, the numbers of patients who HCA said needed more care,
> which would be paid for at significantly higher levels by Medicare, surged.
>
> HCA, which had lagged the industry for those high-paying categories,
> jumped ahead of its competitors and was reimbursed accordingly. The
> change, which HCA's executives said better reflected the service being
> provided, increased operating earnings by nearly $100 million in the first
> quarter of 2009.

Juicing revenue by changing billing codes is, one might say, a rather *creative* solution.

In 2018, R. Milton Johnson, the CEO of HCA, took home $20 million in salary and bonuses.

Tommy Frist, of HCA's founding Frist family, tells Meacham there are "four buckets" that have contributed to Nashville's good fortune. First, there is "employment stability in health care, entertainment, higher education and government." Second, there is "the wealth effect of owner-ship that extends deep into the ranks of some large enterprises, such as HCA, Ingram Industries and Dollar General." Third, the unified metro government aids in "reducing friction in governance and facilitating more private-public partnerships." Finally, Meacham recounts, there is "the more ineffable but no less real issue of livability." Nashville, Frist opines, is "a soulful city in a way that Charlotte or Atlanta just don't seem to be." (Atlanta plays the role of foil in so many stories about how great Nashville is, for little apparent reason, that it's hard not to wonder why that is, exactly.)

Looking past the fuzziness of "livability" and being "soulful"—truly an odd word choice—the buckets mostly contain lots and lots of money. And while Florida became an urban-planning sensation by calling on cities to move past outmoded ideas like sports stadiums and tax incentives and instead start attracting those creatives and their coveted creative-ness . . . well: "The mayor has orchestrated more than a dozen tax incentive deals over the past few years," the *Times'* Kim Severson writes, describing Dean's tenure as of 2013. "Most recently, he arranged a $66 million incentive package to help the health care giant HCA Holdings move part of its Nashville operations to new midtown high-rise buildings." (Incidentally, as part of the deal, the city paid HCA $1 million to buy new office furniture.)

How can this be, that Dean was engaged in the same old boring give-money-to-rich-people strategies while so proudly waving the creative class banner?

"For the average mayor, there are few downsides to making the city safe for the creative class—a creativity strategy can quite easily be bolted on to business-as-usual urban-development policies," Peck writes in "Struggling with the Creative Class." But wait! *GQ*'s "Nowville" spread said that Nashville "used to be just a city of ten-gallon hats and the Grand Ole Opry. Now it's the most electric spot in the South, thanks to a cast of transplanted designers, architects, chefs, and rock 'n' rollers." And *Nylon* said Nashville had "suddenly become a hub for young, emerging creatives." What about the steampunk coffee shops, the small-batch distilleries, the Instagram-able restaurants, the vegan beard oil, all that gleaming subway tile?

"Florida was just describing the 'hipsterization' of wealthy cities and concluding that this was what was causing those cities to be wealthy," Frank Bures concludes in an essay titled "The Fall of the Creative Class." "As some critics have pointed out, that's a little like saying that the high number of hot dog vendors in New York City is what's causing the presence of so many investment bankers. So if you want banking, just sell hot dogs."

Furthermore, Bures writes, "Much of what Florida was describing was already accounted for by a theory that had been well-known in economic circles for decades, which says that the amount of college-educated people you have in an area is what drives economic growth, not the number of artists or immigrants or gays, most of whom also happen to be college educated. This is known as Human Capital theory."

Nashville already had human capital, in buckets.

"In other words, if there was anything to the theory of the Creative Class, it was the package it came in," Bures laments. "Florida just told us we were creative and valuable, and we wanted to believe it. He sold us to ourselves."

That's not to say some weren't doing exactly what Florida said to do, whether they'd read his book or not: trying to lure creative and valuable people to Music City with the aim of intentionally transforming it. In 2013, while I was reporting a story on the local tech community, a prominent Nashville entrepreneur told me that Nashville still lacked experienced, A-list talent.

"I had a guy call me from Silicon Valley very recently who qualifies in that chief technical co-founder role, who's moving to town," he said. "And you know, he didn't call the Chamber, he called me. And the reason he called me is because the narrative we're crafting, the narrative that I put out there, resonates with the people we're after." So he would have dinner with these prospective transplants, hook them up with real estate agents and "white-glove" them into the city. It was all part of a plan: Recruit and retain talent from the Valley and other strongholds, change the culture of Nashville, and make it a world-class tech city in the process.

Not so different, really, from flipping a neighborhood.

"For years, Richard Florida and other urban life pundits have espoused the creative class as the secret to city success," Susie Cagle wrote in *Grist* in 2013. "When the creative class wins, their logic goes, we all win. Gentrification has essentially become America's favored urban redevelopment strategy."

As time wore on, Florida acknowledged the unevenness of gains in cities where his creative class exemplars thrived.

"The trickle-down effect disappears once the higher housing costs borne by less skilled workers are taken into account," he wrote for CityLab in 2013. "The benefits of highly skilled regions accrue mainly to knowledge, professional, and creative workers. While less-skilled blue-collar and service workers also earn more in these places, more expensive housing costs eat away those gains. There is a rising tide of sorts, but it only lifts about the most advantaged third of the workforce, leaving the other 66 percent much further behind."

Put another way: The creative class does well where the creative class does well. Florida then points to research by Rebecca Diamond, a graduate student in economics at Harvard. Higher housing costs disproportionately keep lower-skilled workers out of the successful cities whose success affords them modest wage gains over other regions. This creates, as Florida puts it, "an additional level of inequality—inequality of well-being—where more skilled workers not only take home more money, but benefit from better neighborhoods, superior amenities, and better schools."

Talking about his recent Silicon Valley recruit, the tech entrepreneur I spoke with cited him as a leading indicator: "And when he defects into the red state—the gun-crazy, idiot-ass, Republican—into the blue dot in the red state? His buddies go, 'Hmm, I wonder what's going on there.'" The start of a trickle that he hopes to turn into a wave.

"And, y'know, in 10 to 15 years the town's ruined," he said with a laugh. "But we'll all have made a bunch of money."

Perverse Incentives

BETSY PHILLIPS, 2019

ONE OF THE STRANGER things about Nashville's rise to It-City status has been what's *not* changed. You'd think that as Nashville became a
more desirable city to live and do business in, it would hand out fewer
incentives to developers. After all, now that Nashville is so popular, the
incentive is that you get to be here.

The value that simply being in Nashville has seems not to have registered to city administrators, though. They're still handing money to
developers as if we're lucky to have their interest in our city, instead of
the other way around.

Maybe one of the most recent controversies is the most illustrative.
In 2018, the city agreed to give real-estate developer Tony Giarratana the
small park in front of the downtown library in exchange for his oddly
shaped parking lot next to the Morris Memorial Building.

As William Williams of the *Nashville Post* reported at the time:

> Giarratana and Metro officials are discussing a land deal that would see
> Giarratana Nashville LLC develop a tower of an undisclosed height at
> the city's Church Street Park site between Sixth Avenue and Anne Dallas
> Dudley Boulevard.

In exchange for that property, the company would develop an affordable housing apartment building and homeless services facility (anchored by the Metro Homeless Commission) of eight stories on a distinctively shaped property that Giarratana Nashville-affiliated entity JRP Partners LLC owns at 301 James Robertson Parkway.

The preposterousness defies explanation. Giarratana has a parking lot that is so weirdly shaped he can't figure out how to develop it into anything of more value than a parking lot. The city has a park two blocks from the state capitol, right across the street from the downtown library, in the heart of the city. If Giarratana's parking lot had any value, he'd either develop it himself or sell it.

The city's property has value because it's a park in an area of town with not much greenspace. I'm philosophically opposed to selling any parks, but, if the city was in such dire financial straits that it needed to sell a park to pay for homeless services, at the time this deal was first reported, the cheapest downtown lot available for sale I could find was almost $30 million, and that was down by the river where there'd been flooding in 2010. This park is on high ground. So why would we swap a lot worth at least $30 million for a lot Giarratana can't figure out how to monetize? If we need the money, that's just poor stewardship of our resources. If we don't need the money, why sell a park?

The public backlash to the land-swap deal was so great that, as of this writing, it seems unlikely to happen. But I think that's only because the unfairness of it was so egregious.

Take the new soccer stadium being built at the fairgrounds. Rich Nashvillians, including business tycoon John Ingram, put together a plan to bring a soccer team to Nashville. Considering how popular soccer is in the city, that made good sense. In order for Major League Soccer to consider the city, the team owners had to come up with a soccer-specific stadium. In other words, even though many a professional soccer game has been played there—not to mention friendlies involving the US national team—we couldn't just use Nissan Stadium, where the Titans play football, and which the city forked over some $144 million to help build.

What about the fairgrounds? It's between downtown and Nashville's largest immigrant neighborhood, which is full of soccer fans. There's easy access to the interstates and the fairgrounds could use a little love.

It seemed like a win-win for the whole community.

Until the team owners demanded an additional 10 acres of fairground land to put a mixed-use development on. Which the city gave them.

Wait. *What?*

The city didn't want a soccer team in the first place. The team owners came up with the idea and the city agreed to help them out. The city was doing these rich guys a favor. How did that turn into the city needing to give them 10 acres of land or we don't get a soccer stadium we never wanted in the first place? How was our answer anything other than, "Oh, well, that's too bad. Have fun having no soccer team"?

We did something similar for Ryman Hospitality, the company that used to be called Gaylord, which runs the Ryman Auditorium, the Grand Ole Opry House, and Opryland Hotel among other properties. The fact that the company changed its name from Gaylord to Ryman shows you how tied they are to Nashville, specifically, and how valuable the ability to brand itself as a Nashville place is.

In 2017 the city gave Ryman $14 million in incentives to open a water park in their entertainment complex out in Pennington Bend, on the east side of the city. There are already two waterparks in that side of town—Nashville Shores and Wave Country, which is literally the next exit south of the Ryman properties. What do taxpayers need with another waterpark?

Well, it turns out most Nashvillians will never know—because in order to use the waterpark at the Opryland Hotel, you have to be staying at the hotel and also purchase the special package that includes the waterpark. The least expensive rate I found for this package was $229 a night.

Nashville helped pay for a waterpark most Nashvillians can't afford to use.

This raises the same kinds of questions the soccer deal raises: What was Ryman going to do if we didn't subsidize their waterpark? Not build it? OK, most people in Nashville's lives would have been no different. Put the waterpark at one of their non-Nashville hotels? Again, most people in Nashville wouldn't have noticed. Would fewer people have come to Nashville if they couldn't stay at a hotel with a water park? Every other hotel in Nashville lacks a waterpark and yet plenty of people stay in them. They needed the waterpark to be in Nashville more than Nashville needed the waterpark. So, why did we pay for part of it?

But that's not the only level of weirdness. Though $14 million is a lot to us as a city, it's pocket change to Ryman. In 2018, according to a press release they put out, their consolidated net income was $264.7 million. They also claimed they had $103.4 million in unrestricted cash and $172.7 million available in credit.

They had 20 times the amount we gave them just sitting around, doing nothing.

So, it's not like they were having money troubles and we helped them finance this venture so that they could get back on their feet. That would have been understandable, at least. Ryman and the city have been good partners for a long time. If we were helping out a friend who'd fallen on hard times, that would have some value to us as a city. But the Opryland Hotel is in no danger of going out of business.

In fact the parent company is doing so well that our tax incentives are chump change. To put this in more human terms, say you had a friend who had $100 in his pocket and almost $200 on his debit card. Would you give him $14 to go to the movies without you?

My examples are fairly recent because it's so bizarre that, after everything that has happened to the city to make us hot and popular, everything that has people clamoring to live and work here, we're still acting like we have to entice developers to build here and give in to all their demands.

Let's talk about an older decision Nashville made to let developers do whatever stupid thing they want and how the city then continues to pay for those decisions.

The trendy SoBro area downtown—short for "South of Broadway"—is filled with some of the crown jewels of the It-City years of Nashville. From the Country Music Hall of Fame and Museum to the Schermerhorn Symphony Hall to the upscale restaurant Etch to numerous new hotels and office buildings, this area is one of Nashville's great redevelopment successes. Before the Country Music Hall of Fame moved to this location in 2001, the area consisted of one somewhat charming old apartment building, a firehall, and loads of small warehouses that either were abandoned or looked it.

In fairness to developers, the area seemed ripe for redevelopment.

But still, we might have hoped that developers asked themselves one question: why was this area so close to the parts of downtown that were doing OK not also doing OK? To put it another way, when you look at the buildings in the blocks north of Broadway, even the oldest buildings are three and four stories tall. And they are still standing, many going back to the post-war revival of downtown in the 1870s and 1880s. Why were there old buildings like this lining Broadway (see the Acme Feed

& Seed building or Merchant's) but no old buildings like that one block south? Why, instead, was that area filled with, basically, short, empty, cheaply built boxes?

The hint to the answer to this question lies in the old name for the area south of Broadway near the river—Black Bottom. *Bottom.* As in the low-lying wetland you find along a creek or river.

And any old map can show you that there's a creek that runs to the river from up near Mercy Lounge. It meanders down toward the round-about, under the Music City Center, and then down Demonbreun to the river. In fact, you can tell by where French fur trader and the white guy who was here when Nashville's "first" settlers arrived in 1779, Timothy Demonbreun, put his house—somewhere in the area of what's now Demonbreun and Sixth Avenue South—how far away from the river and that creek bottom you have to be before you're on dry ground.

In other words, the fact that this area "floods" is not now and never has been a secret. It's right in the name of the neighborhood. For centuries Nashvillians who could afford not to live there kept their houses out of the area. Businesses that went into the area were easily replaced plain boxes. And, truly, is it even fair to call what happens in a bottom "flooding"? It's wetland.

If it's wet, then, well, it is what it is.

During one of the great public work projects of the 1880s, the city put the creek underground, in a sewer tunnel. But it's still there. If you are out boating on the Cumberland or hanging out on the east bank of the river, you can see the mouth of the tunnel that lets the creek flow to the river below Ascend Amphitheater.

Because we so rarely say "no" to development, we put some of our most valuable cultural artifacts in a creek bottom. And then we, as a city, had the audacity to be surprised when it flooded in 2010. Every couple of years, So-Bro businesses push for the city to build a floodwall along the Cumberland. Part of this plan includes the ability to cap the tunnel that now contains that creek so that floodwater from the river can't back up into it. Where, then, will all the water from the creek go? The other part of the plan is a series of pumps that will put that water into the Cumberland. And what will happen to all of the homes and businesses on the east side of the river, who also live and work on land that is marked "Bottoms" on old maps?

So far no answer has been satisfactory enough to get the Metro Council to approve paying for the project. But another question hangs out there as well. If developers and downtown businesses want a floodwall, why don't they pay for it? They're the ones that put their buildings in a bottom. They're also the ones most benefitting from all the downtown tourism. So, they have the money and it's their mistake. Why is it on the city to fix it for them?

One terrible, hilarious reason is that the city helped them build there. The city regularly loans businesses money through tax increment financing (TIF). TIFs vary but in general, they work by funneling some tax money collected in certain areas back into the development of those areas. So, say a city wanted to put sidewalks in a business district. It could designate that business district a TIF area and part of the tax it collects from those businesses could go specifically to funding those sidewalks.

In Nashville, we've used TIFs to fund low interest loans for developers. A 2017 report by the Metropolitan Development and Housing Agency lists the places we've lent money to through TIFs. This report showed that, as of 2016 the ACME building owed the city $346,867 on a 5 percent interest loan initiated in 2014. The Omni Hotel connected to the Country Music Hall of Fame owed the city $45,711,197 on a 3.9 percent interest loan initiated in 2013. Two years later, we initiated another loan for their parking garage for almost a million dollars. All those places flooded in 2010. We, the city, not only let them build on land we knew floods, we lent them the money to do it.

Why? Because otherwise they might what? Not build where it floods? OK.

And let's talk Amazon. In 2018, Amazon reportedly made $50 billion in revenue, $3 billion in profits. Nashville made an enormous pitch for Amazon's second headquarters. We promised the company $500 per job they created here, 50 percent off property taxes for 15 years, and a free connection to a transportation system we don't have. In late 2018 we found out we wouldn't be getting their second headquarters, but we would be getting a regional hub. In exchange, we're giving them $17.5 million over seven years, including property tax breaks and $500 per job for the 5,000 jobs it claims it will be creating.

Again, $17.5 million is an enormous amount for the city. It's nothing for Amazon. It's barely a blip on their financial radar. Since it doesn't materially benefit Amazon, I'm left to think that the benefit to the company has to be in knowing that the city is desperate to have them and thus will be desperate to keep them.

But why are we so desperate to get Amazon? Don't get me wrong. I'm not saying that we should be unhappy about Amazon moving here. I'm saying that we have a booming economy, a smart workforce, one of the largest tech communities away from the coasts, and the ability to reach almost everything east of the Mississippi in a day's drive. Compared to Seattle (Amazon's current headquarters), it's cheap to live here and we don't have volcanoes or earthquakes. Plus, we just happen to have this prime real estate downtown available for office space. We're a really ideal place for a company to put a second headquarters.

With all that going for us, and with $3 billion burning a hole in Amazon's pocket, what's with the $17.5 million we're giving them? It certainly seems like it's ceremonial in some way, like the city is just showing Amazon that we will do whatever they want us to do, even if it costs the city. In any case, the last time we invited a behemoth to town and also said we'd pay them for every job they "created," we didn't do so well. "Based on city data, the deal has cost Nashville roughly $39 million so far," Jamie McGee writes in the *Tennessean*. The deal in question is the one that brought Dell to Nashville in 1999. It made a certain kind of sense at the time; Dell's stock had reportedly risen in value by 91,000 percent over the course of the '90s. So, sure. But by the 2010s, the company had trouble staying above the 1,500-employee threshold the city had set to qualify for additional incentives. "While property tax values and employee counts going forward are unknown, the deal could cost about $33 million more over the next two decades, for a total of $72 million," the story continues. In other words, the track record for this kind of deal is less than great.

If the city had been better managed overall, this tendency to continue to throw money at developers would be less galling. But there's long been simmering resentment that there's money for developer incentives but not for schools, that we'll give money to profitable multinational corporations like Amazon, but people had to fight to keep the city from shutting down the safety-net hospital in town. And now, with all the new buildings and the downtown packed with tourists—all the money pouring into the city that isn't making the lives of ordinary Nashvillians better—that resentment is beginning to boil over.

ACKNOWLEDGMENTS

IN ADDITION TO ALL the contributors, with whom it is truly an honor to share a place among these pages, I'm thankful to Zack Gresham for letting me run with the idea—and for copious soothsaying along the way. How many scrambled emails can an editor field from a single author without flipping over his desk? Zack knows. This book would not be possible without him, nor without the efforts of Joell Smith-Borne, Betsy Phillips, Gianna Mosser, Jenna Phillips, Drohan DiSanto, and everyone at Vanderbilt University Press.

I'm grateful to Edwin Willmore, Joel Farran, Margaret Renkl, Mary Laura Philpott, the Rev. Gail Seavey, David Dark, Renata Soto, and Kendra DeColo for their input and encouragement. And to my family for their patience as I stole away for many hours to sit in front of a computer.

I can't imagine Nashville's literary landscape without Ann Patchett, Karen Hayes, and everyone at Parnassus Books, where the idea for this book first took hold. (To the gentleman from Chicago who wandered in wanting to know what happened to the quaint little city you first visited years ago, I hope you're reading this.) The same goes for Maria Browning, Serenity Gerbman, and all at Humanities Tennessee and Chapter16.

Similarly, though I am certainly biased by the seven years I spent working there, I can't imagine Nashville without the *Nashville Scene*. Thanks to D. Patrick Rodgers, Erica Ciccarone, and everyone working to keep the alt-weekly ethos kicking and punching and straining for the sky. Local journalism is under threat, and it's an institution we simply cannot afford to lose or see diminished any further.

The title of this book is a nod to Jason & the Scorchers's 1986 song "Greetings From Nashville," written by Tim Krekel. We are once again, as the song says, entering the great unknown.

CONTRIBUTORS

TED ALCORN is a journalist, researcher, and educator with expertise in gun violence prevention policies and programs. An associate at Columbia University's Mailman School of Public Health, he also reports on health and justice for the *New York Times*, the *Wall Street Journal*, and other national publications. He was a founding employee of Everytown For Gun Safety, where he was the research director and then the director of innovation, and he previously served as a policy analyst in the Office of the Mayor of New York City. He earned graduate degrees as a Bill & Melinda Gates Foundation Fellow at the Johns Hopkins Bloomberg School of Public Health and their School for Advanced International Studies (SAIS), and lived in Beijing, China, as a Henry Luce scholar.

BOBBY ALLYN is an NPR Silicon Valley reporter based in San Francisco, focused on breaking news and criminal justice. For more than four years, he was a reporter for WHYY in Philadelphia covering law enforcement, courts, and usually the big story of the day. He has been a staff reporter at the *Oregonian* and the *Tennessean*, and his work has appeared in the *Washington Post* and the *New York Times*.

STEVE CAVENDISH grew up in and around Nashville, and after graduating from Belmont University, he began his journalism career at the

Nashville Banner. After working at a number of outlets around the country, including the *Chicago Tribune* and the *Washington Post*, he returned home to edit the *City Paper* and the *Nashville Scene*.

TIANA CLARK is the author of the poetry collections *I Can't Talk About the Trees Without the Blood* (University of Pittsburgh Press, 2018), winner of the 2017 Agnes Lynch Starrett Prize, and *Equilibrium* (Bull City Press, 2016), selected by Afaa Michael Weaver for the 2016 Frost Place Chapbook Competition. Clark is a 2019 National Endowment for the Arts Literature Fellow and a recipient of a 2019 Pushcart Prize, as well as a winner of the 2017 Furious Flower's Gwendolyn Brooks Centennial Poetry Prize and 2015 Rattle Poetry Prize. Clark is a graduate of Vanderbilt University and Tennessee State University. Her writing has appeared in the *New Yorker*, *Poetry*, *VQR*, *Tin House* Online, *Kenyon Review*, Buzz-Feed News, *American Poetry Review*, and elsewhere. She teaches creative writing at Southern Illinois University at Edwardsville.

ANSLEY T. ERICKSON is an associate professor of history and education policy at Teachers College, Columbia University. She researched Nashville's schools for her book *Making the Unequal Metropolis: School Desegregation and its Limits* (University of Chicago Press, 2016). Her writing has appeared in numerous scholarly and public venues, including the *Nashville Scene*, the *Washington Post*, and *Dissent*.

BEN FOLDS is widely regarded as one of the major music influencers of our generation. He's created an enormous body of genre-bending music that includes pop albums with Ben Folds Five, multiple solo albums, and numerous collaborative records. For over a decade he's performed with some of the world's greatest symphony orchestras, and he currently serves as the Artistic Advisor to the National Symphony Orchestra at the Kennedy Center. In addition to solo rock and orchestral touring, Folds has recently written the critically acclaimed memoir *A Dream about Lightning Bugs*, which debuted as a *New York Times* Best Seller. An outspoken champion for arts education and music therapy funding in our nation's public schools, Ben has served for over five years as an active member of the distinguished Artist Committee of Americans for the Arts (AFTA), and serves on the board of AFTA's Arts Action Fund. He is also chairman of the Arts Action Fund's ArtsVote2020 national initiative to advocate for a greater commitment to the nation's creative economy through improved public policies for the arts and arts education.

STEVEN HALE is a staff writer for the *Nashville Scene*, where he's covered Metro government, criminal justice, and the effects of the city's rapid growth. His work has also appeared in the *Washington Post* and the *Daily Beast*. He is writing a book about Tennessee's death row.

STEVE HARUCH is a writer, editor, and filmmaker. He worked as a staff editor at the *Nashville Scene* from 1997–2014, covering music, art, film, politics, and culture. His writing has since appeared at the *New York Times*, the *Atlantic*, NPR's *Code Switch*, the *Guardian*, *Gravy*, and Chapter16, among other outlets. His audio stories have aired on Nashville Public Radio and WBUR's *Here and Now*. In 2018, Haruch edited the collection *People Only Die of Love in Movies: Film Writing by Jim Ridley* (Vanderbilt University Press), which was first runner-up for the Ray and Pat Browne Award for Best Reference/Primary Source Work in Popular and American Culture from the Popular Culture Association. He lives in Nashville.

MERIBAH KNIGHT is a reporter for Nashville Public Radio and producer of the podcast *The Promise*. Before moving to Nashville she lived in Chicago, where she covered business, the economy, housing, crime, and transportation. Her writing has appeared in the *New York Times*, the *New Yorker*, *Chicago Magazine*, *Crain's Chicago Business*, and the *Chicago Reader*. Her radio and multimedia work has been featured on NPR, WBEZ, The PBS *News Hour*, and Chicago Public Television. A native of Cambridge, Mass., Meribah has a Masters of Journalism from Northwestern University and a BA from New York University. She lives in Nashville with her husband, a photojournalist with the *Tennessean*, their young son, and six cats.

J. R. LIND is a native Middle Tennessean and has covered the region since 2006, reporting on sports and other, less important topics for the *Lebanon Democrat*, *Nashville Post*, *Nashville Scene*, and the *City Paper*. The Navy veteran wears his love for his local teams on his sleeve, literally: He has a tattoo of a catfish on his left arm. His daughter's favorite stuffed animal is named for a former Predators back-up goalie. Over the past two decades, the Titans and Predators have brought him hours of joy and taken years off his life. He lives in West Nashville.

RICHARD LLOYD is associate professor of sociology at Vanderbilt University. He is the author of *Neo-Bohemia: Art and Commerce in the Postindustrial City* (Routledge, 2010) and has written extensively for academic and popular outlets on the arts, urban development, and American politics.

ANN PATCHETT is the author of eight novels, most recently *The Dutch House*, and three books of nonfiction. In 2019, she published her first children's book, *Lambslide*, illustrated by Robin Preiss Glasser. Patchett has received numerous awards and fellowships, including England's Orange Prize, the PEN/Faulkner Award, the Harold D. Vursell Memorial Award from the American Academy of Arts and Letters, a Guggenheim Fellowship, the American Bookseller's Association's Most Engaging Author Award, and the Women's National Book Association's Award. Her work has been translated into more than 30 languages. In November 2011, she opened Parnassus Books in Nashville with her business partner Karen Hayes. In 2012 she was named by *Time* magazine as one of the 100 Most Influential People in the World. She lives in Nashville with her husband, Karl VanDevender, and their dog, Sparky.

BETSY PHILLIPS is the marketing manager at Vanderbilt University Press. Her writing has appeared in the *Nashville Scene* and the *Washington Post*. She is the author of *Dynamite Nashville: The KKK, the FBI, and the Bombers beyond Their Control*.

MARGARET RENKL is the author of *Late Migrations: A Natural History of Love and Loss*. She is also a contributing opinion writer for the *New York Times*, where her essays appear each Monday. Her work has also appeared in *Guernica*, *Literary Hub*, *Oxford American*, *River Teeth*, and the *Sewanee Review*, among others. A graduate of Auburn University and the University of South Carolina, she lives in Nashville.

ASHLEY SPURGEON is a columnist and longtime contributor to the *Nashville Scene*. Her work has appeared in magazines *NME* and *NYLON*, and websites *The Hairpin* and *The Toast*. She is co-host of the podcasts

Hott Minute and *Chris Gaines: The Podcast.* She lives in Nashville with her boyfriend Dave and dog Gilda.

ZACH STAFFORD is an award-winning journalist, editor, and television host. Most recently he worked as the anchor of the BuzzFeed News morning show *AM2DM* and the editor-in-chief of the *Advocate* magazine. Prior to these roles, he served as the chief content officer of Grindr and editor-in-chief of INTO, the award-winning LGBTQ digital magazine. He has also served as the editor-at-large of *Out Magazine* and was an award-winning journalist at the *Guardian.* Zach regularly provides commentary on radio and podcasts and has appeared on the BBC, CNN, and *The Daily Show with Trevor Noah.* He is the co-editor of the book *Boys: An Anthology*, the co-author of the forthcoming children's book *When Dogs Heal*, and host of the recent documentary *BOYSTOWN*. In 2019, he was named to the *Forbes* 30 Under 30 and to the Root 100 list of most influential African Americans.

CARRIE FERGUSON WEIR moved to Nashville in 1991. A long-time local newspaper journalist, she now works in communications for the public school system, after stints with a local nonprofit and state government. She still owns all the antiques she bought from Nolensville Road salvage stores of the early '90s.

RON WYNN is currently sports and entertainment editor for the *Tennessee Tribune*, a columnist for the Tennessee Jazz and Blues Society, executive editor of the online publication *Everything Underground*, and a frequent contributor to the *Nashville Scene.* He has been co-host of the radio show "Freestyle" on WFSK-FM 88.1 since 2000. He previously worked at several newspapers, among them the *Bay State Banner* in Boston, the *Bridgeport Post-Telegram* (now *Connecticut Post*), the Memphis *Commercial Appeal*, and the *Nashville City Paper.* He was nominated for a liner notes Grammy for *From Where I Stand: The Black Experience in Country Music*, and contributed to the Grammy-winning *Night Train to Nashville.*

CPSIA information can be obtained
at www.ICGtesting.com
Printed in the USA
LVHW030210190221
679489LV00006B/591